Diversity of Experimental Methods in Economics

Toshiji Kawagoe · Hirokazu Takizawa
Editors

Diversity of Experimental Methods in Economics

Institute of Economic Research, Chuo University
IERCU
中央大学経済研究所
1964

Springer

Editors
Toshiji Kawagoe
Future University Hakodate
Hokkaido, Japan

Hirokazu Takizawa
Chuo University
Hachioji, Tokyo, Japan

ISBN 978-981-13-6064-0 ISBN 978-981-13-6065-7 (eBook)
https://doi.org/10.1007/978-981-13-6065-7

Library of Congress Control Number: 2018967418

This Springer imprint is published by the registered company Springer Nature Singapore Pte Ltd.
The registered company address is: 152 Beach Road, #21-01/04 Gateway East, Singapore 189721, Singapore

Contents

Diversity of Experimental Methods in Economics: An Introduction

Toshiji Kawagoe and Hirokazu Takizawa

1 Economics and Experiments

Experimental methods have long been thought of as irrelevant and useless to economic research. To the best of our knowledge, this idea was explicitly stated for the first time by John Stuart Mill in the middle of the nineteenth century. In his treatise on economic methodology, he clearly referred to the impossibility of *experimentum crucis* in economics (Mill 2007/1836). For him, it is this fact that differentiates the methodology of economics from that of natural sciences. Thus, he proposed method a priori for economics that is mainly based on deduction from basic premises. The edifice of economics should be deductively built upon the premise that humans desire to possess wealth, and are capable of thinking of efficient means to that end, which itself is obtained through introspections.

In 1985 when plenty of experimental works had already been in currency, the same idea was expressed in the most celebrated textbook as follows:

> Economists … cannot perform the controlled experiments of chemists or biologists because they cannot easily control other important factors. Like astronomers or meteorologists, they generally must be content largely to observe (Samuelson and Nordhaus 1985, p. 8).

In retrospect, it is somewhat surprising to see the similarity of those ideas after a lapse in time of more than 100 years. In fact, similar ideas have been in currency, such as in Friedman (1953)'s methodology of positive economics.

The recent development of experimental methods in economics, however, shows that there has turned out to be some room for the improvement in the control of "other factors," and that economics has something, actually a lot, to learn from experiments.

T. Kawagoe
Future University Hakodate, Hokkaido, Japan
e-mail: kawagoe@fun.ac.jp

H. Takizawa (✉)
Chuo University, Hachioji, Tokyo, Japan
e-mail: hirokazu.takizawa@gmail.com

T. Kawagoe and H. Takizawa (eds.), *Diversity of Experimental Methods in Economics*,
https://doi.org/10.1007/978-981-13-6065-7_1

Mill, Samuelson and Nordhaus, among others, failed to see these points. It may be that the ideas on the nature of economics as well as of experiments have undergone a major revision among economists in recent years.

By now, experiments are accepted as a legitimate method in economics as exemplified by the awarding of Nobel Prize in economic sciences 2002 to Vernon Smith who "developed methods for laboratory experiments in economics, which has helped our understanding of economic behavior." Nevertheless, the question of what the experiment is and what and how we learn from experiments are not yet so obvious, even if confined to the realm of natural sciences, and still invite new insights.

Our stereotypical image of experiments seems to have been formed by the experiment conducted by Galileo Galilei that led him to the discovery of the law of falling body (the experiment conducted at the Tower of Pisa seems now to be regarded as fictional, but the experiment with falling bodies along a slope as authentic). This stereotypical image arouses a feeling that there exists a strong tie between experiments and laws; laws are found inductively from experimental results. However, as far as current economic experiments are concerned, they do not seem to purport to discover laws. After all, in economics, we have few laws that are comparable with those in natural sciences, and it seems that economists today are more interested in uncovering and understanding mechanisms behind economic phenomena.

In spite of the wide recognition of the validity of experiments, how they are relevant to economic reasoning is not so straightforward. In fact, there seems to be a diversity in the ways that experimental methods are relevant to economics. With the main focus on laboratory experiments, one of the most notable practitioners in this field attempts to classify the purposes of economic experiments into the following categories (Roth 1986):

(1) speaking to theorists (testing and modifying formal theories);
(2) whispering into the ears of princes (providing information for the policy-making process); and
(3) searching for facts (finding interesting phenomena).

Roth made this classification mainly with laboratory experiments in mind, but this classification seems to apply beyond the laboratory experiments. Thus, we will also rely on this classification as needed in what follows.

This book aims to show that the use of experimental methods depends deeply upon the reasoning researchers employ in their respective research. It also attempts to show the limits of experimental methods by examining in wider perspectives what experimenters are actually doing.

That said, this chapter aims to introduce readers to the subsequent chapters by delineating the overall picture concerning the experimental practices in economics, and then to provide information concerning each chapter so that the readers with specific interests may go directly to the relevant parts.

2 Vernon Smith's Market Experiment

It is difficult to identify the first attempt at the economic experiment, but it is increasingly becoming common to cite Edward Chamberlin's market experiment in 1948 as the one that has triggered the ensuing rise of experimental economics (Chamberlin 1948).[1] In fact, it is the participation in this experiment that provided a spark for Smith to embark on serious experimental research along his own research interests. Chamberlin's experiments were market experiments in a classroom, with which he tried to criticize the validity of the theory of perfectly competitive markets.

Chamberlin's innovation in this experiment was that he successfully created in the classroom an economic environment similar to the one supposed by the market theory, in this case, the partial equilibrium theory with discrete goods or service. For this, it would suffice that we can create buyers and sellers with arbitrary amounts of reservation value. For example, a buyer with value v for the good would be created, if his/her reward is set at $v - p$ when he/she buys the good at the price of p. A seller with the reservation value of c would be created if his/her reward is $p - c$ when he/she sells the good at the price of p. Thus, in an experiment, each participant individually receives information ex ante as to whether he/she is a buyer or seller and the amount of his/her own reservation value, and then instructed how the reward is determined. With buyers and sellers thus created, we can draw the demand and supply curves for the market and compute its competitive equilibrium price and quantity. We can then compare the theoretical prediction with experimental outcomes.

Vernon Smith's early experimental study also focused on markets.[2] However, unlike Chamberlin, his interest was not in refuting the theory of competitive market, but in exploring issues that cannot be dealt with by the mathematical models for this theory. The models of competitive equilibrium theory do not necessarily provide the description of how the competitive equilibrium is attained. However, an influential version presupposes a fictitious auctioneer, who works to search for prices that equate demand and supply for goods and services, a process known as *tatonnement*. Of course, there is usually no such a person in the real market. Therefore, it is worthwhile to explore the conditions that ensure rapid convergence to the theoretical equilibrium with actual human subject learning through time in experimental markets. Thus, the objective of Smith's experiments was not simply to test a theoretical hypothesis in the sense of confirming or refuting it, but to discover the way of organizing markets that achieves theoretically predicted outcomes in an efficient way. He then discovered the "double auction" method, now commonly used in classroom market experiments, as the way of organizing markets that closely simulates the prediction of the competitive market theory. This is a method of transaction where *both* sellers and buyers with their own reservation value, unbeknownst to other market parameters however, quote their asking prices to one another.

---

[1]See Roth (1986) as well as Roth (1993). He cites E. Chamberlin, A. Hoggatt, H. Sauermann and R. Selten, M. Shubik, S. Siegel and L. Fouraker, and J. Friedman as independent early contributors to economic experiment. See also Svorenčik and Maas (2016).

[2]Smith's first supply and demand experiment was done in January 1956 (Smith 1989).

In general, any market outcome can be regarded as jointly produced by human subjects' behavior and the specific market institution surrounding them. Since the focus of Smith's experiment was on the performance of various market organizations, he wanted to make the behavioral aspect as constant as possible. Thus, with the competitive market theory in mind, he needed to make the preferences of experimental subjects as close to those supposed in the theory as possible. It was at this specific point that the traditional problem of controlling experimental environments arises.

Smith deliberately contrived his *induced value theory* in this context. Note that, in times when the axiomatic/deductive methodology was the orthodoxy, he had to fend off any possible criticism from those unfamiliar with experimentation in economics. The induced value theory aims to identify the right ways to create incentives the theory assumes in the laboratory, but usually cited as the following precepts for experimentation (Smith 1976, 1982):

(1) non-satiation: making subjects always choose the alternative with the most reward;
(2) saliency: relating rewards appropriately to experimental outcomes;
(3) dominance: making the reward structure dominate any other subjective value/cost that may affect a subject's choice;
(4) privacy: subjects are only informed of their own payoffs; and
(5) parallelism: the choice tendency observed in the experiment also holds in outside environments.

According to this theory, reward system has to be structured so that subjects have clear-cut and sufficient incentives in making their choices in the experiment, as presupposed by the theory to be tested. This is ensured by the arrangement where the points they obtained in the experiment are converted in monetary units and paid in cash immediately after the experiment. This is regarded as the main reason that the experiments reported in published papers have usually followed this practice.[3]

3 The Rise of Behavioral Economics

It is indispensable to mention, at this point, the rise of behavioral economics since the 1970s, which also makes use of experimental methods, and to touch upon its relation to the experimental economics advanced along the line of Vernon Smith.

Behavioral economics analyzes actual human behavior and explores its implications for understanding economic phenomena. This area of study has already produced two Nobel laureates, Daniel Kahneman in 2001 (jointly with Vernon Smith) and Richard Thaler in 2017. Given that traditional economics generally used to

[3]It is interesting to know that historically this practice comes from a laboratory experiment for psychological learning by Siegel (1953). See Svorenčik and Maas (2016, p. 87) for this.

assume that human agents are rational and usually selfish as well, the rise of behavioral economics may be regarded as marking a fundamental transformation of the nature of economic sciences in the recent decades.

It is important to note that the research agenda of behavioral economics greatly differ from experimental economics as aforementioned. As the adjective "behavioral" indicates, it is focused not only on actions but rather also on behaviors in general.[4] This means that it is closely connected to cognitive sciences and/or experimental psychology. In fact, Kahneman was a psychologist when he started his academic career in the 1960s. Recall that Smith was focused on the performance of the market institutions. The difference in focus also implied the difference in the specific methods used. In fact, it was survey questionnaires that Kahneman and Tversky used when they elaborated upon the theory of heuristics and bias, and its subsequent elaboration of the prospect theory (Kahnemann and Tversky 1979).

Heukelom (2014) describes the process, where psychological research by Kahneman and Tversky was gradually acquired by economists such as Richard Thaler in the 1980s. The process required a deliberative "marketing" strategy to establish the field within economics that had had very conservative methodological thinking. Thaler, together with Kahneman and Eric Wanner, set up research programs funded by Alfred P. Sloan Foundation as well as Russel Sage Foundation, carefully organizing the members so that the projects include almost equal numbers of economists and psychologists. In the setting-up process, Smith was also invited, but he did not participate in the project, possibly due to the difference of philosophy.[5]

By now the differences seem to be fading, and the border between the two fields blurring. This may be partly because game theoretic experiments have become increasingly common since the 1990s, and they tend to be more focused on behavioral anomalies observed in social interactions. However, it should be noted here that different research motivations have developed different experimental methods.

4 Behavioral Economics, Neuroeconomics and Naturalism

The rise of behavioral economics has had enormous impacts on economics. For one thing, it revolutionized economics in that it extended the traditional scope of economics to the analysis of the real human behavior. For another, it has made economics an interdisciplinary field of research by introducing research methods that had been adopted outside economics such as psychology. Let us explain these points in turn.

---

[4]According to Heukelom (2014), it was in the US in the early 20twentieth century that the word "behavior" began to be used for comprehensive activities not only of human beings but also of animals.

[5]Smith seems to be somewhat critical against behavioural economists' search for anomalies "in the tails of distributions." See Smith (2008, p. 22, ff. 6).

The structure of traditional economics is basically deductively constructed. Setting several plausible axioms on the behavior of economic agents, economists usually deduce theorems/propositions useful for understanding the working of an economy. As we saw in Mill's statement at the beginning of this chapter, this fundamental character of economics partly followed from the presupposition that conclusive experiments are impossible in economics. The elegant mathematical edifice of competitive equilibrium theory built in this approach has long made most economists refrain from doubting the very foundation of this theoretical construct. From this point of view, the rise of behavioral economics was revolutionary in that it began to focus on the human behavior as such, which constituted the foundation of the whole system of economics.

The rise of behavioral economics also means that economics has now imported different methodological strategies from other disciplines. It is well known that the mainstream economics opted for separating itself from psychology as it establishes itself as an autonomous scientific endeavor in the first half of the twentieth century. This is best exemplified by the statement in Robbins (1932) that economics will not get involved in psychological issues of human agents. This has enabled economics to exclusively engage in the study of resource allocations mainly through the market mechanisms.

Viewed from the historical perspective, however, there have been two distinct approaches to the explanation of human mind and behavior. One approach tries to understand and explain human behavior in terms of such intentional states as preference and belief.[6] This approach to human behavior is not so greatly different from the folk psychology we use in our daily life; we usually justify our behavior by explaining our own preference and belief, and attribute them to understand someone else's behavioral choice.[7] The traditional economics has also adopted this approach. The other approach to the human behavior is naturalistic in the sense that it attempts to understand it in terms of the causal relationship as usually practiced in physical sciences, explicitly excluding teleological elements from the explanation (von Wright 2004).

Human mind and behavior are unique in that they can be subject to analysis under both approaches. If one of the two approaches were reducible to the other, there is no essentially difficult problem. However, there is an influential argument by Davidson that there cannot be laws connecting the mental states and physical states, implying the fundamental incommensurability of the two approaches (Davidson 1980).

---

[6]Here the term "intentionality" should be taken as a philosophical terminology referring to the characteristic of some mental states that they are always "about" something, and intentional states are mental states with such a property. Intentional states include such mental states as perceiving, believing, wanting, hoping and so on.

[7]However, this way of understanding human behaviour has been philosophically sophisticated by some philosophers and social scientists including Max Weber. In their discourse, an action is distinguished from a sheer behaviour such as yawning, because it is based on intentional states and thus regarded as rational choice of an agent. Weber (1978) restricted the object of sociology to the study of actions with rational motives, because we can only understand actions with rationality. Of course, Weber's sociology includes the discipline of economics in our modern parlance.

It seems that both approaches are dispersed within the field of behavioral economics. For example, the prospect theory proposed by Kahneman and Tversky explains the choice behavior under risk by combining preference and belief, although both preference and belief used there are different from such standard ones in the expected utility theory; in the prospect theory, they are both ridden with considerable biases. Despite these differences in the formulation of preferences and beliefs, however, we may be able to regard the prospect theory in line with the intentional approach. In contrast, most of the economic experiments presented in Ariely (2008) utilize "priming," a technique frequently used in psychological experiments, where exposure to one stimulus influences a response to a subsequent stimulus without consciousness, to find out a causal relationship without reference to any mental states.

The naturalistic approach to human mind/behavior is even more obvious by the rise of neuroeconomics since the 1990s. This period saw a rapid development of technologies to measure brain activities in non-invasive ways, such as the functional magnetic resonance imaging (fMRI). With this, some researchers began to investigate which parts of the subjects' brain are activated when they make economic decisions. Most, if not all, of such research has shared the question formulated in behavioral economics. In this sense, neuroeconomics can be regarded as part of behavioral economics, pursuing the same subject matter with different tools.

The emergence of the naturalistic approach gave rise to a controversy in the methodology of economics in the early 2000s. The debate was ignited by Gul and Pesendorfer's (2008) argument that neuro-scientific evidence is irrelevant to economic research. Economics is, they assert, essentially a science of making choices that enables us to understand how people make choices, for which such categories as preference, belief and constraint are relevant and neuro-scientific data does not provide any useful information. In the same volume, Schotter (2008), in contrast, argues that neuro-physiological data can be useful to economic modelling in some instances. As an example, he raises the interpretation problem regarding the outcomes observed in laboratory experiments of first-price, sealed-bid auction. It has been known that, in such experiments, subjects tend to submit higher bids than the theoretical prediction. To explain the phenomenon, theorists may have two options. One strategy is to adopt a behavioral model where human subjects want to feel the "joy of winning." The other is to assume that humans want to avoid the "fear of losing." The physiological data might help us identify which is the right underlying cause for the observed behavior.

The meaning of the rise of naturalism into economics is a very interesting question as such. However, back to our current context, it is interesting to observe that experimental methods are not only related to the so-called "naturalistic" investigation of the causal relationship. It has been also useful in research programs that assume that human decision-making is based on intentional states.

5 Behavioral Game Theory

It is well known that game theoretic experiments were already conducted in 1950, soon after the theory had been launched by Von Neumann and Morgenstern; Melvin Dresher and Meryl Flood experimented with a game that would be later known as "prisoner's dilemma" at RAND Corporation (Flood 1958). The aim of the experiment was to compare the performance of alternative solution concepts for non-cooperative games, including Nash equilibrium. They reported that the experimental results did not necessarily support the prediction of Nash equilibrium. However, John Nash himself gave a critical comment that their experimental design was such that subjects had been actually playing a repeated game, rather than a one-shot game. This is an interesting episode that tells us about the importance of experimental designs.

As game theory became increasingly common among economists in the 1980s, economists soon became interested in conducting game theoretic experiments. This may be partly because it is relatively easy to conduct a game experiment, if casually, in a classroom. It should be noted, however, that game theoretic experiments require a somewhat different consideration than the market experiments. Since, in game theory, common knowledge of the rule of the game and rationality of players is usually assumed, game experiments need to realize that assumption in a laboratory. Recall that the above-described induced value theory included "privacy" as one of the sufficient, if not necessary, conditions for a good experiment. Obviously game experiments, if they are to test a theory, have to ignore this maxim.

Nevertheless, except the privacy requirement, game theoretic experiments have been conducted mostly following the norms of induced value theory. However, their role in game experiments seems to be somewhat different from that in the market experiments. Whereas the market experiments were mainly focused on the performance of various ways of organizing markets, game experiments came to be increasingly driven by the discovery of various anomalous behaviors in game-theoretic social interaction. This is the reason why Colin Camerer coined the word "behavioral game theory" (Camerer 2003). In this context, strict compliance with the standard norm was necessary for researchers to clearly identify deviation from theories.

Examples of anomalies are abundant, but let it suffice to mention one-shot prisoner's dilemma, public goods game and ultimatum game among others. In these games, subjects seem to be affected by consideration of social contexts in which they usually live, even though they are given strong appropriate incentive in the laboratory environments. This naturally led to the proposal of a variety of social preferences or other-regarding preferences, such as altruism, fairness concern, inequality aversion, as well as behavioral model based on bounded rationality such as quantal response equilibrium and level-k model. To date, however, the dispute over which has the most explanatory power has not been resolved. Rather, models with most explanatory power seem to depend on specific contexts, such as whether the situation considered involves a distribution problem. Researchers in this subfield seem to rely on the model comparison method developed in statistics.

Game theory also launched a subfield called market design, which aims to design artificial markets that have not existed in history. Laboratory experiments are also utilized in this ambitious enterprise, as best exemplified by the process, where FCC introduced auctions for the allocation of the microwave spectrum. Newly proposed market mechanisms are usually examined in laboratory experiments before being implemented in reality. For example, experimental results here can offer information as to whether players can "game" the rules in an unexpected manner. The purpose of experimentation here is "whispering into the ears of princes."

6 From Testing Theories to Informing Policies

So far we have mostly seen laboratory experiments, which have the obvious advantage that researchers can make experimental environments close to those supposed by theoretical models. Actually, laboratory experiments, in general, do not necessarily aim to predict what will happen in the real world. Rather they aim to find answers to the question posed by theoretical models. Recall that Smith's question was under what conditions human behaviors well simulate the competitive equilibrium theory, and game theoretic experiments are meaningful only with regard to theoretical predictions. Even if we know that subjects divide pies on the 50–50 basis in the ultimatum game, it will not attract people's interest unless we also know that theory predicts the proposer's taking almost all the pie. Thus, laboratory experiments are deeply involved with theories, and aim to "speaking to theorists," or "search for facts" to be explored by theories, to use Roth's classification.

Then how can we "whisper into the ears of princes"? Intuitively speaking, for this kind of purposes, it seems that we need to get out of laboratories and get closer to the real-world environments where policies are implemented. Furthermore, it does not usually suffice that we only have information about the correlation between relevant variables. It may be that increasing money supply does not cause inflation, even if we know the correlation between them is very strong. Thus, in order to make an effective policy, we need information regarding causality rather than correlation.

In the early 1990s, there emerged the movement of "evidence based medicine" in the UK, which asserts that medical treatments should become more systematic and scientific, relying less on "soft" evidence such as doctors' experiences and gut feelings and more on "hard" evidence. This idea was soon generalized to "evidenced based policies" in the UK and USA, in such areas as social care (the UK Sure Start program) and education policy (No Child Left Behind Policy, USA). It also permeated economics very soon, especially in development economics. The movement regards randomized controlled trial (RCT) as the "gold standard" for obtaining "hard" evidence.

In a typical RCT, all subjects are randomly divided into two groups. The reason that the assignment is random is to make the two groups have identical characteristics from a statistical point of view. One group, called "treatment group," receives treatment, whereas the other group, called "control group," either remains untreated, receives alternative treatment, or is given a placebo, depending on the purpose of the experiment. In order to make the experiment more rigorous, a double-blind method may be adopted, where not only the subjects but also the experimental administrators are given no information as to which is the control group and which the treatment group. This is to avoid the "experimenter effect," whereby the expectation of experimenters regarding the effect of treatment may unknowingly affect the behavior of subjects.

This method dates back to Fisher (1935), but is obviously reminiscent of the "Canon of Inductive Method" that John Stuart Mill crystalized as reliable forms of induction, especially "Method of Difference." Suppose that there are two situations, one of which has some particular phenomenon and the other of which does not. If the two situations are alike except in some other specific factor, then it is judged as an effect or a cause of the phenomenon. The RCT today differs from this method only in that it tries to identify the difference in the effect of a treatment by using modern statistical inferences.

One of the greatest advantages of an ideally implemented RCT seems to lie in the general applicability of its causal inference. Researchers conducting RCTs do not need to have detailed knowledge on the mechanism that causally connects treatments and their effect, although they will have to have specific hypotheses ex ante to design the experiment. In contrast, the use of economic models usually requires us to have detailed knowledge about corresponding mechanisms, but the models as such often rely on dubious assumptions. There are no such worries involved in the implementation of RCTs, because the mechanism is left as a black box as it were.

This methodology, brought into development economics by Abhijit Banerjee, Esther Duflo and others, has achieved significant results in policy-making in developing countries. The introduction of RCT turned the nature of research in development economics from the armchair study that examines the effectiveness of development aid dealing with data econometrically to a kind of research that collects data in the field to investigate the effectiveness of specific policies.

However, even such a powerful method is not without criticism. First, there is the problem of "external validity" (Guala 2005), which questions whether the results obtained in some specific experimental environments also hold in other environments. As this is almost equal to what Smith called "parallelism" in his precepts, external validity is not limited to RCTs, but also problematic in laboratory experiments. However, the problem may become more serious in the context of RCTs, because we might have almost no information as to the causal mechanisms that are working to bring about the obtained results. Thus, we may not be left with enough clues for inferring the possibility that the same results obtain in other contexts.

The second criticism concerns the possible existence of "general equilibrium effects." They may arise when coverage of the policy considered is extended to wider public on a greater scale so that the general implementation of the policy may greatly change the use of other resources in society. The policy might have been effective in a small-scale experiment, because of the *ceteris paribus* conditions that did not affect greatly the use of other resources. As an example, suppose the famous experiment conducted in the USA that examined the effect of a class size on the effectiveness of education. The result was that a smaller class size has better educational outcomes. Would this result continue to hold if we made all the classes in the country smaller? The problem is that we may not be able to keep the quality of teachers constant, if we extend the program to the whole country.

7 Field Experiments and the Identification of Causality

The idea of exploiting high-quality causal information from the RCTs was not confined in development economics, but today is extended to wider areas in economics. As one can easily presume, it is not so easy to conduct RCTs in advanced countries. Nevertheless, there are some situations where we can conduct field experiments even in advanced countries. Furthermore, we sometimes find some contingent situations comparable to ideal experiments in the real-world settings, which is usually called natural experiments. This extension of the basic idea has been made possible by the innovation that occurred in statistics and is today called "statistical causal inference."

Readers might have been taught in an introductory statistics lecture that correlation does not usually imply causal relations, presented with a graph with the values of height and weight taken along horizontal and vertical axes, respectively, in which each subject's data is plotted. Here, obviously the height of a person does not causally determine his/her weight. There is a famous dictum that, in order to examine causality with respect to any system, it is not sufficient to passively observe the data occurring in the system, but it is necessary to intervene into the system to observe the outcomes. The former type of data is called "naturally occurring data," whereas the latter "experimental data." We used to think that it was difficult to grasp causality dealing with statistical data, because we used to have naturally occurring data in mind. However, in the 1970s, innovative statistical research was launched that aims to develop methods for identifying causal relations even using naturally occurring data by regarding experimental data as a benchmark for the identification of causality, Rubin's causal model (Rubin 1974).

In general, to extract causality, we need to compare the outcome when a treatment was applied to an individual/group with the other outcome when it was not. In reality, however, we can only observe either of these. This is the conundrum for identifying causality, called "fundamental problem of causal inference" (Holland 1986). By focusing on causal effects, RCT makes it possible to extract causality by an experimental intervention that randomly assigns subjects to the treatment group, to which a treatment is applied, and the control group, to which it is not, making both groups have the same characteristics from the statistical viewpoint. The point is that, viewed as a random variable, the group assignment is independent of the treatment. This procedure can be regarded as a way to create the counterfactual to measure the causal effect. Although we do not delve into the details here, there are also ways to create the counterfactuals using naturally occurring data. Examples include instrumental variable method, propensity score matching, difference in differences method among others.

Controlled Data			Modeling Naturally-Occurring Data	
LAB	AFE	FFE	NFE	NE, PSM, IV, STR

Where:

LAB: Lab experiment

AFE: Artefactual field experiment

FFE: Framed field experiment

NFE: Natural Field experiment

NE: Natural experiment

PSM: Propensity score matching

IV: Instrumental variables estimation

STR: Structural modeling

Fig. 1 A field experiment bridge (List 2006, p. 7)

Saying that "the goal of any evaluation method is to construct the proper counterfactual," List (2006) thus presents a unified framework that enables us to understand almost all experiments in economics with different degree of control. See Fig. 1.

The horizontal segment in the diagram indicates the degree to which the environments are controlled, with the laboratory experiment at the left endpoint, and natural experiment, propensity score matching, instrumental variable estimation, structural modelling, which deal with naturally occurring data, at the right endpoint. Various kinds of field experiments are located between them. The artifactual field experiment is almost the same as the laboratory experiment, but the group of experimental subjects is set closer to people that the researcher is interested in. The framed field experiment is controlled to the same degree as the laboratory experiment, but the goods traded and/or the information available to the subjects in the experiment are closer to the real world. The experimental environments in the natural experiment are real world, but the subjects are randomly assigned as in the RCT. According to this definition, the RCTs in development economics goes into this category.

According to List, field experiments can function as a bridge between laboratory experiments and the real world, with regard to external validity. That is, the field experiments enable us to check whether the result obtained in laboratory experiments also hold in settings closer to the real world, because they have intermediate characters. For example, the well-known "endowment effects," the phenomenon that people's Willingness to Accept usually exceeds their Willing to Pay (Kahneman et al. 1990), have been shown to dissipate as the exposure of subjects to market experience increases, by a series of field experiments.

8 Looking at Various Experiments as They Arise

Thus, the framework List proposes is very ambitious in that it tries to grasp the very nature of various economic experiments in a unified approach. However, it may not be the whole story. The picture submitted there induces an image that all experimental research in economics share the same motivation, that is, the motivation to identify causality. However, reflecting back on the various ways that experimentation has brought forth new knowledge in social sciences, we may also say that there are diverse motivations for adopting experimental methods.

The nature of a specific problem at hand seems to mostly determine the experimental method to be used. As aforementioned, the laboratory experiment seems to be more related to the examination of specific mechanisms, which we usually express by means of economic models. In contrast, the RCTs are more concerned with identifying causal relationships that are useful for policy-making issues ("whispering to the ear of princes") such as in development economics.[8] Of course, both problems are interdependent on one another, because the knowledge of economics comprises of a complicated network of related hypotheses and models; theories that greatly affect our view of the real world would constrain the hypotheses to be tested.

We will not delve into this issue in this introduction. We hope that the above explanation of the development of various experimental methods sets the ground for the readers to proceed to the subsequence chapters.

9 The Structure of the Book

The book is divided into two parts. Part I: *Diversity in Experimental Methods* and Part II: *Critical Viewpoints*. Let us now give a brief overview of each chapter so that you can go directly to the chapter that you are interested in.

Part I: Diversity in Experimental Methods

Part I mainly describes how various experimental methods have been practiced in such diverse fields as market theory, game theory, development economics, political science, behavioral analysis and evolutionary psychology. These chapters also suggest how it would become possible to have a constructive dialog between diverse fields based on the common language of experimentation.

Chapter 1: Laboratory Experiment in Game Theory

This chapter introduces readers to laboratory experiments in game theory. It begins by briefly reviewing its history. Although one may think of Vernon Smith to hear experimental economics, the experimental game theory has its own origins different

[8]This assertion may not be immediately applicable when we consider designing the actual economic environment by simulating the environment in laboratory experiments.

from his market experiments. With the permeation of game theory into economics in 1990s, experiments on game theory began to increase in number, providing fertile bedrock for economic experimentation.

In this process, experimenters had to slightly change the basic precepts provided by Smith's induced value theory; They had to "ignore" privacy precept, which requires subjects be only informed of their own payoffs, because common knowledge of the rule of the game is usually assumed in game theory. Furthermore, controlling the preferences of subjects gradually came to take on different meanings in game experiments. As the experimental results accumulate, it turned out that subjects do not necessarily behave rationally. In this context however, it was important for experimenters to show that anomaly occurs *in spite of* rigorous controlling procedure of the experimental environments.

With the accumulation of anomalies, the game theory experiment has transformed itself from a tool for testing theory to that for identifying subjects' behavioral model. The behavioral models so far proposed include models based on other-regarding preferences and bounded rationality. The latter half of this chapter explains those models and proceed to ways to compare competing models by using experimental data. One key concept is that of "statistical model" which involves at least one parameter to maximize likelihood function. Experimenters often need to transform a specific theory that provide only point prediction to a statistical model. The other is the criterion of model comparison. AIC and its variants are introduced as a useful tool for model comparison. Unlike other statistical methods, they do not presuppose which hypothesis is true.

Chapter 2: The Field Experiment Revolution in Development Economics

Krugman, a Nobel laureate, stated a quarter century ago that the field of development economics "no longer exists." Beginning with this shocking statement, the chapter describes how the field has been resuscitated with the use of experimental methodology since the turn of the twenty-first century. The key factor to this process has been the use of randomized controlled trials (RCT) in the field, which enable us to examine the causal effect of a policy intervention. The authors not only explain the very basic ideas of RCT and its fruitful applications, but also go further to describe how RCT-based research is enriched by combination with other experimental and/or statistical methods, such as the lab-in-the-field experiment and the structural estimation approach. The reader should feel that a great transformation of economic science is happening now, something that might be properly called "empirical turn" of economics. The authors are aware of this and associate the current development in this field to the general tendency of current economic research, "empiricalization," "scientification" and "team-orientation." The chapter is also rife with informative cases where new experimental methods have come to be used in response to research questions that arise based on the previous experimental research.

Chapter 3: Experimental Research in Political Science

Unsurprisingly, the history of experimentation in political science is almost as old as that of economics, dating back to Gosnell's experiment in the stimulation of voting in 1926. However, it is not until the 1990s that an increasing number of experimental studies began to be published in major American journals. The experimental methodology in politics seems to have invited criticism from those who question how helpful it can be in understanding complex political phenomena. However, the trend has been changing, with the widespread recognition of the usefulness of experimentation.

The author stresses the importance of employing appropriate experimental methods for appropriate research topics. This belief is reflected in the first part of the paper, which surveys advantages and disadvantages of various experimental methods, ranging from field, laboratory, survey and natural experiments and simulation. Thus, this part will serve as a fine introduction of the experimental toolbox to anyone interested in experimental methods. In response to the complex character of the political phenomena, the author advices researchers to break the phenomena down to make them amenable to experimentation, and to integrate the results later.

The chapter also contains the author's own experimental research on people's ideas on distributive justice. This example illustrates how illuminating it can be to combine different experimental methods as well as the importance of deliberately choosing the experimental subjects so as to represent the whole society in the survey experiment.

Chapter 4: Experiments in Psychology: Current Issues in Irrational Choice Behavior

This chapter constitutes, as such, a complete guide to experimental methods in psychology. Readers who consider conducting experiments in this field would find the content of the chapter very useful and informative. The chapter also presents the state-of-the-art research results in behavioral analytic studies, and clearly identifies several research themes that economists and psychologists may profitably pursue in collaboration with each other.

The experiments in behavioral analysis usually use animals as experimental subjects. This means that, unlike economic experiments, the experimenter cannot rely on intentional concepts such as preferences and belief. This might be the fundamental difference between economic experiments and psychological experiments. Thus, there seems to be a hiatus between two subject fields. However, several findings in behavioral analysis, such as in the study of time discounting, have been successfully transferred to behavioral economics. It is interesting to note that the findings are strikingly similar in the two fields in spite of the difference of basic conceptual structure. Knowing how this was made possible would enable us to make further advancement not only in economics and psychology, but also in social sciences in general.

Chapter 5: Evolutionary Psychology and Economic Game Experiments

Chapter 5 examines the relationship between evolutionary psychology and experiments. Evolutionary psychology is a discipline devoted to understanding the human mind in terms of the theory of natural selection. Regarding human mind as a product of adaptation, evolutionary biologists assume that people behave so as to maximize fitness (survival and reproduction) under environmental constraints. Such environmental constraints are often modelled using economic games, such as prisoner's dilemma, enabling evolutionary biologists to use evolutionary game theory, a branch of game theory developed by evolutionary biologists. This creates some similarity in reasoning between economics and evolutionary psychology.

The authors, however, note that there are also important differences. Evolutionary psychologists do not assume that people rely on rational deliberations, whereas economists usually do so. As a result, they may disagree in their interpretation of the same behavioral observation. Evolutionary psychologists are more concerned about the underlying mechanisms yielding particular behavioral responses. Simply observing behavior is not sufficient. Examining both cases where economic game experiments are informative and uninformative, the authors suggest that experiments can often select from among competing hypotheses about the underlying mechanism when they yield the same observed behavior.

Part II: Critical Viewpoints

Part II goes deeper into the experimental methodology in social sciences. It deals with such questions as follows. Is it possible to design a rewarding system that meets all the conditions of the induced value theory? Are RCTs really worth huge investment? Do economic experiments provide us with objective properties of human behavior? Does the performativity of economic experiments make them as useless as they were once supposed to be? How is the "experimental turn" related to the current overall changes in economics?

Chapter 6: Reconsidering Induced Value Theory

As described in Chap. 1, the *induced value theory* developed by Vernon Smith has had enormous impacts on the design of economic experiments until now. It has long been supposed that complying with the precepts in the theory is mandatory, if experimenters want to control experimental subjects' preferences. However, there are several reasons to reconsider the utility of the theory.

Chapter 6 deals with this issue. In the first half of the chapter, the author identifies three approaches to economic experimentation that differ in their aim in conducting experiments, and considers each approach's relation to induced value theory. The approaches identified there are neoclassical approach, "old school" of behavioral economics, and "new school" of behavioral economics.

The argument proceeds by formulating the basic common structure of an economic model, which can be thought of as a mapping that takes the agent's (1) utility function and (2) decision environment as *explanans* to yield (3) observed behavior as *explanandum*. The functional form of this mapping is also important, and may be called a "principle of decision making." The neoclassical economists assume that the principle of decision-making is utility maximization and the utility is the canonical expected utility. Therefore, for them, observed differences in behavior should be explained by some differences in environments. New school in behavioral economics shares with the neoclassical approach the assumption that the principle of decision-making is maximization, but it tries to explain the observed differences in behavior with reference to the differences in the utility function. Finally, the old school of behavioral economics tries to attribute the observed behavioral difference to different principles of decision-making. From this perspective, the author asserts that controlling preference in the sense of the induced value only matters for the neoclassical approach and old school of behavioral economics, because these two approaches assume the subjects' utility is fixed. For the new school of behavioral economics, the important thing is not to control the preferences, but to identify them.

The simple belief in the induced value theory has recently been shaken by debates among experimental economists as well. The "all-pay system," where all subjects are rewarded for all tasks they fulfilled in an experiment, has long been regarded as the gold standard. However, this system is vulnerable to "wealth effect," i.e., subjects who have eared enough in the early rounds of an experiment might lose interest in later tasks. As a more robust rewarding system, some experimentalists proposed to adopt "random payment system," where payment is made for randomly selected tasks and/or subjects. However, this system is also known to be problematic in some experimental context. Then, we are naturally led to asking if there is any rewarding system that incentivizes subjects in an undistorted manner in any context. Citing recent works on this subject, the author says the answer is "No," as long as the experiment involves more than one round of decision-making.

Chapter 7: Billions of Dollars Worth of Experiments: Calibrating Clinical Trial Investments

As Chap. 2 indicates, in spite of its known limitations, RCTs still provide the strongest method for experimentation, especially in the context of identifying causal factors. Some may even say that RCTs are "gold standard" of experimentation. However, conducting RCT, especially in clinical trials, requires a huge investment. Thus, we may ask whether this social movement, the so-called evidence-based policy, is really worthwhile to continue to pursue. In this chapter, the author tries to calibrate the total clinical trial investments in North America, relying on the most recent studies that estimate the average cost of a single clinical trial. The results, presented with four scenarios, are a stunningly huge amount. Based on this research, the author is going to embark on a more challenging task to put these figures in the context of comprehensive cost–benefit analysis.

Chapter 8: New Wines into Old Wineskins? *Methodenstreit*, Agency and Structure in the Philosophy of Experimental Economics

Admitting that experiments have become part and parcel of today's economics, the author tries to put this trend in the context of the history of economics. It is well known that the methodological controversies on economic science have revolved around the question, whether it should basically be a deductive or an inductive science. The most famous example is the *Methodenstreit* that took place at the turn of the 19th and 20th century between the German Historical school and the Austrian school. While the latter emphasized the universal character of economics, the former regarded economics as a historical science dealing with particular values and cultures. The author argues that current economics is becoming more local and ad hoc, and more *empirical*, implying some affinity with the idea of Historical school. He also notes that the current rise of experimental economics fits into this general picture, as he stresses the local and context-dependent nature of the knowledge obtained by means of economic experimentation.

Chapter 9: Creating Social Ontology: On the Performative Nature of Economic Experiments

The conventional view on economic experiments has been that the use of experimental methods enables experimenters to identify objective properties of human behavior, independent from the experimental settings. However, this view is wrong, because economic experiments are *performative* in the sense that subjects, experimenter and experimental designs are inextricably entangled with one another. The author especially focuses on the use of monetary incentives in the laboratory experiments, which most economists have regarded as the only useful device for controlling preference and as contributing to the de-contextualizing of experimental results. He argues that the use of money, in fact, constrains the universalization of laboratory results, because it is a very strong "priming" procedure from the perspective of psychology. However, his insight into the performative nature of experiments does not lead to a negative view of experimentation in economics.

At this juncture, relying on Karen Barad, he turns to Niels Bohr's view on the controversy about the Copenhagen interpretation of quantum mechanics. Bohr suggested that the fundamental ontological units are phenomena that realize in an experimental setting. According to this view, there is nothing such as an immutable and fully autonomous object that could be separated from the phenomena emerging in the laboratory. The author argues that this also applies to economic experiments. Viewed in this manner, the results obtained in economic experiments are regarded as capturing reality in the sense that under similar environmental conditions, people will manifest similar property. Thus, it is meaningless to ask whether experiments can finally provide evidence on which kind of preferences human beings have in general. Economic experiments can identify certain performative mechanisms that generate a particular kind of preference in a particular context.

References

Ariely, D. (2008). *Predictably irrational: The hidden forces that shape our decisions*. New York: HarperCollins.

Camerer, C. (2003). *Behavioral game theory: Experiments in strategic interaction*. Princeton, NJ: Princeton University Press.

Chamberlin, E. H. (1948). An experimental imperfect market. *The Journal of Political Economy, 56*, 95–108.

Davidson, D. (1980). *Essays on actions and events*. Oxford: Clarendon Press.

Fisher, R. (1935/1971). *The design of experiments* (9th ed.). London: Macmillan.

Flood, M. (1958). Some experimental games. *Management Science, 5*, 5–26.

Friedman, M. (1953). The methodology of positive economics. In *Essays in positive economics* (pp. 3–43). Chicago, IL: Chicago University Press.
Guala, F. (2005). *The methodology of experimental economics*. Cambridge; New York: Cambridge University Press.
Gul, F., & Pesendorfer, W. (2008). The case for mindless economics. In A. Caplin & Andrew Schotter (Eds.), *The foundations of positive and normative economics* (pp. 3–41). Oxford: Oxford University Press.
Heukelom, F. (2014). *Behavioral economics: a history*. New York: Cambridge University Press.
Holland, P. (1986). Statistics and causal inference. *Journal of the American Statistical Association, 81,* 945–960.
Kahneman, D., Knetsch, J., & Thaler, R. (1990). Experimental tests of the endowment effect and the Coase theorem. *Journal of Political Economy, 98,* 1325–1348.
Kahnemann, D., & Tversky, A. (1979). Prospect theory: An analysis of decision under risk. *Econometrica, 47,* 263–291.
List, J. (2006). Field experiments: A bridge between lab and naturally occurring data. *Advances in Economic Analysis & Policy, 6*, Article 8.
Mill, J. S. (2007/1836). On the definition of Political Economy; and on the Method of 'Investigation Proper to It. In *Collected works of John Stuart Mill* (Vol. 4). Indianapolis, IN: Liberty Fund.
Robbins, L. (1932). *An essay on the nature and significance of economic science*. London, UK: McMillan & Co.
Roth, A. (1986). Laboratory experimentation in economics. *Economics and Philosophy, 2,* 245–273.
Roth, A. (1993). The early history of experimental economics. *Journal of the History of Economic Thought, 15,* 184–209.
Rubin, D. B. (1974). Estimating causal effects of treatments in randomized and nonrandomized studies. *Journal of Educational Psychology, 66,* 688–701.
Samuelson, P., & Nordhaus, W. (1985). *Economics*. New York: McGrow-Hill.
Schotter, A. (2008). What's so informative about choice? In A. Caplin & A. Schotter (Eds.), *The foundations of positive and normative economics: A handbook* (pp. 70–94). Oxford, UK: Oxford University Press.
Siegel, S. (1953). *Certain determinants and correlates of authoritarianism*. Department of Psychology, Stanford University.
Smith, V. (1976). Experimental economics: Induced value theory. In *The American Economic Review, Paper and Proceedings of the Eighty-eighth Annual Meeting of the American Economic Association* (Vol. 66, pp. 274–279).
Smith, V. (1982). Microeconomic systems as an experimental science. *The American Economic Review, 72,* 923–955.
Smith, V. (1989). Theory, experiment and economics. *Journal of Economic Perspectives, 3,* 151–169.
Smith, V. (2008). *Rationality in economics: Constructivist and ecological forms*. Cambridge, UK: Cambridge University Press.
Svorenčik, A., & Maas, H. (2016). *The making of experimental economics: Witness seminar on the emergence of a field*. Cham: Springer.
von Wright, G. (2004). *Explanation and understanding*. Ithaca, NY: Cornell University Press.
Weber, M. (1978). Economy and society: An outline of interpretive sociology. In G. Roth & C. Wittich (Eds.), *University of California Press*. Berkeley: CA.

Part I
Diversity in Experimental Methods

Laboratory Experiments in Game Theory

Takizawa Hirokazu

This chapter discusses several issues in experimental game theory. Since its inception in the 1950s, experimental game theory has now grown into a field with large literature, still attracting many young researchers (Kagel and Roth 1995; Camerer 2003). Thus, it is becoming increasingly difficult to look over all specific issues by themes (for example, see a bulky book, Dhami (2016). Readers eager to know the cutting-edge discussions for various specific themes should consult this book).

Instead, the chapter intends to introduce readers who may consider conducting experiments in game theory. Thus, its focus has to be selective: the basic information regarding the history of experimental game theory; what kinds of care have to be taken when conducting experiments in this field; basic behavioral models submitted thus far for explaining human behavior in the social contexts; and what we can do with experimental data. I also discuss some philosophical problems inherent in this enterprise.

I had to narrow down the range of topics to be dealt with even further by focusing only on laboratory experiments, where the experimental environment is made close to theoretical games to be examined. In such games as auctions, a host of research has been submitted with real data obtainable in eBay, say (Steiglitz 2007). However, the objectives are rather different between laboratory and field experiment, as we stated in the introduction to this book.

The organization of this chapter is as follows. In the first section, we briefly summarize the emergence and development of experimental game theory. Section 2 describes another strand of experimental economics, market experiment as initiated by Vernon Smith. This is to turn attention to differences in aims and methods employed between market experiments and experimental game theory. Section 3 briefly explains the basic models that have been proposed to explain human behavior in games. Section 4 explains statistical techniques to deal with data obtained in game experiments. Section 5 concludes the chapter.

T. Hirokazu (✉)
Faculty of Economics, Chuo University, Hachioji, Japan
e-mail: hirokazu.takizawa@gmail.com

T. Kawagoe and H. Takizawa (eds.), *Diversity of Experimental Methods in Economics*,
https://doi.org/10.1007/978-981-13-6065-7_2

1 A Brief History of Game Experiments

It has been well documented that the publication of Von Neumann and Morgenstern (1944) had enormous impact on psychology as well economics. Their expected utility theory, along with Savage's (1954) version of it, shaped the decision theory as we know today, by providing the normative standard of the rational behavior (Heukelom 2014). However, in our context, it is more important that it spawned the subject field of game theory that has tremendously flourished since then.

The game experiment often cited as the earliest one is that conducted at Rand Corporation by Melvin Dresher and Merrill Flood in 1950 (reported as Case 3 in Flood 1958). It was the time when several competing theories, including Nash (1951), were submitted to give a most plausible solution to nonconstant-sum games, and they aimed at testing alternative theories with experimentation. The game they experimented with was one hundred repetition of the game that later came to be known as the prisoner's dilemma (see Table 1). The observed outcomes were reported to be not only far from the Nash equilibrium of the game, (Row 2, Column 1), but also from the fully cooperative behavior, (Row 1, Column 2). Nash commented on this experiment that the experimental subjects were actually playing one large multi-move game in this experiment. This comment is of interest because it does not only lead to the study of repeated games, but also points out the importance of careful designing in game theory experiments.

The 1980s saw a thorough penetration of game theory into economics, which turned the main subject matter of the discipline from the working of the market mechanism to strategic interactions among economic agents and/or institutions that shape these interactions. Game theory allows us to rigorously define each game and give sharp prediction of the outcome, albeit quite often with multiple equilibria. Thus, we were able to talk about the working of diverse institutions (not only of the market) by rigorous mathematical standards that most economists were satisfied with.

Exemplar games dealt with in a course on game theory typically involve only a small number of agents. Thus, it is very natural for many economists to conduct experiments with games to compare the experimental results with theoretical predictions. As we will see later, the main objective of the early experimental economics had been the understanding of market mechanism. Offering new bedrocks to experiments, game theory thus turned the main focus of experimental economics by 1990s.

Eventually, economists found that behaviors of subjects reported in game experiments did not necessarily endorse rational choices predicted by game theorists. The

Table 1 The prisoner's dilemma game experimented with by Dresher and Flood

		Column player	
		Column 1	Column 2
Row player	Row 1	−1, 2	1/2, 1
	Row 2	0, 1/2	1, −1

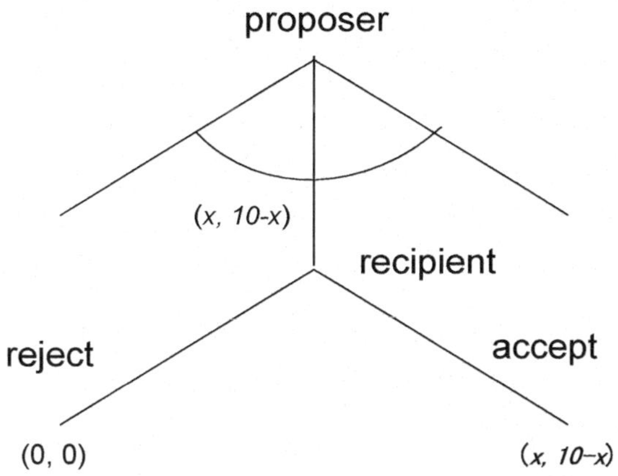

Fig. 1 Ultimatum game

most famous example is the ultimatum game experiment (Fig. 1), where a unique subgame-perfect equilibrium predicts that the proposer takes all of the pie. Roth et al. (1991) report however that the experimental results greatly differed from this prediction. Typically, the proposer offered 50:50 division of the pie, and the recipient rejected "unfair" division proposal. They also report about 25% of plays resulted in the rejection. This experiment aroused great interest because the study reported significant differences in the observed distribution of the pie among countries where the experiments were conducted, USA, Yugoslavia, Israel, and Japan.

The accumulation of "anomalies" naturally gave impetus to the rise of behavioral economics, which had mainly focused on behavior of a single agent in the face of uncertainty (Kahneman and Tversky 1979). The problem of how to explain the anomalous behavior observed in *strategic* interactions came to be recognized widely among economists. Thus, the penetration of game theory into economics had an enormous impact on experimental economics as well as behavioral economics since the late 1980s.

2 Some Reflections on the Purposes and Methodology of Market Experiments

It is always difficult to identify the "first" attempt of the practices or ideas that later became a "norm" in scientific investigation. This common fact also applies to the experiment in economics (for a comprehensive survey including earliest achievements, see Roth 1995). However, it seems to be increasingly common to cite the experiment conducted by Edward Chamberlin in 1948 as the earliest trial that has had enormous impacts on the current experimental economics (Chamberlin 1948). In fact, it is the participation in this experiment that Vernon Smith, who received

2002 Nobel Prize in economics for "having established laboratory experiments as a tool in economic analysis," began to seriously engage in experimental research.

It is important to recall that, in those days, most economists had thought that experimentation was almost useless or irrelevant for economics. We can trace this idea back at least to John Stuart Mill's methodology of economics (Mill 2007/1844). He thought that the fundamental difference between natural sciences and economics is that it is impossible to conduct *experimentum crucis* in economics.[1] Thus, economics has to adopt what he calls the "method *à priori*," which means "reasoning from an assumed hypothesis" (Mill 2007/1844, p. 325). Mill thought that economics should begin with a hypothesis that humans prefer a greater portion of wealth to a smaller, which can only be obtained by introspection and not amenable for direct refutation through empirical evidence.

This idea was even reinforced under the strong influence of logical empiricism, while the neoclassical economics became increasingly dominant in the twentieth century based on the axiomatic approach. The most important and influential achievement of the neoclassical economics is the (first) fundamental theorem of welfare economics proved by Arrow and Debreu, which states that the resource allocation realized in a competitive equilibrium, if any exists, is always Pareto-efficient. The system of neoclassical economics is based on the assumption that economic agents act rationally combining their own preferences and beliefs, the supposition on which almost no economist cast doubt.

This is the general background against which Vernon Smith embarked on his own experimental research. In retrospect, it is interesting to know that, unlike Chamberlin, he did not try to contend with the competitive equilibrium theory, or the assumption that agents are rational in the market. Rather he tried to complement the theory by examining through experimentation what the theory itself cannot explore. In the competitive theory, Walrasian tâtonnement is supposed to equilibrate markets instantly, whereas in the real markets, there is no such a thing as tâtonnement and transactions therein take place through time. This led Vernon Smith to ask the conditions under which the real markets can simulate the behavior of the theoretical competitive markets.

Thus, his purpose of experimentation is not simply to "test" hypotheses derived from theories but to discover how to organize a market in order to preserve the theoretical prediction (Smith 1962).[2] For this purpose, Vernon Smith invented what is now known as the "double auction," where both sellers and buyers, only knowing their own reservation prices, quote prices, and compared its performance with the "posted offer" mechanism where only sellers are allowed to quote prices. The market performances he examined include the speed of convergence to the theoretical equilibrium price of the experimented market. Markets with various information conditions were also compared.

---

[1] We will later see that the absence of crucial experiments also applies to natural sciences in a sense, a claim known as Duem-Quine thesis.

[2] In a sense, this idea is similar to the one held by current market designers.

In this endeavor, Smith had to keep the laboratory environment as close to theory as possible. We may think of observed outcomes as produced from the combination of human behavior and an institution. Thus, comparing the working of variable institutions requires fixing the human behavior part. This is why his main concern was how to create and control in the laboratories the preferences that are typically assumed by economic theory (Smith 1976, 1982). He thus tried to devise rigorous methodology for economic experiments. The most significant aspect of this is "[s]uch control can be achieved by using a reward structure to induce prescribed monetary value on actions" (Smith 1976, p. 275). The *induced value theory* provides sufficient conditions for a good experimental environment. The commonly cited version of the precepts is summarized as follows (See Friedman and Sunder 1994):

> *Non-satiation*: Subjects always choose the alternative that yields most reward. Hence, utility is a monotone increasing function of the monetary reward.
>
> *Saliency*: Rewards are related appropriately to the realized experimental outcomes.
>
> *Dominance*: The reward structure dominates any subjective costs (or values) associated with participation in the activities of an experiment.

These precepts put economic experiments in sharp contrast with experimentation in psychology. The rewards for participants in economic experiments are usually paid in cash in proportion to the payoffs they earned in the experiment, whereas, in most psychological experiment, they are paid a fixed amount of money regardless of their choice. The important part of a whole experiment that an experimenter is actually interested in may not be open to the participants in psychological experiments, whereas the procedure should basically be open to them in economic experiments.

In fact, Vernon Smith included *privacy* and *parallelism* in addition to the above precepts. To quote Smith himself (Smith 1982, pp. 935–936),

> *Privacy*: Each subject in an experiment is given information only on his/her own payoff alternatives.
>
> …
>
> *Parallelism*: [p]ropositions about the behavior of individuals and the performance of institutions that have been tested in laboratory microeconomies apply also to nonlaboratory microeconomies where similar *ceteris paribus* conditions hold.

Smith considered privacy condition as important because he thought it was "a pervasive characteristic, in varying degrees, of virtually all market institutions in the field" (op. cit.). Recall that his main focus was the study of market mechanisms. Parallelism corresponds to external validity in today's parlance.

Note that it simply does not make sense to create an experimental environment with privacy in experiments in games because most game situations involve direct externality among players' choices. Furthermore, game theory usually assumes that the rule of the game is common knowledge among all the players. This means especially that it is common knowledge among players that the payoffs of all players are known to each other. Thus, experiments in game theory have to embrace precepts slightly different from those in market experiments. However, it is safe to say that game theory experiments have mostly conformed to the induced value theory with this exception.

3 Explanatory Strategies in Experimental Game Theory

It seems that early experiments in game theory aimed at "testing" the validity of equilibrium theories, as exemplified by Dresher and Flood's experiments. This was done by carefully designing experimental environments so that they replicate the theoretical assumptions. As to the key issue of controlling preferences, experiments mostly complied with the precepts given by the induced value theory, so that rewards were usually paid in cash to create enough incentive to seriously maximize their payoffs. Furthermore, since the standard game theory assumes that the rule of the game is common knowledge among players, it was written as clearly as possible in an instruction, which is usually read aloud in front of all participants.

As stated in the history part, however, it soon became clear that experiments in game theory have revealed substantial deviations from theoretical predictions. In retrospect, this is natural, since game theory is inseparably intertwined with agents' behavior, although at a first sight it looks like an equilibrium prediction for an aggregate outcome. In this sense, experimental game theory is closer to behavioral economics than to market experiments. At the same time, however, experimental game theory is different from standard behavioral economics in that game theory necessarily deals with human behavior in *social contexts*.

This is why experiments in game theory constitute a rather self-standing subfield of behavioral game theory (Camerer 2003). In experimental game theory, we have to face two problems simultaneously in order to explain observed behavior in experiments. One is how the *social* contexts may affect people's plays in games. The other is how people with cognitive limits and emotions would behave, the bounded rationality of players in parlance of behavioral economics.[3]

Corresponding to the twofold problems described above, experimental game theory has proposed two different strands of models for explaining observed behavior: (1) models of social preferences, (2) models of bounded rationality. I will now explain both of them in turn.

3.1 *Models of Social Preferences*

As aforementioned, we cannot exclude the influence of social consideration from the game experiments, especially in games involving cooperation and bargaining, such as the ultimatum game, the trust game, the gift exchange game, and the public goods game. That is, however carefully we set up laboratory environments to make them

[3]The concept of bounded rationality was coined and has been developed by Herbert Simon. Thus, the term was accompanied by Simon's own connotations. Richard Thaler used the term "quasi rationality" rather than bounded rationality in the 1980s and 1990s. However, bounded rationality has been increasingly accepted by behavioral economists since the early 2000s. Heukelom (2014, p. 182) vividly describes the historical process where the dichotomy between the descriptive and the normative in terms of Kahneman and Tversky's legacy was transformed to the current one between rationality and bounded rationality in behavioral economics.

resemble the situations modeled by game theory, subjects seem to consider something other than the maximization of their own payoffs. This lead researchers to develop a theory with agents that have other-regarding preferences or social preferences.

In general, those models distinguish players' utility from their own payoff specified in the game, often called material/monetary payoff. Whereas purely self-regarding preferences do not explain the observed behavior in the above games, purely altruistic preferences usually cannot fully explain it. Thus, any proposed models have a mixture of selfishness and altruism. All the models that follow assume that players are rational in the other respects than the specification of their utility. Thus, they all employ equilibrium concepts.

Inequality aversion

Fehr and Schmidt (1999) assumed that agents have inequality-averse preferences. Denoting the material payoff vector of n players by $x = (x_1, \ldots, x_n)$, the Fehr-Schmidt utility function of player i is expressed as

$$U_i(x) = x_i - \alpha_i \frac{1}{n-1} \sum_{j \neq i} \max\{x_j - x_i, 0\} - \beta_i \frac{1}{n-1} \sum_{j \neq i} \max\{x_i - x_j, 0\},$$

where $\alpha_i \geq \beta_i$ and $0 \leq \beta_i < 1$. If the players' payoffs are equal, their utility is maximized at just their own payoff. Thus, this formulation means that the player feels disutility from the difference of payoff among players. The second term of the RHS expresses the disutility from envy, which the player feels when the payoffs of the others are greater than their own. The third term means that the player is altruistic to some extent because he/she feels disutility when he/she earns more than others. Thus, $\alpha_i \geq \beta_i$ implies that envy is greater than altruism.

The prediction of this model depends on the values of parameters α_i and β_i. Fehr and Schmidt (1999) devise a method to statistically estimate these values with experimental data. In general, it is known to explain many findings in games involving social redistribution, such as the ultimatum game, the gift exchange game, and public goods games. Bolton and Ockelfels (2000) offer a related model, where players care about the absolute value of their payoff and their payoff relative to the total payoff of other players.

Theory of Reciprocity

The models of inequality aversion are consequentialist, in that the players modeled their care exclusively about the resultant payoffs of players; they do not care about the perceived type (e.g., altruistic or selfish type) of other players or specific procedures that determine their payoffs. However, in the experiments of the ultimatum game, the responder in the game changes his/her rejection rate depending on the proposal because he/she naturally perceives the intention/motivation of the proposer in the proposal.

To take this aspect into consideration, Rabin (1993) proposes an equilibrium concept, fairness equilibrium, that purports to express the intention-based reciprocal relation between players. Consider a two-player strategic-form game with two choices for each player. Let a_i represent player i's strategy, b_j represent player i's belief about player j's strategy, c_j represent player i's belief about player j's belief about player i's strategy choice, and $\pi_i(a_i, b_j)$ represent the payoff of player i in the original game. The utility function of player i is formulated as follows:

$$u_i(a_i, b_j, c_i) = \pi_i(a_i, b_j) + f_j(b_j, c_i) * [1 + f_i(a_i, b_j)].$$

Here, the reciprocal relation is expressed by $f_j(b_j, c_i)$ and $f_i(a_i, b_j)$. The former is player i's belief about how player j is kind to him/her and given by

$$f_j(b_j, c_i) = \frac{\pi_i(c_i, b_j) - \pi_i^e(c_i)}{\pi_i^h(c_i) - \pi_i^{\min}(c_i)},$$

where $\pi_i^e(c_i) = [\pi_i^h(c_i) + \pi_i^l(c_i)]/2$ is the average of player i's highest and lowest payoffs among points that are Pareto-efficient when he/she plays c_i. $\pi_i^{\min}(c_i)$ is player i's worst payoff. The latter is player i's kindness to player j's, and similarly given by

$$f_i(a_i, b_j) = \frac{\pi_j(b_j, a_i) - \pi_j^e(b_j)}{\pi_j^h(b_j) - \pi_j^{\min}(b_j)}.$$

It is easy to check that $f_i(a_i, b_j)$, $f_j(b_j, c_i) \in [-1, \frac{1}{2}]$. In this utility function, each player i is better off by responding favorably ($f_i(a_i, b_j) > 0$), if player j is also favorable ($f_j(b_j, c_i) > 0$). Similarly, each player i is better off by responding unfavorably ($f_i(a_i, b_j) < 0$), if player j is also unfavorable ($f_j(b_j, c_i) < 0$).

A pair of strategies (a_1, a_2) is a fairness equilibrium if, for $i = 1, 2$, $j \neq i$,

$$a_i \in \arg\max_{\mathrm{a}} u_i(a_i, b_j, c_i); \text{ and}$$
$$c_i = b_i = a_i.$$

The first condition means that each player responds optimally to his/her belief, and the second means their beliefs are consistent.

3.2 Models of Bounded Rationality

In the standard decision theory, agents are supposed to combine two intentional states to come up with a rational behavioral choice: beliefs and preferences. With this framework as a benchmark, we can divide models with bounded rationality into two classes. One introduces "noises" to the preferences of players, the other to their beliefs. We first look at models where noises are introduced to preferences.

Table 2 Prisoner's dilemma game

		Player 2	
		C	*D*
Player 1	*C*	1, 1	−1, 2
	D	2, −1	0, 0

Quantal Response Equilibrium

Solution concepts in game theory usually give "deterministic" prediction of game outcomes. Consider the prisoner's dilemma game as in Table 2, where the actions are labeled as *C* (Cooperation) and *D* (Defect) as usual. The standard theory predicts that players will play the unique dominant strategy *D*. Note that this is a "point prediction" with probability 1 assigned to the strategy profile (D, D), whereas the other outcomes have zero probability of occurrence. This can create a problem when we compare the performance of one prediction with that of another by calculating likelihood using observed data because the value of log-likelihood of probability zero is minus infinity. In statistics, the model to be tested should allocate nonzero probability to any possible outcomes. Another problem from the viewpoint of statistics is that the concepts do not themselves constitute statistical models, which should "contain adjustable parameters" (Sober 2008, p. 79).

The concept of quantal response equilibrium (QRE) proposed by McKelvey and Palfrey (1995) allows us to avoid this problem. The QRE is an equilibrium concept based on boundedly rational strategic behavior, assuming that players play a noisy best response in such a way that a higher frequency is assigned to a strategy that yields higher payoff. One interpretation for the probabilistic play is that players calculate the expected payoffs but makes calculation errors according to some random process, which is the reason for classifying this model into the boundedly rational model of preferences.

For example, the probability of choosing *C* for player 1 in the prisoner's dilemma is formulated as

$$p = \frac{\exp(\lambda \times EU(C))}{\exp(\lambda \times EU(C)) + \exp(\lambda \times EU(D))},$$

where $\lambda \in [0, \infty)$ is supposed to represent the degree of rationality of players and $EU(s)$ denotes expected utility for playing strategy s. A similar equation is formulated for player 2. QRE is the fixed point of these simultaneous equations. Note that if $\lambda = 0$, then players play each of their strategies with equal probability, which is usually called the centroid of the simplex of the strategy space. McKelvey and Palfrey (1995) show that (1) the correspondence QRE(λ) is upper hemicontinuous, (2) the number of QREs is odd for generic values of λ, and (3) generically, the graph (λ, QRE(λ)) contains a unique branch which starts at the centroid and converges to a unique Nash equilibrium as λ goes to infinity. The limiting point of this principal branch is called limiting (logit) QRE.

Thus, limiting QRE can serve as an equilibrium selection criterion. Furthermore, it is indeed easy to calculate with the homotopy approach as developed by Turocy (2005). However, what is important in the present context is that QRE is a statistical model that allows for statistical estimation. Suppose, for example, that N_C is the number of instances in which C is chosen in the prisoner's dilemma experiment, N is the total number of choices, and $p(\lambda)$ is the choice probability of C in QRE corresponding to λ. Then, in the QRE estimation, the following log-likelihood function is maximized with respect to λ:

$$LL = N_C \log p(\lambda) + (N - N_C)\log(1 - p(\lambda))$$

Agent quantal response equilibrium (AQRE) is a model adapted for use in extensive-form games from the QRE for normal-form games (McKelvey and Palfrey 1998). For applications of this concept to centipede games, see McKelvey and Palfrey (1992) and Kawagoe and Takizawa (2012).

Level-*k* and Cognitive Hierarchy models

In contrast with QRE, the level-*k* model finds boundedly rational elements of players in their specification of beliefs. It is a nonequilibrium theory, where players are supposed to identify their preferences correctly and play the best response but may have incorrect beliefs. During the early rounds of experiments, there is no reason that players hold consistent beliefs. Thus, this model is usually interpreted as suitable for explaining players' initial responses to games, reflecting their strategic thinking.

More specifically, the level-*k* model assumes that each subject's decision rules follow one of a small set of a priori plausible types and tries to estimate the distribution of player types that best fits the subject's observed behavior. The types are defined inductively as follows. Type Lk ($k \geq 1$) anchors its belief in type $L0$ and adjusts its belief through thought experiment. More specifically, the $Lk(k \geq 1)$ player responds optimally to the $L(k-1)$ player. This procedure implies that specifying type $L0$, called the anchoring type, is the key to the analysis. Type $L0$ could be fictitious and exist only in the mind of type $L1$ players. Typically, $L0$ is supposed to play all the strategies with equal probabilities. However, a specific strategy may be used for $L0$ if there is an obvious naïve candidate strategy in the game examined.

The level-*k* model has been applied to various games (Stahl and Wilson 1995; Nagel 1995; Ho et al. 1998; Camerer et al. 2004; Costa-Gomes et al. 2001; Costa-Gomes and Crawford 2006; Ellingsen and Östling 2010; Crawford 2003; Kawagoe and Takizawa 2009). In some games, the higher types yields the same strategies used by lower types, which can create an identification problem. Furthermore, when applied to dynamic games, how to determine a best response in the off-the-play path can become problematic. Kawagoe and Takizawa (2012) thus introduced an element of QRE by supposing that players play probabilistically. This technique allows the model to be a statistical model in the sense stated above. Although it is rather difficult to state the findings generally, most results show that the greatest proportion of players is of type $L1$, with $L2$ and $L3$ becoming increasingly rare.

The cognitive hierarchy model (CH) is a generalization of the level-k model (Camerer et al. 2004). In this model, type Lk player assumes that there is a distribution (typically Poisson) of all the lower types of players $L0, \ldots, L(k-1)$. Each type then plays a best response to the distribution of those types.

4 Dealing with Experimental Results

Having conducted experiments and collected data, we are left with the task of stating experimental findings in terms of definite hypotheses. This process is achieved with the help of a wide variety of statistical techniques. Which technique to employ depends on the kind of hypothesis that a researcher has in mind. I divide the basic techniques into three kinds: treatment test, structural models, and the model selection. The system of statistical methods for evaluating experimental results has long been sorted out and is now called *Experimetrics*. I refer the readers to Moffat (2016) for a more comprehensive treatment.

4.1 Treatment Tests

The most basic technique is treatment test. The key feature of the experimental design relevant to the treatment test is whether the experimenter adopts the "between-subject" design or "within-subject" design. In the former case, the subjects are divided into two groups: treatment group, to which the treatment is applied, and control group, to which no treatment is applied. In this case, the focus of interest is the effects of the treatment on the experimental outcomes. Thus, there should be no differences in any characteristics between the treatment group and control group except for the application of the treatment. This is usually implemented by the random assignment of subjects into the two groups, which is why this design is often called randomly controlled trial (RCT). It may be often useful to introduce a third group with a different treatment. If the third group does not show any sign of the effect observed in the treatment group, then the conclusion will be reinforced that the effect observed in the treatment group is attributable to the treatment.

In the within-subject design, each subject participates in experiments with and without treatment or with two different treatments. In this case, experimenters should be careful of the "order effect." Suppose there are two different conditions, *A* and *B* and the observed behavior differed across the two conditions. However, this result may be due to the specific order of the treatments. Thus, in this case, we need to create two randomly assigned groups, one with the order of *AB* and the other *BA*, and compare the outcomes.

In both designs, simple comparison of outcomes with and without treatment will usually suffice for the identification of the effects of different treatments. The statistical techniques employed are standard in this case, whereas the prior experimental design must be done very carefully.

4.2 Structural Models

If the experimenter has some specific behavioral theory in mind, then he/she will use structural models. A structural model is a model that combines a specific theory with a statistical model. Suppose that the experimenter wants to test the level-k model in the previous section, where there is supposed to be a distribution of types with different depths of strategic thinking. In this case, the structural model includes parameters for the depth of strategic thinking as well as those determining a specific distribution of types from the observed data. If agents are supposed to be boundedly rational as in QRE models, then the degree of rationality parameter also has to be included as a parameter.

4.3 Model Selection Theory

Any experimental attempt to test a hypothesis, not only in social sciences but even in natural sciences, is plagued by a difficult problem posed by Duem-Quine thesis. A easy-to-understand version of this thesis states that we cannot test a single hypothesis in isolation because any experimental outcome is the result produced by the mixture of the hypothesis to be tested and auxiliary hypothesis. The experimental environments we set up do not only include the conditions that the hypothesis to be tested presupposes (denoted as A), but also extra conditions (denoted as B) such as specific experimental settings and devices. Suppose we theoretically expect to have $A \supset C$ and experimental results show $\neg C$.[4] Under the actual experimental conditions, however, what we actually tested is not $A \supset C$, but $A \bigwedge B \supset C$. Thus, even if the experimental data clearly suggests $\neg C$, this does not necessarily mean that we should refute the target hypothesis. The results may have come from the presence of extra conditions B. In addition, it may be extremely difficult to enumerate all the conditions in B in reality.

Furthermore, even if there are two alternative hypotheses that are against each other and evidence suggests the falsity of one of them, we cannot convincingly conclude that the other hypothesis is true. This is because, in empirical sciences, there can always be a third hypothesis. This situation makes it very difficult to identify the single most plausible behavioral model from among the ones we overviewed in the previous section.

The problems described above are so fundamental that any researcher cannot escape from them by any means. However, this does not mean that we cannot say

[4]Here $\supset$ denotes implication.

anything conclusive. As Duem himself thought, scientific findings are up to the judgement of scientists who try to find the mechanism behind observed phenomena with their own "sense."

One way out of this conundrum is to employ the techniques developed in the model selection theory in statistics, of course with appropriate qualifications. According to Sober (2008), Akaike (1973) is the seminal paper that founded this area of research. Akaike's basic idea is that we can compare statistical models by looking at the relative information lost when a given model is used to represent the process that generated the data. The Akaike information criterion (AIC), based on information theory, is an estimator of the relative quality of statistical models for a given data set. Thus, we can compare the performance of models, even if we do not know the true model.

Suppose we have a statistical model, as defined in Sect. 3.2 that has adjustable parameters. Let k be the number of estimated parameters in this model and $\hat{L}$ be the maximized value of the likelihood function. The value of AIC is defined as follows:

$$\mathrm{AIC} = 2k - 2\ln\,\hat{L}.$$

The lower the value of AIC, the relatively better the model is. It is interesting to note that this criterion not only rewards goodness of fit in terms of likelihood function but also penalizes using more parameters. Its derivation implies, unlike the usual supposition, that AIC can be used to compare models that are not nested with each other. The Bayesian information criterion (BIC) is similar in spirit to AIC but has a slightly different formula for penalizing overfitting, $\ln(n)k$ instead of $2k$. Kawagoe and Takizawa (2012) used AIC and BIC to compare the performance of a group of models related to level-k as well as AQRE and its variant models with altruistic type.

5 Conclusion

The present chapter has outlined the main issues arising in the laboratory experiment in game theory with the focus on its own aim and methodology. Experimental game theory is similar to behavioral economics in that it aims to elucidate real human behaviors, but the main difference lies in its focus on behaviors in the social contexts. This adds to some complication to this subject. Nevertheless, we have accumulated a host of experimental results in game experiments, finding stylized facts in various games. We also have invented techniques to muddle through the identification difficulties, and several candidate behavioral models, such as models with social preference or bounded rationality, have been submitted for explanation of experimental results. Admittedly, plausible models differ depending on contexts; generally, social preference models perform better than models based on bounded rationality in the context that involve cooperation and social redistribution.

In spite of those difficulties, however, I believe that elucidating human behavior in social contexts is gaining importance, especially because it is related to the deepest nature of human being, i.e., creating institutional facts. Thus, I would like to invite many young researchers to this field of study, looking forward to its further development.

References

Akaike, H. (1973), Information theory as an extension of the maximum likelihood principle. In B. Petrov, & F. Csaki (Eds.), *Second international symposium on information theory* (pp. 267–81). Budapest: Akademiai Kiado.

Bolton, G., & Ockenfels, A. (2000). ERC: A theory of equity, reciprocity, and competition. *American Economic Review, 90,* 166–193.

Camerer, C. (2003). *Behavioral Game Theory: Experiments in Strategic Interaction*. Princeton, NJ: Princeton University Press.

Camerer, C., Ho, T.-H., & Chong, J.-K. (2004). A cognitive hierarchy model of games. *Quarterly Journal of Economics, 119*, 861–898.

Chamberlin, E. H. (1948). An experimental imperfect market. *Journal of Political Economy, 56,* 95–108.

Costa-Gomes, M., & Crawford, V. (2006). Cognition and behavior in two-person guessing games: An experimental study. *American Economic Review, 96,* 1737–1768.

Costa-Gomes, M., Crawford, V., & Broseta, B. (2001). Cognition and behavior in normal-form games: An experimental study. *Econometrica, 69,* 1193–1235.

Crawford, V. (2003). Lying for strategic advantage: Rational and boundedly rational misrepresentations of intentions. *American Economic Review, 93,* 133–149.

Dhami, S. (2016). *The Foundations of Behavioral Economic Analysis*. Oxford, UK: Oxford University Press.

Ellingsen, T., & Östling, R. (2010). When does communication improve coordination? *American Economic Review, 100,* 1695–1724.

Fehr, E., & Schmidt, K. (1999). A theory of fairness, competition, and cooperation. *Quarterly Journal of Economics, 114,* 817–869.

Flood, M. (1958). Some experimental games. *Management Science, 5,* 5–26.

Friedman, D., & Sunder, S. (1994). *Experimental Methods: A Primer for Economists*. Cambridge, UK: Cambridge University Press.

Heukelom, F. (2014). *Behavioral Economics: A History*. New York, NY: Cambridge University Press.

Ho, T.-H., Camerer, C., & Weigelt, K. (1998). Iterated dominance and iterated best response in experimental 'P-Beauty contest'. *American Economic Review, 39,* 649–660.

Kagel, J. H., & Roth, A. E. (Eds.). (1995). *The Handbook of Experimental Economics*. Princeton, New Jersey: Princeton University Press.

Kahneman, D., & Tversky, A. (1979). Prospect theory: An analysis of decision under risk. *Econometrica, 47*, 263–291.

Kawagoe, T., & Takizawa, H. (2009). Equilibrium refinement vs. level-*k* analysis: An experimental study of cheap-talk games with private information. *Games and Economic Behavior, 66,* 238–255.

Kawagoe, T., & Takizawa, H. (2012). Level-*k* analysis of experimental centipede games. *Journal of Economic Behavior & Organization, 82,* 548–566.

McKelvey, R., & Palfrey, T. (1992). An experimental study of the centipede game. *Econometrica, 60,* 803–836.

McKelvey, R., & Palfrey, T. (1995). Quantal response equilibria for normal form games. *Games and Economic Behavior, 10,* 6–38.

McKelvey, R., & Palfrey, T. (1998). Quantal response equilibria for extensive form games. *Experimental Economics, 1,* 9–41.
Mill, J. S. (2007/1844). On the definition of political economy; and on the method of 'investigation proper to it. In *Collected works of John Stuart Mill* (Vol. 4). Liberty Fund, Indianapolis, Indiana.
Moffatt, P. (2016). *Experimetrics: Econometrics for Experimental Economics*. Palgrave: London, UK.
Nagel, R. (1995). Unraveling in guessing games: An experimental study. *American Economic Review, 85,* 1313–1326.
Nash, J. (1951). Non-cooperative games. *Annals of Mathematics, 54,* 286–295.
Rabin, M. (1993). Incorporating fairness into game theory and economics. *American Economic Review, 83,* 1281–1302.
Roth, A. E. (1995). Introduction to experimental economics. In Kagel, & Roth (Eds.), *The handbook of experimental economics* (pp. 3–109). Princeton: NJ: Princeton University Press.
Roth, A. E., Prasnikar, V., Okuno-Fujiwara, M., Zamir, S. (1991). Bargaining and market behavior in Jerusalem, Ljubljana, Pittsburg, and Tokyo: An experimental study. *American Economic Review, 81*, 1068–1095.
Savage, L. (1954). *The Foundations of Statistics*. New York: Wiley.
Smith, V. (1962). An experimental study of competitive market behavior. *Journal of Political Economy, 70,* 111–137.
Smith, V. (1976). Experimental economics: Induced value theory. *American Economic Review, 66,* 274–279.
Smith, V. (1982). Microeconomic system as an experimental science. *American Economic Review, 72,* 923–955.
Sober, E. (2008). *Evidence and Evolution: The Logic behind the Science*. Cambridge, UK: Cambridge University Press.
Stahl, D., & Wilson, P. (1995). On players' model of other players: Theory and experimental evidence. *Games and Economic Behavior, 10,* 218–254.
Steiglitz, K. (2007). *Snipers, Shills, and Sharks: eBay and Human Behavior*. Princeton, NJ: Princeton University Press.
Turocy, T. (2005). A dynamic homotopy interpretation of the logistic quantal response equilibrium correspondence. *Games and Economic Behavior, 51,* 243–263.
Von Neumann, J., & Morgenstern, O. (1944). *Theory of Games and Economic Behavior*. Princeton, NJ: Princeton University Press.

The Field Experiment Revolution in Development Economics

Yasuyuki Sawada and Takeshi Aida

1 Introduction

"Once upon a time there was a field called development economics"—by this Paul Krugman started his review article on development economics a quarter century ago (Krugmran 1993). "That field no longer exists," he also added. The 1940s and 1950s were the eras of "high development theory" when development economics became one of the top fields in economics armed with a distinctive set of new ideas stressing pecuniary externalities arising from increasing returns technologies and imperfect market competition (Krugman 1993). Aspiration for economic independence among newly independent countries around the world also facilitated emergence of development economics as a unique and highly policy-oriented field in economics. Unfortunately, the high development theory could not continue due to its failure in formulating consistent mathematical models. Also, during the 1970s and 1980s, the main ideas had rejected empirically because the high development theory's policy recommendation of the import-substituting industrialization did not work in the real world. Development economics as a distinctive field was crowded out of the mainstream of economics. Indeed, until the end of the twentieth century, development economics definitely ranked lower than other fields of economics. To endorse this, Leijonfhufvud (1973) stated in his celebrated article titled "Life among the Econ" that:

> The priestly caste (the Math-Econ) for example, is a higher "field" than either Micro or Macro, while the Develops just as definitely rank lower. Second, we know that these caste-rankings (where they can be made) are not permanent but may change over time. There is

Y. Sawada (✉)
Asian Development Bank and Faculty of Economics, University of Tokyo, Tokyo, Japan
e-mail: ysawada@adb.org

T. Aida
Institute of Developing Economies, Japan External Trade Organization (IDE-JETRO), Chiba, Japan
e-mail: Takeshi_Aida@ide.go.jp

T. Kawagoe and H. Takizawa (eds.), *Diversity of Experimental Methods in Economics*,
https://doi.org/10.1007/978-981-13-6065-7_3

evidence, for example, that both the high rank assigned to the Math-Econ and the low rank of the Develops are, historically speaking, rather recent phenomena. The rise of the Math-Econ seems to be associated with the previously noted trend among all the Econ towards more ornate, ceremonial models, while the low rank of the Develops is due to the fact that this caste, in recent times, has not strictly enforced the taboos against association with the Policies, Sociogs, and other tribes.

As we can see, economics research has placed its fundamental emphasis on the formal model making. Inevitably, interdisciplinary approach with other areas of social sciences, which were much less formal than economics, was not welcomed in economics. Mathematical modeling approach did not flourish in development economics. Rather the filed engaged in interdisciplinary research with political science, sociology, and anthropology for more policy- or field-oriented studies. Accordingly, development economics became discriminated substantially by the mainstream filed in economics.

Entering into the twenty-first century, development economics was resuscitated, becoming one of the most popular and prestigious fields in economics. Professor Esther Duflo of Massachusetts Institute of Technology (MIT) won the John Bates Clark medal, so-called a stepping-stone of the Nobel economics prize, in 2010 for her definitive contributions to the field of development economics. Many academic papers in development filed started appearing in top five economics journals, i.e., *Econometrica*, *American Economic Review*, *Journal of Political Economy*, *Quarterly Journal of Economics*, and *Review of Economic Studies*. Furthermore, development economics papers have been published not only in these top economics journals but also in general science journals such as *Science*, *Nature*, and *PNAS* (e.g., Banerjee et al. 2013, 2015a, b, c; Dupas 2014; Guiteras et al. 2015). Moreover, best Ph.D. candidates in economics department at top institutions such as MIT, Yale, and Harvard now specialize in development economics.[1] Development economics definitely became one of the very top fields in economics.

What happened? This chapter aims to uncover determinants of this drastic change in the academic status of development economics. The main driving force behind the restoration of development economics is the dominance of experimental approach exemplified by the impact evaluation of development projects using randomized control trials or RCTs (Banerjee and Duflo 2011; Karlan and Appel 2011). Field experiments revolutionized development economics.

2 The Field Experiment Revolution in Development Economics

The most notable approach in modern development economics is employing a field experiment as a scientific method to experimentally examine the causal effect of

[1] In 2013, 6 out of 18 job candidates at MIT, and 5 out of 15 at Yale majored in development economics.

Table 1 Papers in top five economics journals

Year	Total # of papers	# of development papers	# of which are RCTs
2015	271	32	10
2000	215	21	0
1990	278	17	0

http://live.worldbank.org/the-state-of-economics-the-state-of-the-world

a (policy) intervention D on an outcome Y in the real world rather than in the laboratory. The policy intervention is often formalized by a discrete variable with an indicator function taking one if the argument is true and zero otherwise, $1[.]$: $D = 1$ [a policy is placed]. A most straightforward way to measure the causal effect of a policy is to regress Y on D. However, as is well known, we cannot recover the average treatment effect on the treated (ATT) by this approach. This regression coefficient is basically the observed mean difference of outcome with treatment, Y_1, and that without treatment, Y_0: $E[Y_1|D=1] - E[Y_0|D=0] = (E[Y_1|D=1] - E[Y_0|D=1]) + (E[Y_0|D=1] - E[Y_0|D=0])$. Hence, the mean difference is a summation of the true policy effect, $\delta = E[Y_1|D=1] - E[Y_0|D=1]$ which is called the average treatment effect on the treated (ATT), and the selection bias, $\gamma = E[Y_0|D=1] - E[Y_0|D=0]$. In other words, the simple regression coefficient gives us a mixture of the ATT and selection bias, making it difficult to identify the true policy effect unless we can eliminate the selection bias. RCT is a method which, by nature, sets zero selection bias by randomly assigning the treatment. The selection bias becomes zero due to the law of large numbers, $\gamma = E[Y_0|D=1] - E[Y_0|D=0] = 0$. Hence, data obtained from an RCT enables us to estimate an ATT parameter by simply regressing an outcome, Y, on a treatment dummy, D.[2]

Indeed, the introduction of the RCT-based research strategy has improved the status of development economics within economics science substantially. Table 1 summarizes the number of papers in top five economics journals. The total number of articles is almost the same in 1990 and 2015. However, the number of development economics papers has nearly doubled over the 25 years. Among these development papers, ten articles employed RCT—most of the increase in development economics papers can be explained by the advent of RCT-based research projects.

In the real world, however, people in a policy treatment may not comply with the treatment. Then, a natural question is what will happen if an RCT is implemented with imperfect compliance, i.e., the actual participation to the program is endogenous even if the assignment to treatment and control group is exogenous. In this case, a comparison between treatment and control groups yields the intention-to-treat (ITT)

[2]Glewwe et al. (2004) compared the impact of using "flip charts" in Kenyan schools, finding that the estimated impact was significantly positive for non-RCT data, whereas the impact for RCT data was insignificant, implying that the selection bias is very serious.

effect, which can be very different from ATT of the program. However, even in this case, we can estimate the ATT among the compliers. Under certain assumptions, Imbens and Angrist (1994) show that the local average treatment effect (LATE) can be estimated as LATE $= \frac{E[Y|Z=1]-E[Y|Z=0]}{E[D|Z=1]-E[D|Z=0]}$. Note that even if an RCT is implemented with imperfect compliance, we can estimate the LATE as the ITT divided by the difference between the probability of being treated for those who are in the treatment group and those who are in the control group. An important implication of this theorem is that we can estimate LATE using the random assignment of the program (Z) as an instrumental variable for the actual program participation (D). Therefore, RCT can also be interpreted as creating strictly exogenous instrumental variables to estimate a policy effect we are interested in.

Making the ATT visible, a powerful nature of RCTs is that they allow policy-makers to use the scientific evidence from these rigorous evaluations by comparing cost-effectiveness of different policy interventions. Figure 1 compares cost-effectiveness of projects and programs in education, measured in terms of extended years of schooling with 100 US Dollars spending in each intervention. Studies include deworming programs in Kenya, conditional cash transfers in Mexico, providing free uniforms in Kenya, and providing information to parents in Madagascar showing a variety of cost-effectiveness in extending years of schooling. We should note that these cost-effectiveness comparisons by themselves do not necessarily provide sufficient information for policy-makers to make actual policy decisions because they often take into account multiple objectives and policy feasibility at the same time. For example, even with a relatively high unit cost in extending years of schooling, the conditional cash transfers would be considered positively because such transfers will also act as broader social protection. In any case, rigorous evidence created by RCTs facilitates evidence-based policy-making process through constructive collaboration between policy-makers and researchers.

3 Lab-in-the-Filed Experiment

Another important strand in development economics to employ experimental method can be traced back to the dominant view of "poor but efficient" in neoclassical economics toward the poor in developing countries (Schultz 1964). In this view, the poor are poor because of the constraints, not because they are irrational and do not try very hard. Market frictions and other binding constraints on rational agents can also explain the common paradox of peasant household behavior which is characterized by coexisting "external stability" of low elasticity of supply response to price incentives and "internal stability" of large swings in the shadow prices of labor and food (de Janvry et al. 1991).

The "poor but efficient" view also induced lab-in-the-field experiments approach (Gneezy and Imas 2017) in investigating people's behavior in developing countries in accordance with the development of behavioral and experimental economics. The role of nonstandard, as well as standard, preference parameters has become popular

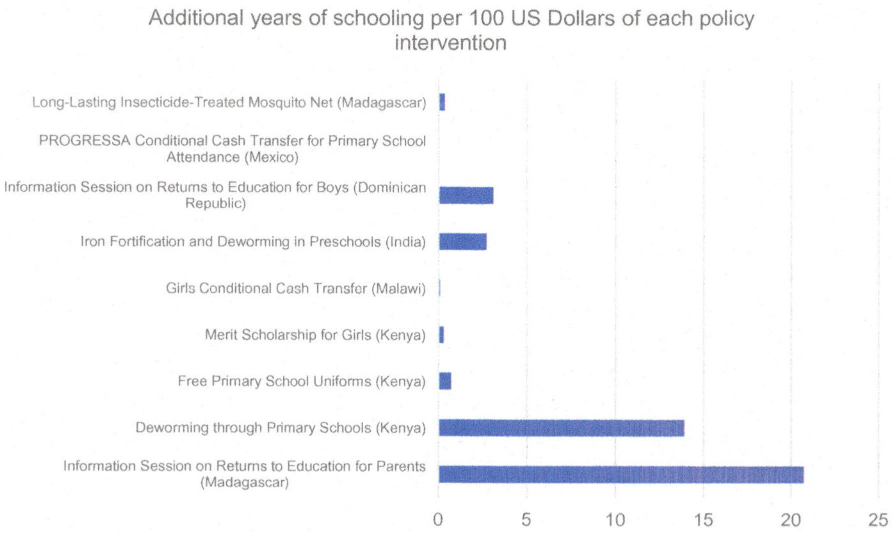

Fig. 1 Comparison of cost-effectiveness of different education interventions (*Source* Dhaliwal et al. 2013; Yamasaki et al. 2018)

in recent development economics. One of the earliest works to elicit preference parameter by economic experiment is Binswanger (1980). In this study, he employed a gambling game to calculate the risk aversion parameter of farmers in South India, finding a negative but insignificant relationship between risk aversion parameter and wealth. After this seminal study to elicit preference parameters in the field, numerous lab-in-the-filed experiments have been conducted in developing countries (Cardenas and Carpenter 2008). For example, Pender (1996) elicited subjective discount rate in rural India, the same areas studied by Binswanger (1980), finding a negative correlation with wealth level. Tanaka et al. (2010) conducted risk and time preference experiments in Vietnam and found that household income is correlated with the degree of patience but not with risk parameters.

Another set of important nonstandard preference parameters is social preferences which include various prosocial components of preferences such as altruism, trust, reciprocity, and fairness, which have been set out of scope in the traditional neoclassical economics. However, these social preferences can be an essential instrument to complement market and government failure in developing countries (e.g., Bowles and Herbert Gintis 2002; Hayami 1989). In behavioral and experimental economics, there is an established correspondence between each type of social preference and experimental games to measure them: dictator game for altruism, ultimatum game for fairness, public goods game for voluntary reciprocal cooperation, and trust game for trust and trustworthiness (Camerer and Fehr 2004; Levitt and List 2007). Basically, these games elicit different prosocial behaviors by measuring deviation from the Nash equilibrium of each game played by egoistic individuals. As case studies from developing countries, Barr (2003) found that trust tends to be lower in communities where trustworthiness is low. Aoyagi et al. (2014) showed that being embedded in an irrigation system foster trust among farmers. Sawada et al. (2016) found that implementation of a school-based management program in education significantly increases social capital between parents and teachers. A systematic review by Cardenas and Carpenter (2008) surveyed the results of these experimental games around the world, finding that the amount sent in trust game is positively correlated with GDP growth rate and negatively correlated with poverty, Gini coefficient, and unemployment rate. These results suggest that prosocial behavior plays a critical role in facilitating a country's development, amending market and government failures.

In addition to the abovementioned type of study focusing on the determinants of risk, time, and social preferences, there is a type of study which uses the preference parameters elicited by economic experiments to predict various kinds of socioeconomic behavior and outcomes. Specifically, this type of study uses the results of economic experiments as independent variables of regression models to capture the direct relationship between preference parameters and real-world behavior and outcomes. From a viewpoint of estimating econometric models, this use of experimental results is also important because exclusion of these variables potentially causes omitted variable bias in estimated regression coefficients. For example, Ashraf et al. (2006) showed existence of sophisticated hyperbolic discounters in the Philippines: those who have time-inconsistent preference tend to take up commitment device for saving. Using experimental data from China, Liu (2013) found that risk averse and loss averse farmers tend to adopt a new technology, i.e., genetically modified variety of cotton, later. As for social preferences in developing countries, it has been demonstrated that the degree of prosocial behavior elicited by experimental games has positive correlation with common pool resource management (Bouma et al. 2008; Fehr and Leibbrandt 2011; Kosfeld and Rustagi 2015; Sawada et al. 2013; Aida 2018): the repayment rate in microcredit (Karlan 2005); workers' earnings and productivity (Barr and Serneels 2008; Goto et al. 2015); and household expenditure (Carter and Castillo 2011).

Yet, the literature of lab-in-the-field experiments in developing countries is still its infancy. Continued efforts to validate the experimental results must be needed. In contrast to these existing studies, a recent paper by Chuang and Schechter (2015) test the stability of individuals' choices in panel data of experiments and surveys from rural Paraguay over almost a decade. They found that while answers to preference survey questions are quite stable, experimental measures of risk, time, and social preferences do not exhibit much stability, suggesting that in a developing country context researchers should explore designing simpler experiments and including survey questions in addition to experiments to measure preferences.

4 Modern Empirical Methods in Economics

As we have seen, new experimental methods such as RCT and LATE play an extremely significant role in modern development economics. However, this trend is not specific to development economics: instead, it reflects more profound "revolution" in the entire empirical economic research. Hamermesh (2013) shows the long-run shift of economic research from theory-driven approach to empirical-oriented research by summarizing the articles published in top three journals in economics, i.e., *American Economic Review*, *Journal of Political Economy*, and *Quarterly Journal of Economics*. Figure 2 shows his data on number of articles published in these top three economics journals, classified by methodological type. While we see that theory papers dominated in economics in the 1960s, 1970s, and 1980s, the share of theoretical studies has declined substantially and become less than half over the five decades. In contrast, the share of empirical studies using own data has grown especially in the last 20 years. In addition, the steady increase of experimental studies should also be noted.

After the 1990s, indeed, these social experiments have gained popularity in labor, public, medical, and environmental economics as well as development economics. Recent features of the experiments are not only to test economic theories, but also to evaluate the impacts of a policy intervention and to reflect the results into the actual policy-making. Behind this trend are the controlled experiments in natural science and evidence-based medicine (EBM). In the field of development economics, this trend can be also found from the fact that World Bank's flagship publication, *World Development Report*, featured experimental and behavioral economics in 2015 (World Bank 2015).

In order to better understand this drastic "empiricalization" in economics, we can set up an encompassing picture of the modern empirical economics methodologies. Figure 3 extends the taxonomy of empirical economic studies made by Levitt and List (2009). The vertical axis classifies the relationship with economic theory: subjective or partial equilibrium and general equilibrium approaches. The horizontal

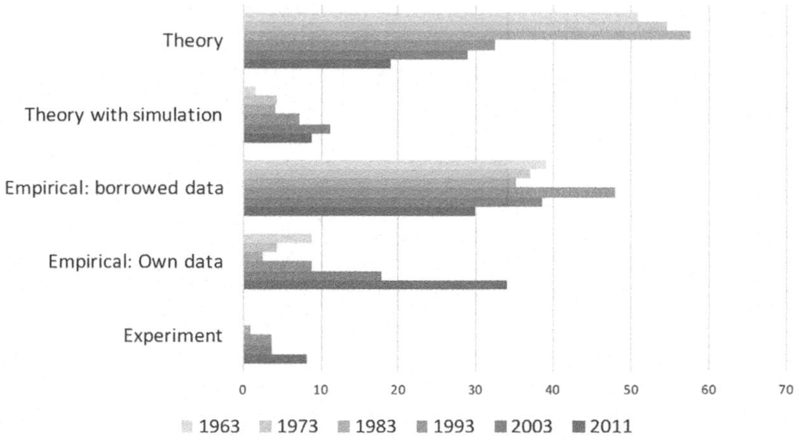

Fig. 2 Number of articles published in top three economics journals by methodological type (*Data source* Hamermesh 2013)

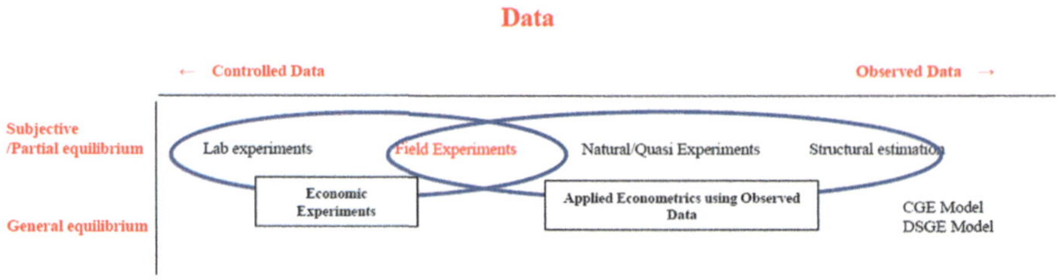

Fig. 3 Typology of empirical economic research (*Source* The authors' augmentation of the typology of Levitt and List 2009)

axis classifies the type of data used for the analysis. The left side is the data collected under a controlled situation, and the right side is the observed data occurring from natural context.

In a lab experiment located on the left end, a researcher can assign the treatment and control groups in the most controlled situation, and thus there is comparatively little room for other factors to confound the outcome. In a lab experiment, therefore, a high level of the internal validity can be achieved more or less. The research using lab experiments have often rejected the assumptions and results of the conventional economic theories, leading to evolution of new theories especially in the area of behavioral economics. In this way, behavioral economics research has progressed substantially, going hand in hand with development of experimental economics.

However, the main limitation of the lab experiment is in external validity of its findings because there is no guarantee that the behavior in lab experiments can be extended to the real-world behaviors. Especially, lab experiment tends to rely on subjects of college students in developed countries which are called "Western, Educated, Industrialized, Rich, and Democratic (WEIRD)" societies, limiting its external validity to other societies and subjects (Henrich et al. 2010). Also, the topics that can be analyzed by lab experiments are rather narrow by nature. For example, it is difficult to design and implement experiments to test the long-term, aggregate impact of a policy intervention.

In order to overcome these problems of the lab experiment at least partially, the methods of field experiments have been developed further. A field experiment is defined as an experiment where researchers manipulate to create exogenous variations in a naturally occurring situation rather than in a laboratory setting (Harrison and List 2004). Following Levitt and List (2009), field experiments can be classified into three categories: artefactual field experiment (AFE), framed field experiment (FFE), and natural field experiment (NFE). AFE refers to lab experiments employing "nonstandard," i.e., non-student subjects such as traders and farmers.[3] In contrast to this artificiality of the experimental intervention in AFE such as risk, time discounting, and other experiments on social preferences, FFE introduces interventions in a natural situation where subjects are asked to take more realistic tasks in experiments.

[3]This type of experiment also includes lab-in-the-field experiment (Gneezy and Imas 2017).

However, in FFE, subjects are basically aware that they are subjects to an experiment, causing them to behave differently from the everyday real-world setting. A notable example of such a deviation from a real-world behavior is the Hawthorne effect studied in social phycology. To avoid this effect, NFE conduct interventions without letting the subjects know that they are part of an experiment. Policy interventions using RCTs fall into the category of FFE and NFE.

Although RCT is a powerful tool to evaluate development programs, it is far from a panacea in pursuing evidence-based development policy-making. There are several fundamental limitations about RCT-based program evaluation (Ravallion 2012). First, even if a project has a significantly positive impact on the people's welfare, it does not necessarily mean that the project has the same effect in different time and different place. Basically, this is an issue of external validity of experimental results. To discuss the external validity problem, it is imperative to carry out systematic replication studies or systematic reviews (Banerjee and Duflo 2009). The general equilibrium effect is a serious lack of external validity when an intervention is scaled up. For example, Mobarak and Rosenzweig (2014) showed that providing insurance only to land-owning cultivators can aggravate the welfare of wage laborers through the changes in labor market conditions. Therefore, even if the impact of a project is confirmed by RCT, verifying a significant partial equilibrium effect, scaling up the project requires careful consideration on this issue of general equilibrium effect created through feedback mechanisms in an actual social and economic system. Second, there are several important issues in which conducting RCT is very difficult by nature. For example, construction of large-scale infrastructure is difficult to randomize, although its effect is expected to be quite extensive. In contrast, RCT is more suitable for small-scale interventions such as training, education, health care, and financial services. Third, ethical issues about RCT should be noted carefully. Strict implementation of RCT forces unwilling subject in the treatment group to participate and willing subject in the control group not to participate. Therefore, it is essential to share enough information on the intervention with the subjects and to obtain informed consent from them.

Considering the pros and cons of these experimental approaches, it is also important to identify the causal effect from nonexperimental "observed data" without making a full-fledged RCT-based experiment. Econometric methods have been developed to analyze observed data, and standard econometrics textbooks have a list of available methodologies to analyze these observed data (Griliches 1986). A recent trend of analyzing observed data is to employ a carefully designed reduced-form model by setting a set of clear identification assumptions (e.g., Angrist and Pischke 2010; White and Raitzer 2017). Such quasi-experimental methods include regression discontinuity design (RDD), difference in difference (DID), propensity score matching (PSM), and instrumental variable approach (IV). Among these, the method which takes advantage of a naturally occurring exogenous change is called a natural experiment (e.g., Rosenzweig and Wolpin 2000). When successful, precision of these empirical approaches has been regarded as being comparable to that of RCT.

In broader empirical economic research, these experimental and quasi-experimental methodologies have brought so-called "credibility revolution," which demands more clearly articulated research design to identify casuality (Angrist and Pischke 2010). This revolution corresponds to the conventionally controlled experiments in natural science and evidence-based medicine (EBM) in medical science. Economics has a long tradition of positive and normative approach to analyze socioeconomic issues. The recent development of experimental and quasi-experimental approaches has added "active" analysis to this tradition, i.e., the collaboration of proactive research and actual policy interventions. In this sense, the field of economics has been moving forward to a more rigorous, full-set "science" field (Chetty 2013).[4]

The development of (quasi) experimental approach in economics has brought a significant change not only in the research topic or methodologies but also how to carry out actual research. Rath and Wohlrabe (2016) showed the time trend of relative shares of co-authorship in economics. In the year 1991, the average number of authors per paper in economics was 1.56 in 1991, which has increased to 2.23 in 2012. There has been a continuous decline in the share of single-authored papers and an increase in the papers written by two or more authors. This trend indicates the clear surge of team orientation in conducting economic research. One of the most decisive reasons behind this trend is credibility revolution in empirical economics.

As we have seen above, both experimental and quasi-experimental approaches are the main driver of "emipiricalization," "scientification," and "team-orientation" in economics. However, in many cases, it is not straightforward to conduct experiment or to find quasi-experimental situation to analyze and understand mechanisms behind the impact of a project. A natural response to this limitation of experimental approaches is to superimpose a "structure" of economic theories on the observed data set and uncover the causal mechanisms empirically. More specifically, researchers can formulate a mathematical model of agents' decision-making and recover the "deep parameter" of the model from observed data, which can be used to understand the causal impact of a project. This approach is called "structural estimation' approach (e.g., Keane and Wolpin 2009).

There has been a hot debate between "structuralist" and "experimentalist" on the credibility of the estimation results (Keane 2010). While RCT and quasi-experimental approaches have a high level of internal validity in the estimation results, structuralists criticize that these highly reduced-form approaches do not have external validity as the causal mechanisms are treated as a black box. In contrast, since the results from structural estimation rely on the assumed theoretical model, experimentalists have been criticizing the use of untested strong assumptions. However, these two approaches are not necessarily competing nor conflicting with each other. Instead, recent literature tries to overcome the limitation of both sides by consolidating RCT and structural approaches. For example, Todd and Wolpin (2006) validated out-of-sample performance of a dynamic structural model for counterfactuals using control

[4]Chetty (2013) stated that economics became a science: *These examples are not anomalous. And as the availability of data increases, economics will continue to become a more empirical, scientific field. In the meantime, it is simplistic and irresponsible to use disagreements among economists on a handful of difficult questions as an excuse to ignore the field's many topics of consensus and its ability to inform policy decisions on the basis of evidence instead of ideology.*

group data of an RCT-based experiment. This hybrid approach also enables us to compute the general equilibrium effect using RCT which was not possible only with RCT-based data (Attanasio et al. 2012; Duflo et al. 2012; Chetty 2009; Todd and Wolpin 2006). After all, it is important for researchers to reaffirm the fact that a field experiment is just one of the many methodologies available in empirical economics. Depending on the topic and issues to be investigated, a researcher should adopt mixed research strategies by combining different methods optimally.

Most of the abovementioned methods are subjective or partial equilibrium approaches, in the sense that researchers (implicitly) focus on the direct causal effect between the treatment and outcome. While it is beyond the scope of this chapter, there are several general equilibrium approaches such as traditional models of computable general equilibrium (CGE) and more recently developed dynamic stochastic general equilibrium (DSGE) models which have been developed in macroeconomics to tackle general equilibrium effects explicitly.

5 Poverty Trap

Let us illustrate how this revolution in experimental approach has extended the scope of development economics. As the first theorem of welfare economics states, equilibrium in a perfectly competitive market is Pareto efficient. However, in reality, markets are far from perfect due to legitimate reasons such as asymmetric information, externalities, missing markets, imperfect property rights, and so on. In addition, even if the markets are perfect, the first theorem does not assure the socially desired level of equality in the resource allocation. Therefore, the problem of poverty cannot be solved by the market basically. In order to fix these market failures and poverty issue, governmental interventions are called for.

While a variety of experimental or quasi-experimental approach enables us to identify cost-effective policy interventions in a rigorous manner, it does not necessarily mean that these interventions actually reach to the end users in the real world. For example, in the area of preventive health care, several effective interventions such as bed nets for malaria, immunization for infectious diseases, and oral rehydration solution for diarrhea have been identified scientifically. However, there is no guarantee that these technologies are delivered to the people who are in need for sure. Indeed, the price elasticities of these services are known to be very high (Dupas and Miguel 2016), letting people shy away from their use. Inventing these effective treatments and delivering these interventions to end users involve quite different issues. This issue is so-called "the last one-mile problem" (Dupas 2014). The last one-mile problem highlights importance of considering effective interventions to correct market failure and to tackle psychological factors which prevent the poor from moving out of poverty.

Broadly speaking, poverty has always been a central issue in development economics. Typically, poverty has been captured by the incidence of poverty, i.e., the proportion of people whose income is below a well-defined poverty line. Now, 1.9

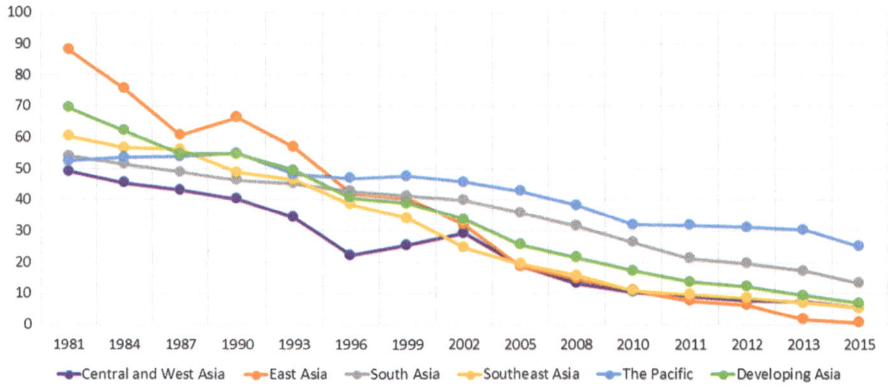

Fig. 4 Trend of incidence of poverty in Asia and the Pacific region (in %; 1.9 USD Poverty Line) (*Data* PovcalNet: the online tool for poverty measurement developed by the Development Research Group of the World Bank. http://iresearch.worldbank.org/PovcalNet/povDuplicateWB.aspx)

USD a day per person is taken as an international poverty line. As we can see from Fig. 4, there has also been a significant reduction in poverty incidence in all subregions of Asia and the Pacific region. From 1981 to 2015, poverty incidence fell really dramatically in East Asia from 88.2 to 0.7%. Yet, we still observe persistent poverty, especially in the Pacific and South Asia subregions. Also, issues such as rising inequality, growing environmental pressures, and rapid urbanization should be addressed. In eradicating extreme poverty, it will be imperative to understand a poverty trap.

Traditionally, wide variety of both theoretical and empirical studies have been conducted to uncover the underlining mechanisms of a poverty trap, describing how poverty causes further poverty. The concept of poverty trap originally dates back to Rosenstein-Rodan (1943), Leibenstein (1954), and Nelson (1956) who formulated a model of a poverty trap created by some type of nonlinear technologies such as increasing returns to scale or inverted S-shaped production function. Figure 5 shows the persistency of poverty in macro-level in the manner of Kraay and McKenzie (2014). The horizontal axis shows the log of GDP per capita in 1960 and the vertical axis shows that in 2014. The observations above the 45-degree line are the country which got better off; in contrast, the observation below the line are the countries which got worse off, and therefore trapped by poverty. These trapped countries are sub-Saharan African countries: Central African Republic, Democratic Republic of the Congo, Guinea, Niger, and Zimbabwe.

More recently, researchers formalized the poverty trap in micro-level arising from incomplete insurance market (Barrett and Carter 2013; Bryan et al. 2013), food market failure (Ravallion 1997; Kraay and Raddatz 2007; Mazumdar 1959; Dasgupta and Ray 1986), credit market failure due to, for example, asymmetric information between lenders and borrowers (Banerjee and Newman 1993), and systematic psychosocial bias (Haushofer and Fehr 2014; Shah et al. 2012).

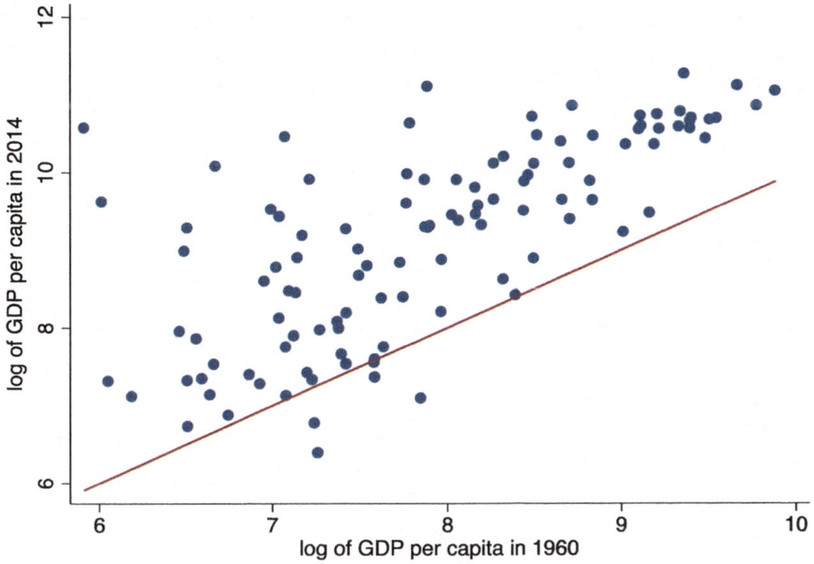

Fig. 5 Real GDP per capita growth 1960–2014 (in 2011 USD adjusted for purchasing power) (*Source* Penn World Table, Version 9.0. https://www.rug.nl/ggdc/productivity/pwt/)

5.1 Credit Market Failure and Microcredit

Let us take an example of microfinance and microcredit programs, which are celebrated policy interventions to complement the credit and other financial market failures, making the poor moving out of the poverty trap. Microfinance is defined as a variety of programs of providing small-scale financial services to the poor, typically without collateralizable assets, who have been excluded from the formal banking and other financial services. Such financial services include credit, saving, insurance, and money transfers of migrants. Among these, "microcredit," a mode of microfinance has attracted wide attention where a typical "microcredit" program is defined as a collateral free small-scale loan program, popularized by Grameen Bank of Bangladesh led by Professor Muhammad Yunus.

As is well known, there is asymmetry in information between lenders and borrowers in credit transactions. This asymmetric information generates three different problems: adverse selection, (ex-ante) moral hazard, and strategic default (or ex-post moral hazard) problems. For adverse selection, lenders cannot distinguish safe borrowers from risky ones. Thus, lenders have to set unified interest rate which makes expected net losses for safe type but expected net gains for risky type due to the limited liability constraint, making only risky borrowers stay in the credit market. In the case of moral hazard, lenders cannot observe borrowers' effort level or cannot enforce the proper use of the loan. Thus, under the limited liability, borrowers have an incentive to invest in high-risk high-return projects and the likelihood of default increases, making borrowers take larger risks with access to the credit program. As for strategic default, lenders cannot observe borrowers' ability to repay the loan, and borrowers have an incentive to default if the penalty is small due to limited liability.

Despite these fundamental asymmetric information problems in credit market, the repayment rate of microfinance is known to be very high even without taking collaterals for enforcement of loan repayment. Researchers have been working to uncover the secret behind this seeming puzzle both theoretically and empirically. The first strand of approach, mostly theoretical, focuses on the role of group lending with joint liability as a mechanism to mitigate asymmetric information problems (Armendáriz de Aghion and Morduch 2005). A typical microfinance requires the borrowers to form repayment groups with joint liability. This scheme exploits the feature that information asymmetry is much less salient among the borrowers than between a lender and a borrower. More specifically, previous studies can be classified into three types of models: peer screening (Armendariz de Aghion and Gollier 2000; Gangopadhyay et al. 2005; Ghatak 1999; Guttman 2008; Van Tassel 1999), peer monitoring (Stiglitz 1990; Banerjee et al. 1994), and peer enforcement by social sanction (Armendariz de Aghion 1999; Besley and Coate 1995). In the peer screening model, borrowers have an incentive to form a group with the same type (i.e., safe–safe or risky–risky type), which mitigates the adverse selection since the groups of risky people cannot make profit due to joint liability. As for peer monitoring, group members will monitor each other's effort level for their investment projects to mitigate moral hazard. This peer monitoring will be incentive compatible because of joint liability nature of the credit program. In the model of peer enforcement, group members will use threat of social ostracism to mitigate strategic default.

In a broader perspective, market failures can be regarded as a standard type of prisoner's dilemma game, where *laissez-faire* cannot achieve social optimal as a Nash equilibrium. A direct way to achieve social optimal is to enforce cooperative behavior by the third party, which is the government in many cases. However, in many developing countries, the enforcement by government is limited. Under such cases, repeated interaction among people and other regarding preferences play an important role to complement the market failure. Therefore, the role of the community, as well as market and government is especially important in developing countries (e.g., Bowles and Herbert Gintis 2002; Hayami 1989; Hayami and Godo 2005). Theoretically, the success of microcredit program can be understood as an effective use of community enforcement mechanisms by the joint liability system in overcoming market and government failures. In fact, Karlan (2005) indicated that high repayment rate of a microcredit program in Peru has been supported by trustworthiness quantified in an incentivized trust game.

In order to test which mechanism is the main channel for the high repayment rate, several studies employ RCT-based field experiments. The results are largely mixed in supporting theoretical implications. Karlan and Zimman (2009) conducted a large-scale RCT in South Africa, finding strong evidence for moral hazard. In contrast, Kono (2014) found that joint liability rather induced strategic default in a field experiment in Vietnam. Furthermore, Giné and Karlan (2014) found no clear difference between group lending and individual lending in an RCT-based field experiment, a finding against the theoretical results of peer screening, monitoring, and enforcement. These findings are in line with the fact that Grameen Bank has shifted its lending scheme from group lending (Grameen I) to individual lending (Grameen II).

Reflecting this issue, more recent strand of the study has been focusing dynamic incentive scheme, which have been employed by many microfinance institutions. In the dynamic incentive scheme, the amount of money they can borrow increases as the loan cycle proceeds, providing borrowers with an incentive to invest in safer projects and to repay honestly and mitigate moral hazard and strategic default. In fact, Karlan and Zinman (2009) found that dynamic incentive scheme had a positive impact on the repayment rate. Giné et al. (2012) also found a supportive evidence for mitigating asymmetric information problems by randomly introducing fingerprinting that can make dynamic repayment incentives more effective.

Overall, the experimental approach has provided a very powerful tool to formally test the theoretical mechanisms behind the remarkably high repayment rate in microfinance. However, a more fundamental problem is whether microfinance really has an impact on poverty reduction. Experimental and quasi-experimental approach play an important role to answer this question as well. A classical work on the poverty reduction effect of microfinance is a celebrated study by Pitt and Khandker (1998) on microcredit programs in Bangladesh including the ones supplied by Grameen Bank, BRAC, and the government. They employed regression discontinuity design (RDD) using the quasi-experimental condition where the eligibility to the microfinance program is determined by the land size, finding a significant impact on consumption level, consumption smoothing, and female education (if a loan is given to female). However, their approach caused a long dispute on poverty reduction effectiveness of microfinance (Morduch 1998; Roodman and Morduch 2009).

More recent approach employs RCT to evaluate the impact of microfinance programs in reducing poverty rigorously. For example, *American Economic Journal: Applied Economics* organized a special issue, featuring the impact of microcredit programs around the world (Banerjee et al. 2015a, b, c; Tarozzi et al. 2015; Attanasio et al. 2015; Crépon et al. 2015; Angelucci et al. 2015; Augsburg et al. 2015). Banerjee et al. (2015b) summarized the experiments in this journal issue conducted in six developing countries (Bosnia & Herzegovina, Ethiopia, India, Mexico, Mongolia, and Morocco) with different conditions. They showed that none of the studies found a significant impact of microcredit on income. The impact on consumption is even significantly negative in the cases in Bosnia and Herzegovina as well as in Ethiopia. In contrast, most of the studies confirmed significant improvement in credit access and business activity.

5.2 *Targeting Ultra Poor*

While microcredit programs can serve as an important instrument to mitigate credit market imperfection, it is known that the ultra poor cannot access such programs. To tackle more fundamental problem of poverty, there is another innovative program called a targeting ultra poor (TUP) or a multifaceted graduation program, which was initially developed by a Bangladeshi NGO, BRAC.[5] This program aims to provide the extremely poor with a combination of an initial productive asset grant, training and support, life skills coaching, temporary cash consumption support, and typical access to savings accounts and health information or services. By doing so, this program aims to salvage the ultra poor to a client of usual microcredit and microfinance programs. Using an RCT approach, Banerjee et al. (2015c) analyze the effect of this multifaceted program replicated in six developing countries, Ethiopia, Ghaha, Honduras, Pakistan, India, and Peru. Their evaluation results are impressive with statistically significant cost-effective impacts on a variety of welfare outcomes such as consumption and psychosocial status, which lasted 1 year after all implementation ended. Their results suggest that with TUP or a multifaceted graduation program, it is possible to provide the chance for the poorest to escape from the poverty trap with a relatively short-term intervention.

5.3 *Psychological Poverty Trap*

In addition to the classical poverty traps driven by market failures, possibilities of psychological or behavioral poverty trap have gained attention recently.[6] This type of poverty trap focuses on the interplay between poverty and behavioral parameters such as risk and time preferences. For example, Shah et al. (2012) argue that scarcity limits people's attention by concentrating on some problems while neglecting others, leading to behaviors that reinforce poverty.[7] Haushofer and Fehr (2014) showed that poverty causes a higher level of stress, leading to impatient and risk-averse decision-making, which in turn limits attention and favors habitual behaviors.

In order to cope with this behavioral poverty trap, we need to design interventions which change people's behavior without forcing or forbidding any options, i.e., nudge (Thaler and Sunstein 2008). In the literature on development economics, the effectiveness of nudge has been confirmed repeatedly. For example, in the case of farmers in developing countries, their income has seasonality: they have the cash right after harvest but their liquidity constraint tends to bind at the beginning of the next cropping season. This situation generates procrastination problems resulting from hyperbolic discounting, leading to underinvestments or low take up of insurance, making the poor stay poor and vulnerable. Duflo et al. (2011) offered small time-limited discounts on fertilizer just after harvest, showing that it significantly

[5]BRAC is the largest NGO in the world in terms of the number of employees. Its activity covers wide range of issues such as microfinance, education, public health, and disaster relief.

[6]This is often labeled as the conflict of "Econ's versus Human's," where Econ means a rational agent assumed in the neoclassical economics and Human means nonrational agent modeled in behavioral economics (Thaler 2016).

[7]Mullainathan and Shafir (2013) also discuss that the mind is occupied with forefront issues when the resources (e.g., time or money) are scarce, crowding out other important issues. This "tunneling" effect can prevent the poor from moving out of poverty.

increases fertilizer use. Casaburi and Willis (2018) offered insurance with pay-at-harvest, i.e., deducting the premium from the sales to the contractor at harvest, finding that it significantly increases the take up of insurance. These examples suggest that it is possible to cut the behavioral poverty trap by nudging the poor with carefully designed interventions.

6 Concluding Remarks

Development economics, once stagnated at the bottom of economics, resuscitated at the turn of this century. The main driving force behind the restoration of development economics is "field experiments revolution," i.e., the dominance of experimental approaches in the field exemplified by the impact evaluation of development projects using randomized control trials or RCTs. It is also important to notice that such revolution in development economics is nested in broader "credibility revolution" in economics. Once economics has been criticized due to its unrealistic assumption and too much theoretical orientation. "Under the streetlight" story can highlight such a drawback of traditional economics:

> A police officer is patrolling a neighborhood when he sees a man, disheveled and reeking of alcohol, crawling around underneath a streetlight. The officer walks over to the man and asks if there is a problem. The drunkard turns to the officer and conveys that he dropped a quarter and was trying to find it. The officer peruses the area and after observing nothing in the light emanating from the streetlight, he asks the man where exactly he dropped it. With this, the drunken man replies that he dropped it two blocks away. When the police officer asks him why he is looking for his money all the way over here, the man replies, "Because the light is better here." (Battaglia and Atkinson 2015)[8]

This story caricatures observational bias or cherry-picking tendency of economics where economists only look for whatever they are searching by looking where it is easiest. In the 1980s, game theory brought about a revolution in economic theory which expands the scope and power of the "streetlight" substantially, enabling to model strategic interaction in a variety of economic analyses (Kandori 1994). In the twenty-first century, it is the field experiment that has been expanding the scope of the streetlight further. Traditional empirical economists, searching for instrumental variables, confined themselves to address economic issues which can be investigated by available instruments. Now, we have research agenda of designing and creating instrumental variables using experimental methods such as RCTs. Even quasi-experimental methods are now armed with big data sets such as newly available remote sensing data and computerized administrative data from the governments and private companies. "A man searching for IVs" now has a variety of empirical methods and data to overcome traditional constraints in empirical economics. The field of economics has become a rigorous full-fledged "science" field, emphasizing pre-analysis plan and replicability of scientific evidence.

[8] Although the historical origins of this joke are subject to debate, this citation is based on the comic strip Mutt & Jeff (Fisher 1942).

References

Aida, T. (2018). Social capital as an instrument for common pool resource management: A case study of irrigation management in Sri Lanka. *Oxford Economic Papers*, forthcoming.

Angelucci, M., Karlan, D., & Zinman, J. (2015). Microcredit impacts: Evidence from a randomized microcredit program placement experiment by Compartamos banco. *American Economic Journal: Applied Economics, 7*(1), 151–182.

Angrist, J. D., & Pischke, J.-S. (2010). The credibility revolution in empirical economics: How better research design is taking the con out of econometrics. *Journal of Economic Perspectives 24*, Spring 2010, 3–30.

Aoyagi, K., Sawada, Y., & Shoji, M. (2014). Does infrastructure facilitate social capital accumulation? evidence from natural and artefactual field experiments in Sri Lanka. *JICA-RI Working Paper*, No.65.

Armendáriz de Aghion, B. (1999). Development banking. *Journal of Development Economics, 58*(1), 83–100.

Armendáriz de Aghion, B., & Gollier, C. (2000). Peer group formation in an adverse selection model. *Economic Journal, 110*(465), 632–43.

Armendáriz de Aghion, B., & Morduch, J. (2005). The economics of microfinance. Cambridge, Mass.: MIT Press.

Ashraf, N., Karlan, D., & Yin, W. (2006). Tying odysseus to the mast: Evidence from a commitment savings product in the philippines. *Quarterly Journal of Economics, 121*(2), 635–672.

Attanasio, O., Augsburg, B., De Haas, R., Fitzsimons, E., & Harmgart, H. (2015). The impacts of microfinance: Evidence from joint-liability lending in Mongolia. *American Economic Journal: Applied Economics, 7*(1), 90–122.

Attanasio, O. P., Meghir, C., & Santiago, A. (2012). Education choices in mexico: Using a structural model and a randomized experiment to evaluate progresa. *Review of Economic Studies, 79*(1), 37–66.

Augsburg, B., De Haas, R., Harmgart, H., & Meghir, C. (2015). The impacts of microcredit: Evidence from bosnia and herzegovina. *American Economic Journal: Applied Economics, 7*(1), 183–203.

Banerjee, A. V., Besley, T., & Guinnane, T. W. (1994). Thy neighbor's keeper: The design of a credit cooperative with theory and a test. *Quarterly Journal of Economics, 109*(2), 491–515.

Banerjee, A., Chandrasekhar, A. G., Duflo, E., & Jackson, M. O. (2013). The diffusion of microfinance. *Science, 341*(6144), 1236498.

Banerjee, A., & Duflo, E. (2009). The experimental approach to development economics. *Annual Review of Economics, 1,* 151–178.

Banerjee, A., Duflo, E. (2011). Poor economics: A radical rethinking of the way to fight global poverty. PublicAffairs.

Banerjee, A., Duflo, E., Glennerster, R., & Kinnan, C. (2015a). The miracle of microfinance? evidence from a randomized evaluation. *American Economic Journal: Applied Economics, 7*(1), 22–53.

Banerjee, A., Karlan, D., & Zinman, J. (2015b). Six randomized evaluations of microcredit: Introduction and further steps. *American Economic Journal: Applied Economics, 7*(1), 1–21.

Banerjee, A., Duflo, E., Goldberg, N., Karlan, D., Osei, R., Parienté, W., et al. (2015c). A multifaceted program causes lasting progress for the very poor: Evidence from six countries. *Science, 348*(6236).

Banerjee, A. V., & Newman, A. (1993). Occupational choice and the process of development. *Journal of Political Economy, 101*(2), 274–98.

Barr, A. (2003). Trust and expected trustworthiness: Experimental evidence from zimbabwean villages. *Economic Journal, 113*(489), 614–630.

Barr, A., & Serneels, P. (2008). Reciprocity in the workplace. *Experimental Economics, 12,* 99–112.

Barrett, C. B., & Carter, M. R. (2013). The economics of poverty traps and persistent poverty: Empirical and policy implications. *Journal of Development Studies, 49*(7).

Battaglia, M., & Atkinson, M. A. (2015). The streetlight effect in type 1 diabetes. *Diabetes, 64*(4), 1081–1090.
Besley, T., & Coate, S. (1995). Group lending, repayment incentives and social collateral. *Journal of Development Economics, 46*(1), 1–18.
Binswanger, H. P. (1980). Attitudes toward risk: Experimental measurement in rural India. *American Journal of Agricultural Economics, 62*(3), 395–407.
Bouma, J., Bulte, E., & van Soest, D. (2008). Trust and cooperation: Social capital and community resource management. *Journal of Environmental Economics and Management, 56,* 155–166.
Bowles, Samuel, & Gintis, Herbert. (2002). Social capital and community governance. *Economic Journal, 112*(483), F419–F436.
Bryan, G., Chowdhury, S., & Mobarak, A. M. (2013). Escaping famine through seasonal migration. *Yale University Economic Growth Center Discussion Paper* No. 1032.
Camerer, C. F., & Fehr, E. (2004). Measuring social norms and preferences using experimental games: A guide for social scientists. In J. Henrich, R. Boyd, S. Bowles, C. F. Camerer, E. Fehr, & H. Gintis (Eds.), *Foundations of human sociality: Economic experiments and ethnographic evidence from fifteen small-scale societies* (pp. 55–95). Oxford: Oxford University Press.
Cardenas, J. C., & Carpenter, J. (2008). Behavioral development economics: Lessons from field labs in the developing world. *Journal of Development Studies, 44,* 311–338.
Carter, M. R., & Castillo, M. (2011). Trustworthiness and social capital in South Africa: Analysis of actual living standards data and artefactual field experiments. *Economic Development and Cultural Change, 59,* 695–722.
Casaburi, L., & Willis, J. (2018). Time versus state in insurance: Experimental evidence from contract farming in Kenya. *American Economic Review*, forthcoming.
Chetty, R. (2009). Sufficient statistics for welfare analysis: A bridge between structural and reduced-form methods. *Annual Review of Economics, 1,* 451–488.
Chetty, R. (2013). Yes, economics is a science. *New York Times*, October 20, 2013.
Chuang, Y., & Schechter, L. (2015). Stability of experimental and survey measures of risk, time, and social preferences: A review and some new results. *Journal of Development Economics, 117,* 151–170.
Crépon, B., Devoto, F., Duflo, E., & Parienté, W. (2015). Estimating the impact of microcredit on those who take it up: Evidence from a randomized experiment in Morocco. *American Economic Journal: Applied Economics, 7*(1), 123–150.
Dasgupta, P., & Ray, D. (1986). Inequality as a determinant of malnutrition and unemployment: Theory. *Economic Journal, 96*(384), 1011–1034.
de Janvry, A., Fafchamps, M., & Sadoulet, E. (1991). Peasant household behaviour with missing markets: Some paradoxes explained. *Economic Journal, 101*(409), 1400–1417.
Dhaliwal, I., Du o, E., Glennerster, R., & Tulloch, C. (2013). Comparative cost-effectiveness analysis to inform policy in developing countries: A general framework with applications for education. In P. Glewwe (Ed.), *Education policy in developing countries* (pp. 285–338). Chicago: University of Chicago Press.
Duflo, E., Hanna, R., & Ryan, S. P. (2012). Incentives work: Getting teachers to come to school. *American Economic Review, 102*(4), 1241–1278.
Duflo, E., Kremer, M., & Robinson, J. (2011). Nudging farmers to use fertilizer: Theory and experimental evidence from Kenya. *American Economic Review, 101*(6), 2350–2390.
Dupas, P. (2014). Getting essential health products to their end users: Subsidize, but how much? *Science, 345*(6202), 1279–1281.
Dupas, P., & Miguel, E. (2016). Impacts and determinants of health levels in low-income countries. *NBER Working Paper* No. 22235.
Fehr, E., & Leibbrandt, A. (2011). A field study on cooperativeness and impatience in the tragedy of the commons. *Journal of Public Economics, 95,* 1144–1155.
Fisher, B. (1942). Mutt & Jeff. Florence Morning News, 3 June 1942, p. 7.
Gangopadhyay, S., Ghatak, M., & Lensink, R. (2005). Joint liability lending and the peer selection effect. *Economic Journal, 115*(506), 1005–1015.

Ghatak, M. (1999). Group lending, local information and peer selection. *Journal of Development Economics, 60,* 27–50.
Giné, X., & Karlan, D. S. (2014). Group versus individual liability: Short and long term evidence from Philippine microcredit lending groups. *Journal of Development Economics, 107*, 65–83.
Giné, X., Goldberg, J., & Yang, D. (2012). Credit market consequences of improved personal identification: Field experimental evidence from Malawi. *American Economic Review, 102*(6), 2923–54.
Glewwe, P., Kremer, M., Moulin, S., & Zitzewitz, E. (2004). Retrospective versus prospective analyses of school inputs: The case of flip charts in Kenya. *Journal of Development Economics, 74*(1), 251–268.
Gneezy, U., & Imas, A. (2017). Lab in the field: Measuring preferences in the wild. In A. V. Banerjee & E. Duflo (Eds.), *Handbook of economic field experiments* (Vol. 1, pp. 439–464). Amsterd: North Holland.
Goto, J., Sawada, Y., Aida, T., & Aoyagi, K. (2015). Incentives and social preferences: Experimental evidence from a seemingly inefficient traditional labor contract. *CIRJE Discussion Paper* F-961. Faculty of Economics: University of Tokyo.
Griliches, Z. (1986). Economic data issues. In Z. Griliches & M. D. Intriligator (Eds.), *Handbook of econometrics* (vol. 3, pp 1465–1514). Elsevier.
Guiteras, R., Levinsohn, J., & Mobarak, A. M. (2015). Encouraging sanitation investment in the developing world: A cluster-randomized trial. *Science, 348*(6237), 903–906.
Guttman, J. M. (2008). Assortative matching, adverse selection, and group lending. *Journal of Development Economics, 87*(1), 51–56.
Hamermesh, D. S. (2013). Six decades of top economics publishing: Who and how? *Journal of Economic Literature, 51,* 162–172.
Harrison, G. W., & List, J. A. (2004). Field Experiments. *Journal of Economic Literature, XLII*, 1009–1055.
Haushofer, J., & Fehr, E. (2014). On the psychology of poverty. *Science, 344,* 862.
Hayami, Y. (1989). Community, market and state. In A. Maunder & A. Valdes (Eds.), *Agriculture and Governments in an Independent World* (pp. 3–14). Amherst, MA: Gower.
Hayami, Y., & Godo, Y. (2005). *Development Economics: From the Poverty to the Wealth of Nations.* Oxford University Press.
Henrich, J., Heine, S. J., & Norenzayan, A. (2010). The weirdest people in the world? *Behavioral and Brain Sciences*, Page 1 of 75.
Imbens, G. W., & Angrist, J. D. (1994). Identification and estimation of local average treatment effects. *Econometrica, 62*(2), 467–475.
Kandori, M. (1994). Game Riron niyoru Keizaigaku no Shizuka na Kakumei (Silent revolution of economics by game theory). In K. Iwai & M. Ito (Eds.), *Gendai no Keizai Riron (modern economic theory)* (pp. 15–56). Tokyo: University of Tokyo Press.
Karlan, D. S. (2005). Using experimental economics to measure social capital and predict financial decisions. *American Economic Review, 95,* 1688–1699.
Karlan, D., & Appel, J. (2011). *More than good intentions: Improving the ways the world's poor borrow, save, farm, learn, and stay healthy*. Dutton Press.
Karlan, D., & Zinman, J. (2009). Observing Unobservables: Identifying information asymmetries with a consumer credit field experiment. *Econometrica, 77*(6), 1993–2008.
Keane, M. P. (2010). Structural versus atheoretic approaches to econometrics. *Journal of Econometrics, 156,* 3–20.
Keane, M. P., & Wolpin, K. I. (2009). Empirical applications of discrete choice dynamic programming models. *Review of Economic Dynamics, 12*(1), 1–22.
Kono, H. (2014). Microcredit games with noisy signals: Contagion and free-riding. *Journal of the Japanese and International Economies, 33*, 96–113.
Kosfeld, M., & Rustagi, D. (2015). Leader punishment and cooperation in groups: Experimental field evidence from commons management in Ethiopia. *American Economic Review, 105,* 747–783.

Kraay, A., & McKenzie, D. (2014). Do poverty traps exist? Assessing the evidence. *Journal of Economic Perspectives, 28*(3), 127–148.

Kraay, A., & Raddatz, C. (2007). Poverty traps, aid, and growth. *Journal of Development Economics, 82*(2), 315–347.

Krugman, P. (1993). Towards a counter-counterrevolution in development theory. *Proceedings of the World Bank Annual Conference on Development Economics*, pp. 15–38.

Leibenstein, H. (1954). *A theory of economic-demographic development*. Princeton: Princeton University Press.

Leijonfhufvud, A. (1973). Life among the Econ. *Western Economic Journal, 11*(3), 327–336.

Levitt, S. D., & List, J. A. (2007). What do laboratory experiments measuring social preferences reveal about the real world? *Journal of Economic Perspectives, 21,* 153–174.

Levitt, S. D., & List, J. A. (2009). Field experiments in economics: The past, the present, and the future. *European Economic Review, 53,* 1–18.

Liu, E. M. (2013). Time to change what to sow: Risk preferences and technology adoption decisions of cotton farmers in China. *Review of Economics and Statistics, 95*(4), 1386–1403.

Mazumdar, D. (1959). The marginal productivity theory of wages and disguised unemployment. *Review of Economic Studies, 26*(3), 190–197.

Mobarak, A. M., & Rosenzweig, M. (2014). Risk, insurance and wages in general equilibrium. *NBER Working Paper* No. 19811.

Morduch, J. (1998). *Does microfinance really help the poor? New evidence from flagship programs in Bangladesh* (Working Papers No. 198). Princeton University.

Mullainathan, S., & Shafir, E. (2013). *Scarcity: Why having too little means so much*. London, England: Allen Lane, an imprint of Penguin Books.

Nelson, R. R. (1956). A theory of the low-level equilibrium trap. *American Economic Review, 46,* 894–908.

Pender, J. L. (1996). Discount rates and credit markets: Theory and evidence from rural India. *Journal of Development Economics, 50*(2), 257–296.

Pitt, M. M., & Khandker, S. R. (1998). The impact of group-based credit programs on poor households in Bangladesh: Does the gender of participants matter? *Journal of Political Economy, 106*(5), 958–996.

Rath, K., & Wohlrabe, K. (2016). Recent trends in co-authorship in economics: Evidence from RePEc. *Applied Economics Letters, 23*(12).

Ravallion, M. (1997). Famines and economics. *Journal of Economic Literature, 35*(3), 1205–1242.

Ravallion, M. (2012). Fighting poverty one experiment at a time: Poor economics: A radical rethinking of the way to fight global poverty: Review essay. *Journal of Economic Literature, 50*(1), 103–114.

Roodman, D., & Morduch, J. (2009). *The impact of microcredit on the poor in Bangladesh: Revisiting the evidence* (Working Paper, No. 174). CGIAR.

Rosenstein-Rodan, P. N. (1943). Problems of industrialisation of eastern and south-eastern Europe. *Economic Journal, 53*(210/211), 202–211.

Rosenzweig, M. R., & Wolpin, K. I. (2000). Natural "Natural Experiments" in economics. *Journal of Economic Literature, 38*(4), 827–874.

Sawada, Y., Aida, T., Griffen, A. S., Kozuka, E., Noguchi, H., & Todo, Y. (2016). Election, implementation, and social capital in school based management: Evidence from a randomized field experiment on the COGES project in Burkina Faso, *JICA-RI Working Paper,* No.120.

Sawada, Y., Kasahara, R., Aoyagi, K., Shoji, M., & Ueyama, M. (2013). Modes of collective action in village economies: Evidence from natural and artefactual field experiments in a developing country. *Asian Development Review, 30*(1), 31–51.

Schultz, T. W. (1964). *Transforming traditional agriculture*. New Haven, London: Yale University Press.

Shah, A. K., Mullainathan, S., & Shafir, E. (2012). Some consequences of having too little. *Science, 338*(6107), 682–685.

Stiglitz, J. E. (1990). Peer monitoring and credit market. *World Bank Economic Review, 4*(3), 351–366.

Tanaka, T., Camerer, C. F., & Nguyen, Q. (2010). Risk and time preferences: Linking experimental and household survey data from Vietnam. *American Economic Review, 100*(1), 557–571.

Tarozzi, A., Desai, J., & Johnson, K. (2015). The impacts of microcredit: Evidence from Ethiopia. *American Economic Journal: Applied Economics, 7*(1), 54–89.

Thaler, R. H. (2016). Behavioral economics: Past, present, and future. *American Economic Review, 106*(7), 1577–1600.

Thaler, R., & Sunstein, C. (2008). *Nudge: Improving decisions about health, wealth, and happiness*. New Haven, CT: Yale University Press.

Todd, P. E., & Wolpin, K. I. (2006). Assessing the impact of a school subsidy program in Mexico: Using a social experiment to validate a dynamic behavioral model of child schooling and fertility. *American Economic Review, 96*(5), 1384–1417.

Van Tassel, E. (1999). Group lending under asymmetric information. *Journal of Development Economics 60*(1), 3–25.

White, H., & Raitzer, D. A. (2017). *Impact evaluation of development interventions: A practical guide*. Asian Development Bank.

World Bank. (2015). *World development report 2015: Mind, society, and behavior*. Washington, DC: World Bank Group.

Yamasaki, J., Ichimura, H., & Sawada, Y. (2018). Mosquito nets and human capital accumulation: The impact on schooling in a developing country, mimeo.

Experimental Research in Political Science

Naoko Taniguchi

1 Introduction

Experiments are a way of verifying the correctness of a theory or hypothesis under an artificial condition. They are especially effective in identifying causalities in a certain situation. Experiments have always been the driving force of natural and biological sciences. To take a simple example, early humans must have done experiments in agriculture: planting seeds in different fields with the same climate conditions and giving varying amounts of water and fertilizers would have led to different yields. Adopting the methods with the highest yields was precisely how agriculture made progress.

Experiments were first adopted in those sciences, then were employed in the field of psychology in the late nineteenth century and helped to describe the microprocesses of the human cognition, mind, and awareness. Social psychology followed the study of an individual's mind in society, which used experiments to understand political attitudes and behaviors. Examples include the experiment of group pressure (Asch 1952) and obedience to authority (Milgram 1974), both of which were highly effective in understanding the relationship between totalitarianism and mass psychology during World War II.

In the 1950s, microeconomics adopted experiments by comparing mathematically derived hypotheses of decision-making and decisions made in the real world, along with an assumption of the rational self, economic equilibrium, and mathematical descriptions. Since then, experimental economics (which examines microeconomic models by means of laboratory experiments) and behavioral economics developed into a major branch of economics; and eventually in 2002, Vernon L. Smith and Daniel Kahneman were awarded the Nobel Prize for Economics for having established laboratory experiments as a tool to verify the model of the rational self.

N. Taniguchi (✉)
Graduate School of System Design and Management, Keio University, Collaboration Complex, 4-1-1 Hiyoshi, Kohoku-ku, Yokohama, Kanagawa 223-8526, Japan
e-mail: naoko.taniguchi@sdm.keio.ac.jp

T. Kawagoe and H. Takizawa (eds.), *Diversity of Experimental Methods in Economics*,
https://doi.org/10.1007/978-981-13-6065-7_4

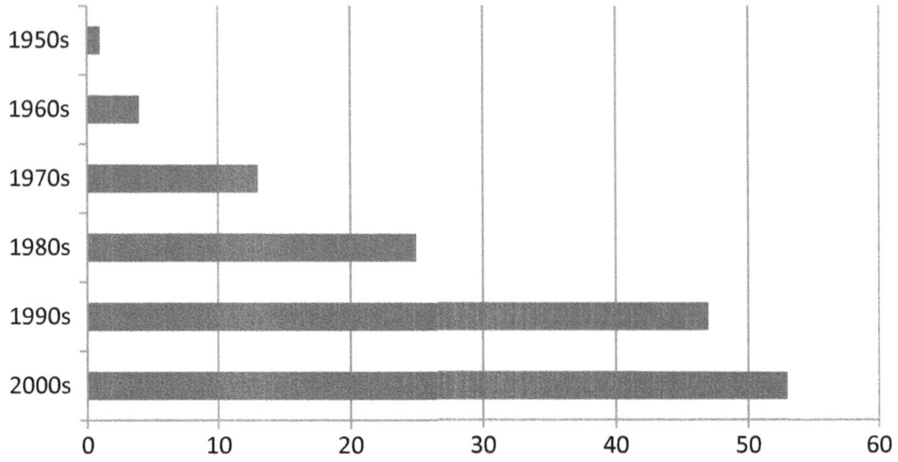

Fig. 1 Number of articles in major American journals on political studies (*Created by Author based on Morton and Williams (2010), p. 4, Fig. 1.1)

When were experiments adopted in political studies? The first political science experiment is older than one might expect; it dates back to Gosnell's experiment in the stimulation of voting (Gosnell 1926). In the following decades, however, experimental studies in political studies were few in number (McDermott 2002). In 1971 a journal *The Experimental Study of Politics* was published but was discontinued in just four years. According to Morton and Williams (2010), from the 1950s to 1980s, only 50 articles on experimental studies were published in the major American journals on political studies (APSR, AJPS, JOP). However, from 1990s to 2007, this number rose to about a hundred, showing a long-term increase (Fig. 1). In 2014, a journal in experimental political studies was relaunched, *The Journal of Experimental Political Science.*

Why is experimental political science now gaining recognition? One factor is the growing trend of interdisciplinary studies. More researchers with a background of experimental studies in economics or psychology are conducting research, in some cases by teaming with political scientists, to create new interdisciplinary fields such as political economics and political psychology. Another factor is that a greater emphasis on empiricism and scientific approach has led to a revival of experimental studies, which is effective in identifying causalities. To add to this, developments in technologies and methods that enable generalization of results (statistical studies and computer simulations) have also contributed to experimental studies.

Despite the growth so far, it is unlikely that we will see further dramatic growth in experimental political studies. Insights from experiment outcomes tend to be looked down on as indirect and seen as an obsolete implication to real-world politics (Lupia 2002). Experiments adds a creative aspect to political studies; on the other hand, they are sometimes avoided due to the following concerns: (1) the risk of oversimplification by applying experiments to complicated political phenomena, (2) experiments may be applied to only a limited area, and (3) the extensive effort and cost required to undertake adequate results from an experiment.

In the face of such concerns, should experiments be further implemented into political studies? This chapter will list the different types of experimentation in social sciences, examples of each type, and the benefits and challenges in adopting experimentation in political studies, by referring to discussions on experimentation in political science by Kinder and Palfrey(1993), Lupia (2002), McDermott (2002), Druckman et al. (2006, 2011), and Morton and Williams (2010). We will also show an experimental study based on discussions on distributive Justice (Ogami et al. 2016) and discuss the differences between a laboratory experiment using students as subjects and a survey experiment with adults as subjects.

2 An Overview of Experimental Studies in Political Science

2.1 What Are Experiments in Political Studies?

As described in Sect. 1, experiments generally refer to a method of testing a theory or hypothesis under an artificial condition. In particular, a set of experiments conducted in an environment where a different factor is assigned to each experiment with all other factors controlled, and the results of all experiments are compared to see the effect of each factor, is called a *controlled experiment*. In Gosnell's classic study (Gosnell 1926), it was hypothesized that stimulating voters will lead to a higher voter turnout, and attempts were made to examine the causality between stimuli encouraging voter registration (independent variable) and increased voter turnout (dependent variable). Twelve districts in Chicago were chosen in the Presidential election of 1924 and cards encouraging voting were sent to citizens. It turned out that voter turnout was higher by 8% on average in districts which received the cards than those which did not. Here the group that received a card (or "treatment") is called the experimental group; those that did not receive a card are called the control group. This method, which compared the experimental group with the control group, dates back to the late nineteenth century, when Darwin implemented this in biological studies. The same method was implemented in social science studies in early twentieth century, and became more common in the mid-twentieth century (Kinder and Palfrey 1993).

Gosnell's experiment in the stimulation of voting was reproduced by Gerber and Green (2000). There they performed a random assignment, where subjects were divided randomly into the experimental group and the control group. Random assignments do not ensure that the experimental group and the control group are identical in quality, but they do ensure that there is no significant difference between the two groups other than the difference in manipulation. This means that if there was a significant difference between the two groups in the first place, then it may lead to different outcome s between the two groups, and manipulation may not be the only factor making the difference. Therefore, in order to claim that the manipulation is the sole cause of the outcome, or that there is a true causality between the independent and dependent variables, an adequate random assignment is required. This has been regarded as a key to a reliable experiment since the mid-1950s, when random assignment became common in social sciences, hence in some cases the term experiment refers only to those controlled by a random assignment, and when random assignment is lacking or insufficient, the term quasi-experiment is used.

2.2 Methods in Experimental Political Science

This section explains the experimentation methods employed in social sciences, in particular, political science.

2.2.1 Field Experiment

Field experiments are experiments that are performed in real-world settings. Examples include studies by Gosnell and Gerber. Experiments conducted in real political activities and phenomena certainly have benefits; however, we must note that mundane realism (the impression of reality based on real-world context) and experimental realism (the reality of the experiment itself) are different things (McDermott 2002).

What is a realistic experiment? The answer to this question is simple: an experiment which leads to a real causality between the treatment and result of an experiment is a realistic experiment. However, in a field experiment, it is difficult for the experimenter to verify whether the treatment really reached the subject (operation check), or to control other intervening factors.

In conducting an experiment, not only realism but also the *internal validity* of the experiment must be considered. In Gerber and Green's experiment, all the residents in the experiment area were personally encouraged by researchers to vote. However, the residents may have talked about the experiment and the encouragement among themselves, since they are neighbors; this conversation might have led to a higher voter turnout, making it difficult to distinguish the motivation to vote. This example implies that when the stimulation from the treatment is weak or irrelevant, or is offset by a different, stronger stimulation, then the experiment will become inadequate, no matter how realistic it is. This is referred to as the problem of *internal validity*.

2.2.2 Laboratory Experiment

To overcome the problem of internal validity, *laboratory experiments* are an effective measure. Laboratory experiments in political studies are conducted in much the same way as those in natural sciences: that is, subjects are invited to a laboratory where there are no stimulants or intervening factors. A laboratory experiment in political studies may consist of an opinion poll where participants are asked questions about their exposure to media and their political attitudes, followed by a relationship analysis of the two responses.

However, it is difficult to use opinion polls to measure the net effect of media exposure on political attitudes. First of all, there is the problem of *self-selection bias*: subjects may choose what they want to know. Those who are interested in politics may actively access news on voting, or supporters of a certain party may choose to expose themselves to news that is favorable to such supporters. Moreover, it is difficult to know in detail how much, and what kind of, news they were exposed to. And of course, the respondent's memory may not be fully trustworthy, or they may have been affected by conversations with friends and colleagues about news coverage on elections.

To overcome this, Iyengar et al. adapted their laboratory experiment. They showed subjects videos from the news, with varying patterns and contents, and measured their effect on political attitudes (Iyengar and Kinder 1987; Ansolabehere and Iyengar 1995). This method is effective in that a laboratory setting allows researchers to control the treatment so that linking the stimulation and the effect becomes much easier.

However, we must note that laboratory experiments in social sciences have several considerations as they study human behavior and attitudes. One is the experimenter bias, where the experimenter's hypothesis affects the subjects' behavior by over-focusing on behaviors or responses that confirm the hypothesis. Another is the demand characteristics, where the subject speculates the experimenter's intentions and attempts to act accordingly. In order to avoid such considerations, several measures are adopted. One is the *double-blind test*, where neither the experimenter nor the subject knows the conditions assigned to each subject.

Another is the *deception* method, where the experimenter communicates false information about the intention or agenda of the study or does not communicate that at all. Examples of deception include adding dummy participants, making subjects believe that they are competing with human opponents when they actually are responding to a computer-based test, and secretly observing subjects' behaviors before and after the experiment. In using the deception method, follow-up of subjects are important, particularly because they may be shocked to know that they have been deceived in the debriefing process after the experiment. Caring for the subject's feelings is ethically important in order not to hurt them mentally or physically.

Some criticize laboratory experiments, saying they are limited in its generality and universality. Laboratory settings are artificial, they say, without external "noise", so there is no guarantee that the results will not be reproduced in real-world politics or society. Another criticism against laboratory experiments is that their subjects are mainly students and neighbors of a university so the results are not representative, nor is it possible to obtain as large a sample as those of opinion polls. Such problems are referred to as the problems of *external validity*: in other words, the difficulty of generalizing the findings of an experiment.

2.2.3 Survey Experiment

As we have seen so far, a relevant experiment requires both internal validity and external validity, and there should be a true causality between the treatment and the result of an experiment. And at the same time, the relevance of an experiment will be limited if its findings cannot be generalized into other experiments or non-experimental situations.

In order to overcome this challenge, the *survey experiment* was developed. Survey experiments conduct multiple surveys with varying methods and questions as experiment conditions, then classifies them (randomly) into samples and compares the overall responses under each condition.

Survey experiment has once become a topic of academic debate, such as Sullivan et al. (1978). This goes back to research by Converse et al., who, based on data from the American National Election Survey (NES), concluded that there are no coherent ideological structures in the general voters' attitudes toward political issues (in the 1950s). This was criticized by Nie et al. (1976), who argued, based on later NES data, that the general voters' attitudes toward political issues have indeed become more coherent since the presidential election of 1964. In the debate, Sullivan et al. pointed to the fact that the questionnaires of NES were revised in 1964, studied the effect of the two type of questionnaire on response patterns, and concluded that the difference in analysis and findings between the two studies derives from the revision of questionnaire styles.

Recently, there are programs in place to promote large-scale survey experiments. Time-Sharing Experiments for the Social Sciences (TESS) is one of them, a program which offers grants to survey experiments in fields including political studies, economics, and psychology. Since its establishment in 2003, TESS has supported over 200 survey experiments.

Political studies, with its long history of survey-based studies, is particularly well suited to survey experiments, partly because the method of survey experiment is well-established as compared to field experiments, partly because the samples are more representative than those of laboratory experiments, and partly because they are efficient in that they can handle a large number of samples at once. On the other hand, survey experiments have drawbacks, too: characteristics of the survey experiment may restrict the content of the survey, and the results do not always correspond with those of laboratory experiments, leading to an occasional debate on their validity.

Another more recent challenge on survey experiments is the nonresponse bias. As the response rate of surveys declines, the nonresponse bias seems to gain significance and cannot be ignored. This bias seems to be of concern particularly when there is a close relationship between the factors that determine the subjects' response/nonresponse and the factors that affect the dependent variables. Moreover, the lower the response rate, the more difficult it is to make statistical adjustments to the effects. In short, survey experiments share the same concerns as those faced by contemporary public surveys.

2.2.4 Natural Experiment

Another experiment method is a quasi-experimentation referred to as the *natural experiment* method. Natural experiments are a method in which we identify multiple cases where all conditions except the exogenous factor (which is the independent variable) are the same, and compare them. They are adopted when experimenters cannot control the various conditions pertaining to real-world phenomena that are (apparently) taking place.

A well-known example of a natural experiment is a labor economics study by Card and Krueger on the effect of minimum wage policies (Card and Krueger 1994). In this study, the authors evaluated the impact of a policy change, by selecting two areas—an area where the minimum wage was raised and an area where it was not—which had similar characteristics in terms of population size, industries, and urbanization rates, and compared the employment trend and wage levels of the two areas. The aim of their study was to identify the effect of a raise in the minimum wage, based on the argument that although the raise apparently is in accord with the well-being of workers, it leads to fewer employment opportunities, resulting in a higher unemployment rate. In conclusion, they showed that an increase in minimum wage does not lead to a higher unemployment rate.

Not only do natural experiments help verify the effects of current government policies, they also help to explore the effects of historical events. We might suggest, for example, that by using this method we may take a number of developing countries with common characteristics (in terms of culture, regimes, and ethnicities) which underwent communist rule and capitalist rule, and compare their development paths. In this way, we may say that natural experiments may lead to valuable case studies, though we must also note that the validity of natural experiments lies all the more in how to choose the appropriated cases to study.

2.2.5 Simulations

A further experimentation method used when the event one wishes to verify is not actually taking place, or is difficult to reproduce, is a simulation. Simulation has been widely used in natural sciences, from the behavior or bacteria or movement of the planets, in order to identify the course of events in a certain set of conditions. Recently, simulation has also been increasingly employed in social sciences, including political studies.

One such study was conducted by Axelrod (1984), who carried out a computer simulation of the iterated prisoner's dilemma (IPD) game. IPD game was traditionally tested in a laboratory setting with human subjects; however, Axelrod recruited strategies from researchers in various fields, tested them in a simulated environment, and calculated the average score of each strategy. In this way, he reached the conclusion that the best strategy was that "Tit for tat" (responding to cooperation by cooperation, and noncooperation by noncooperation) suggested by the psychologist Anatol Rapoport.

One benefit of simulation is its repeatability: whereas it is unrealistic and inefficient to have human subjects participate in the same experiment hundreds and thousands of times, simulations allow for experimenters to conduct tens of thousands of experiments using computer agents. This has led to the wide use of *Agent-based Simulation* (ABS), where the dynamics of interaction between agents and the effects of various parameters are tested. ABS which is based on evolutionary game theory has also been incorporated in Axelrod's study, leading to findings in economics and sociology.

A major benefit of computer-based simulation lies in the fact that it allows researchers to reproduce events that are unobservable in real life or laboratories by using a computer and trace their long-term dynamics and outcomes. For example, if we want to know the long-term effects of a certain election system on party politics in real-life situations, we would have to undergo a sufficient number of elections. On the other hand, if we can express various parameters (election system, election environment, party strategies, preference distribution) adequately enough, then we will be able to confirm various dynamics and outcomes, ranging from which the default value of a parameter will lead to which party system (confirmation of convergence value), whether changing the parameter will change the outcome or not (testing robustness).

Of course, this also means that computer simulations depend heavily on the conditions and algorithms that are predefined by the researchers, and will not express anything beyond such predefinitions. Therefore, it would be safe to say that simulations are one method of thought experiments.

2.3 Experimental Studies in Political Science

What kinds of experimental political studies have been carried out? According to McDermott, who made a list of articles on experimental studies that have appeared in major American journals on political science (McDermott 2002), 80% of them were about American voting behaviors. Other topics were: bargaining (13 articles), game theory (10 articles), international relations (10 articles), committees (8 articles), biases on experiments (6 articles), race/ethnicity (6 articles), field experiments (5 articles), media-related (4 articles), leadership (4 articles), and survey experiment (3 articles). Although the list includes both topics and methodologies, it gives an overview of experiments in political studies.

2.4 Impacts of Experimental Studies in Psychology and Economics

We should also add that psychological /sociological experiments have given a significant impact on experiments of voting behaviors/political attitudes of electorates. Economic studies such as game theory have given an impact too: we are seeing experimental studies in the field of political studies adopting mathematical models. Such influence from other fields sometimes changes the attitudes and processes of experimental political studies.

Experiments in economics and psychology/sociology have some differences. One is the remuneration to subjects: in certain economic experiments, subjects receive a fee, which is based on the assumption that financial incentives affect people's behavior. Alternatively, economic models and experiments are designed with various values translated into a certain amount of money. On the other hand, in psychological or sociopsychological experiments, it is uncommon to give financial rewards to subjects directly, since the impact of remuneration on a subject's responses is also taken into consideration.

Another difference is related to the disclosure of the experiment's "context". In economic experiments, contexts (such as the process of elections, the party system), or the experimenter's interests, are rarely disclosed to subjects, so as to minimize the effect on subjects or the experiment itself. In fact, they tend to employ an abstract situation or incentive. On the other hand, psychological/sociopsychological experiments will not hesitate to disclose its context to their subjects, especially when the aim of the study is to identify the effect of a certain context. Moreover, the latter will sometimes use the deception method.

Experimental studies in political studies are similar to those in economics in some cases, and close to those in psychology/social psychology in some cases, depending on the academic background of the researchers. In any case, it is important for the experimenter to choose an experimental method appropriate to their objective, and to understand the advantages and disadvantages of the method.

3 Advantages and Disadvantages of Experimental Political Science

3.1 Advantages of Experimental Political Science

The greatest advantage of experiments lies in their capacity to test a causality hypothesis, in other words, to identify causality. This capacity is particularly helpful in today's political studies, where inferring and testing causalities is important. That is, there are cases where observation or statistical data is limited or difficult to collect, and this is where experimentation comes in. Experiments allow researchers to create a set of data based on a set of hypotheses, with all the unnecessary bias removed, and test their causality. Moreover, they allow researchers to reproduce findings from observation/statistical data. In fact, in order to understand a complex phenomenon, one must break down a phenomenon into components and identify the causal relationship among them; using experiments plus analysis of observation/statistical data will promote the development of theories, especially when analyzing observation/statistical data is not enough to separate and integrate components. All of this process, we may say, is the driving force of scientific progress.

Another great advantage of experiments is their interdisciplinary nature: experimentation is a common language of science, hence we can expect experiments to stimulate and drive the growth of political science by promoting its interaction with other sciences. In fact, the current growth of experimental political studies is fueled by political scientists who majored in other disciplines, researchers in fields other than political studies, and joint studies with other disciplines; indeed, experimental political studies have become a transdisciplinary field, with specialists in social and natural sciences sharing their academic interests.

Furthermore, experimental political studies are an invaluable means of training in the research methodologies of political science. Of course, knowledge of experimentation may not be a prerequisite for all political scientists, but it is a good way to learn the basics of the discipline of a field which has a larger choice of methodologies than other social sciences (economics and social psychology), and challenges in specialized training.

By having knowledge of experiments, political scientists will have an understanding of what a "verification of causality" is, how should a "relevant comparison" be conducted. Moreover, the basics of experimentation will give one an understanding of how to identify the relevant independent/dependent variables and compare them with all the noise eliminated.

As noted earlier, case studies can be regarded as natural experiments, then the methodologies of experiment planning will be effective in the selection of cases. For example, field experiments on voting participation by Gerber and Green (2000) and Horiuchi et al. (2007) used stimulants (letters, phone calls, visits, movies, the Internet) to the experimental group and analyzed their effects. Lassen (2005) chose as the experimental group areas where there were efforts by the municipalities to increase voting rates, and areas where there were no such efforts as the control group, and made a comparison between the two groups. This is an example of a natural experiment and case study.

It would also be a valuable experience, for those who study political behaviors and attitudes of people, to observe, in an experiment setting, how people make decisions and act under certain conditions, not to mention witnessing raw survey data. Observing a phenomenon directly and creating data from it, rather than just reading articles or analyzing existing data, which is an indirect contact to data, will definitely be a valuable experience, along with fieldwork.

3.2 *Disadvantages of Experimental Political Science*

Experimental political studies may lead to clear-cut studies and revolutionary findings, but they have challenges too. One is the need to establish ethical screening guidelines for experiments. Today, experimental sciences which employ human subjects are required to establish such guidelines, and experimental political studies, although with a relatively long history, has a long way to go in order to present itself as an experimental science. Experiments that impose mental or physical pain on subjects, such as those done by Milgram, must be avoided.

Other challenges include secure management of personal information, and response to complaints from subjects. In American universities and research centers, there are certain measures in place that require researchers to go through an evaluation process on the experiment's content/subjects, information management, and publication channels before they can do an experiment. However, other countries including Japan, political studies lack such an ethical evaluation system, which is seen as a problem (Morton and Tucker 2014). These should be organized by universities, faculties, or academia.

There is also a concern related to specialist education: Is the experimental method an efficient and cost-effective way to train specialists? Experiments require specialist education on both theory and practice, which means that developing a specialist training environment where trial and error leads to reliable experiments. To overcome such concerns, it may be suggested that experimental political studies and neighboring social sciences create a shared opportunities of training on experimentation, or a joint experimentation system be created, which, like TESS, can be shared by a large number of researchers. Some recent papers present a guideline on the kinds of information to be included (Gerber et al. 2014) considering the recent growth in the publication of experimental studies. Such guidelines will be useful for young researchers as well as those trying experimental political studies.

Last but not least, the greatest challenge that the field faces is: how helpful can experimentation be in understanding the complex phenomena and structure of the history, institutions, and behaviors relevant to current politics? Of course, this forms the basis of all sciences; however, in political studies one is faced with the challenge to understand the complexities of various features and context in its entirety. This challenge leads to the issue of internal and external validity as noted earlier: how should experimentation ensure internal validity and generality and expandability (external validity) at the same time? To take an example, if the subjects of an experiment consist only of students, most political scientists would doubt that the subjects have a strong political awareness or belief. If everyone, under the same circumstances, react exactly the same way in a certain setting or topic, is not it useless to conduct political experimentation on such a topic?

There are other concerns relevant to experimentation method as a whole, such as the fact that the research environment/setting or interviews as stimulation are more often artificial and specific than not, and so responses of the subjects may become extraordinary. Also, a small difference in experimental settings leads to different results, which means that results may be unreliable.

To conclude, in order to enhance the external validity of experimental political studies, one should consider choosing a topic which is well suited to be examined by experiments, reproducing the topic appropriately in an experimental setting, repeating and integrating trials, and combining with other empirical methods.

4 Experiments of Distributive Justice

4.1 Student Subjects or General Adult Subjects?

As noted in Sect. 2.1, when the aim of an experimental study is to identify causal inferences (how a treatment affected the subjects), we only have to compare the experimental group and control group randomly, and if there are no systematic differences between to two groups, then any differences that appear after the experiment can be attributed to differences in treatment. In other words, if we wish to know the effect of a treatment, we do not have to use data that is representative of a whole society. This is confirmed by a report that Internet survey experiments, an increasingly common method whose samples are not representative of the whole society, can ensure the external validity of causal inferences (Mullinix et al. 2015). Also, in cases where we wish to examine responses common to most people, or to examine actions that are based on rational calculation, the data need not be representative.

On the other hand, there are cases where we do place importance on the representativeness of data, and this is when we want the *distribution* of a certain matter in real society. Examples of distribution might typically be: to identify the causality between an attribute of a person and the attitude towards a certain issue in an election (voting for a candidate person or party), or the causality between an attitude of a person and the candidate that person votes. In such cases, a more representative data, such as social survey data may be more preferable. Alternatively, in an experiment, if the attribute or characteristic of the subject may affect his or her response or choice, it may be necessary to design the experiment by taking the distribution of such attributes or characteristics into consideration.

4.2 J. Rawls "A Theory of Justice" and Related Experimental Studies

In order to discuss this issue, we will look at the experiments of distributive justice. As it is known, in "A Theory of Justice", Rawls (1971, 1999) states that social or economic inequality is permissible only if they benefit the least well-off positions of society (the difference principle); if people are behind the veil of ignorance (a situation in which they are deprived of all knowledge of the circumstances of themselves and of others), they will arrive rationally and universally to this principle, because one would wish that when the veil is uncovered and one discovers that he or she is in the least well-off positions, the difference or situation be bearable enough.

On the other hand, Frohlich and Oppenheimer (1992) conducted a laboratory experiment to verify if people really chose the principles which Rawls insists, with university students as subjects. They defined the principles of Rawls maximizes the floor (or lowest) income in the society (The Principle of Maximizing the Floor Income). Along with this principle, they showed the subjects the principle of maximizing the average income, the principle of maximizing the average with a floor constraint, and the principle of maximizing the average with a range constraint, and found that the latter two principles were preferred more than Rawls' principle of maximizing the floor income. This led Frohlich and Oppenheimer to doubt the realistic validity of Rawls' principle.

Michelbach et al. (2003) conducted a survey experiment on the same topic. There, the authors chose American university students as subjects and asked the following question: "if you were a member of a third party committee who is in charge of designing the society of another country, which income distribution would you think is the most preferable?" They presented several options of income distribution patterns based on equality, efficiency, necessity, and ability, and found that student subjects most preferred the option in line with Rawls' principle. They also found that by analyzing experiment data, it was the socially vulnerable people in American society, such as women and non-white subjects, who preferred "Rawls' principle" and the principle of equal distribution. This suggests that the preference regarding the distribution principle is affected by the socioeconomic position and the resulting values of each subject, even in an experimental setting reproducing "the veil of ignorance"; in other words, this result shows the real situation of American society, and has limitations in expanding it to a universal finding.

4.3 Comparing Student Subjects and Adult Subjects

Ogami et al. (2016) revised the Rawls' principle and the above experimental setting (how the veil of ignorance is explained), and carried out a laboratory experiment with Japanese university students and a survey experiment with general adult subjects. On the latter, monitors gathered by an Internet survey company were adjusted so that gender, age (20, 30, 40, 50 s and over), city size (large, mid-size, rural) were close to Japan's population composition as appears on the National Census. In using data from Internet surveys, such adjustments are known to produce data which is closer to real life. Also, regarding the veil of ignorance, the expression was revised as follows: "If you were to be born again, what type of income distribution would you want your country to have (provided that you could not know beforehand your household, your ability, or your status).

Table 1 The attributes of subjects

		Internet	University A	University B
Number of subjects		1012	121	75
Gender	% of male	50.0%	95.0%	65.8%
	% of female	50.0%	5.0%	34.2%
Household income	Under 3 million yen	18.4%	4.4%	0.0%
	3–4 miliion yen	15.1%	5.3%	3.5%
	4–5 miliion yen	14.3%	9.7%	7.0%
	5–6 miliion yen	13.0%	10.6%	7.0%
	6–7 miliion yen	8.3%	10.6%	1.8%
	7–8 miliion yen	8.3%	16.8%	12.3%
	8–10 miliion yen	10.6%	8.8%	7.0%
	10–12 miliion yen	6.2%	12.4%	24.6%
	12 miliion yen +	5.7%	21.2%	36.8%
All	All	100.0%	100.0%	100.0%

The aim of this revision was to have the subjects, though without information, have ownership in considering a preferred income distribution. The experiments were conducted in two universities (A and B), both located in Tokyo. Table 1 shows the number of subjects, percentages of each gender and household income class. Note that the almost all subjects of University A are male.

Subjects were shown five charts on household income distribution (Fig. 2), and were asked to grade them on a scale of 1–10. The household income distribution of the five charts A to E differs in the presence of those living below the absolute poverty level (i.e. annual income below 1.3 million yen, four-member family), size of disparity, and average household income.

Based on their preference, subjects were classified into the following four categories:

Egalitarian: those who prefer an equal distribution of wealth, with a reduced difference

$$A \geqq B \geqq D \quad \text{and} \quad A > C > E$$

Rawlsian: those who prefer to improve the situation of the least well-off (i.e. extreme poverty group)

$$A > C \geqq E \quad \text{and} \quad B > C \quad \text{and} \quad D > C$$

Mixed Equality-Efficiency: those who prefer something between Egalitarian and Rawlsian

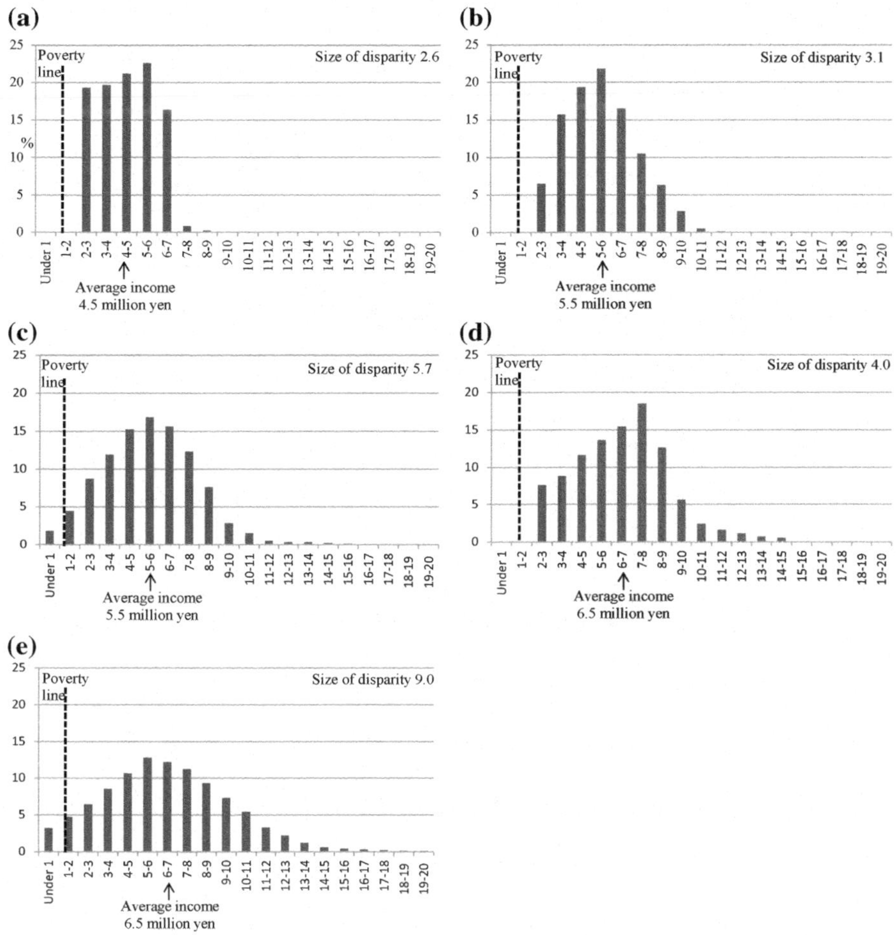

Fig. 2 Household income distributions that subjects evaluate

$$B > D \quad \text{and} \quad B > A \quad \text{and} \quad C > A \quad \text{and} \quad C > E$$

Utilitarian: those who prefer efficiency (maximizing the average)

$$E \geqq C \geqq A \quad \text{and} \quad D > B \geqq A$$

Figure 3 shows the result of the experiment. In response to the question "If you were to be born again, what type of income distribution would you want your country to have", few students in Universities A and B chose the Egalitarian principle; in University A, where most students are male, the Utilitarian principle was preferred most. In University B with a much higher female rate, the Rawlsian principle was

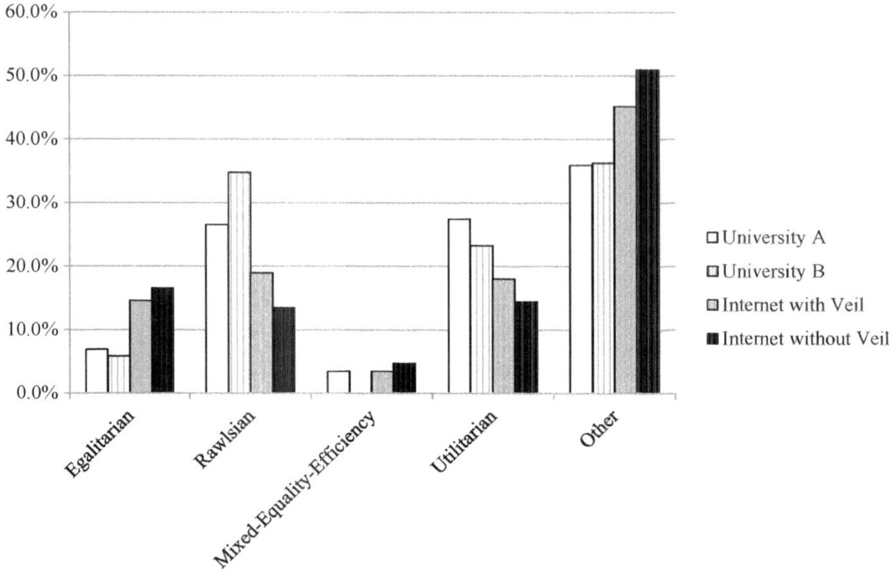

Fig. 3 Experimental results

preferred. Results of the Internet survey were adjusted so that the subjects' attributes resembled that of the Japanese society. These subjects were randomly classified into the two groups, the veiled and the unveiled. In response to the above question, more people chose the egalitarian principle than did university students, whereas the response rates for Rawlsian and Utilitarian were lower. Interestingly, the veiled group of the Internet survey most likely chose the Egalitarian principle, while there were fewer Rawlsians and Utilitarians.

Insights of these results seem twofold. First, even when deliberately placed behind the veil of ignorance, the decision-making of subjects is affected by their positions and attributes. That is, compared to university students, who are in a relatively well-off position, subjects representing the general population have a stronger sense of equality. From this, it seems that asking university students about the preferred form of society, looking at the distribution of the answers, and generalizing the findings, may be problematic.

Moreover, the results imply that the logic behind the response may differ between the position of the subjects: the veiled group of the Internet survey may think "my current income is low, so right now I wish for equality in society, but if I were to be born again, I might be in a better position, so I would prefer a wealthy society with an income gap"—which may mean that "higher expectation" is given priority over "consideration toward the least well-off".

However, it should be noted that many of the Internet survey subjects did not fall into the four categories, meaning that the responses for the Internet survey experiment were not adequate enough to meet the experimenters' intentions. Although Internet surveys enable a large-scale experiment on the general adult population, the problem of ensuring the right operation still remains.

5 Conclusion and Future Directions

In this chapter, we have seen an overview of experimental political studies: its features, advantages, and challenges, and have discussed the issue of external validity by comparing a laboratory experiment and a survey experiment.

Needless to say, experimentation is only one of the many approaches of political studies. In order to utilize this approach adequately and produce meaningful studies, the following would be helpful: (1) choose a topic that is suited to experimentation, (2) understand the experimental method as a whole as well as its advantages and disadvantages, and choose the type of experiment suited to the purpose of study, (3) break down the political phenomenon as you carry out the experiment, and make various attempts to integrate the results, (4) use analyses of other observation/statistical data alongside experimental data.

Modern researches in political science require sophisticated theories, the power to verify, and trans-disciplinarity, and as such, experimentation is also a method that any academic in this field should acquire. In particular, for those who study political behaviors and political attitudes, their aim being an understanding of the political decision-making process, experimentation is an effective methodology so there is no reason not to familiarize itself with it. In this light, it seems that the question has shifted from "Should political science adopt experimentation studies?" to "How can we make the costs related to experimental studies/education more effective?".

Note This chapter is based on Taniguchi (2016) presented for the 2016 Annual Meeting of Japan Public Choice Society.

References

Ansolabehere, S., & Iyengar, S. (1995). *Going negative: How political advertisements shrink and polarize the electorate*. New York: Free Press.

Asch, S. (1952). Effects of group pressure upon the modification and distortion of judgement. In H. Guetzkow (Ed.), *Groups, leadership, and men* (pp. 177–190). Pittsburgh: Carnegie Press.

Axelrod, R. (1984). *The evolution of cooperation*. New York: Basic Books.

Campbell, A., Converse, P., Miller, W., & Stokes, D. (1960). *The American voter*. New York: Wiley & Sons Inc.

Card, D., & Krueger, A. B. (1994). Minimum wages and employment: A case study of the fast-food industry in New Jersey and Pennsylvania. *American Economic Review, 84,* 772–793.

Druckman, J. N., Green, D. P., Kuklinski, J. H., & Lupia, A. (2006). The growth and development of experimental research in political science. *American Political Science Review, 100,* 627–635.

Druckman, J. N., Green, D. P., Kuklinski, J. H., & Lupia, A. (2011). *Cambridge handbook of experimental political science*. New York: Cambridge University Press.

Fisher, R. A. (1935). The design of experiments. Olyver and Boyd Edinburgh.
Frohlich, N., & Oppenheimer, J. A. (1992). *Choosing justice: An experimental approach to ethical theory*. Berkley: University of California Press.
Gerber, A. S., Arceneaux, K., Boudreau, C., Dowling, C., Hillygus, S., Palfrey, T., et al. (2014). Reporting guidelines for experimental research: A report from the experimental research section standards committee. *Journal of Experimental Political Science, 1*(1), 81–98.
Gerber, A. S., & Green, D. P. (2000). The effects of canvassing, telephone calls, and direct mail on voter turnout: A field experiment. *American Political Science Review, 94,* 653–663.
Gosnell, H. (1926). An experiment in the stimulation of voting. *American Political Science Review, 20,* 869–874.
Horiuchi, Y., Imai, K., & Taniguchi, N. (2007). Designing and analyzing randomized experiments: Application to a Japanese election survey experiment. *American Journal of Political Science, 51,* 669–687.
Iyengar, S., & Kinder, D. R. (1987). *News that matters: Television and American opinion*. Chicago: University of Chicago Press.
Lassen, D. D. (2005). The effect of information on voter turnout: Evidence from a natural experiment. *American Journal of Political Science, 49,* 103–118.
Lupia, A. (2002). New ideas in experimental political science. *Political Analysis, 10,* 319–324.
McDermott, R. (2002). Experimental methodology in political science. *Political Analysis, 10,* 325–342.
Michelbach, P. A., Scott, J. T., Matland, R. E., & Bornstein, B. H. (2003). Doing rawls justice: An Experimental study of income distribution norms. *American Journal of Political Science, 47*(3), 523–539.
Milgram, S. (1974). *Obedience to authority*. New York: Harper and Row.
Morton, R. B., & Tucker, J. (2014). Experiment, journals, and ethics. *Journal of Experimental Political Science, 1,* 99–103.
Morton, R. B., & Williams, K. C. (2010). *Experimental political science and the study of causality: From nature to the lab*. New York: Cambridge University Press.
Mullinix, K. J., Leeper, T. J., Druckman, J. N., & Freese, J. (2015). The generalizability of survey experiments. *Journal of Experimental Political Science, 2,* 109–138.
Nie, N. H., Verba, S., & Petrocik, J. R. (1976). *The changing American voter*. Massachusetts: Harvard University Press.
Ogami, M., Taniguchi, N., & Shibutani, M. (2016). If you were to be reborn, which income distribution would be desirable for you?: An experimental study about effects of the veil of ignorance. A paper presented for the 2016 Annual Meeting of Japan Public Choice Society.
Rawls, J. (1999). A theory of justice. Cambridge, Mass: Harvard University Press, rev. ed.
Sullivan, J. L., Piereson, J. E., & Marcus, G. E. (1978). Ideological constraint in the mass public: A methodological critique and some new findings. *American Journal of Political Science, 22,* 233–249.
Taniguchi, N. (2016). Experimental researches in political science (*Seinjigaku ni okeru Jikken Kenkyu* in Japanese). Presented for the 2016 Annual Meeting of Japan Public Choice Society.

Experiments in Psychology: Current Issues in Irrational Choice Behavior

Takeharu Igaki, Paul Romanowich and Takayuki Sakagami

Psychology is the scientific study of behavior and the mind. To scientifically understand behavior and the mind, psychologists use diverse research methods such as experiments, questionnaire surveys, and interviews, among others. The experimental method is the most powerful tool for showing cause-and-effect relationships. Therefore, this chapter focuses on the experimental psychological studies.

Due to its focus on behavior and the mind, psychology also encompasses a wide range of subfields. Some of these subfields primarily utilize experimental research methods for studying behavior and the mind. Among them, behavior analysis is especially concerned with experimentally studying the fundamental principles that underlie organisms' behavior. Behavior analysis shares some common research themes with economics, such as behavioral economics. Specifically, both subfields are interested in the value derived from incentives such as money, and the factors affecting choice or decision-making. Additionally, both fields examine living organisms' behavior through descriptive and experimental approaches, not by normative approaches. Therefore, behavior analysis is an ideal psychology subfield to introduce psychological research methods to economists.

Choice behavior is one of the main research themes for behavior analysts. While principles and laws that control choice behavior have been postulated, examples of irrational choice in which choice behavior deviates from those principles and laws have also recently been studied. Because irrational behavior is a fundamental research subject in behavioral economics, irrational choice is one research theme where behavioral economics in economics and behavior analysis in psychology can significantly collaborate with each other.

T. Igaki (✉)
Ryutsu Keizai University, 3-2-1 Shin-Matsudo, Matsudo-shi 270-8555, Chiba-ken, Japan
e-mail: igaki@rku.ac.jp

P. Romanowich
University of Texas San Antonio, San Antonio, USA

T. Sakagami
Keio University, Tokyo, Japan

T. Kawagoe and H. Takizawa (eds.), *Diversity of Experimental Methods in Economics*,
https://doi.org/10.1007/978-981-13-6065-7_5

In this chapter, we provide a brief overview of experiments in psychology (especially with reference to behavior analysis) by introducing research findings pertaining to irrational choice. We begin with an overview of psychology and general research methodology. Next, we present some of the fundamental findings in behavior analysis. We then describe the main topic for this chapter, irrational choice, concentrating on the particularly intriguing research topics of self-control and suboptimal choice, among others. Lastly, we discuss how cooperation between economics and psychology can be improved, and what experimental methodology means for social science in general.

1 A Brief Overview of Psychology

1.1 What Is Psychology?

Psychology is the scientific study of mind and behavior. The mind refers to processes such as thoughts, feelings, and perceptions that are not directly observable and measurable. That is, mental processes must be inferred from directly observable/measurable action, which is what defines behavior. Examples of behavior include running, talking, and laughing.

Some fields of psychology, while measuring a behavior as the dependent variable, also try to explain this behavior change through psychological constructs or internal intervening variables such as will, intention, or representation. Behavior analysis, as described below (Sect. 2.1), focuses on the functional relationship between behavior and environmental variables, and does not use psychological constructs or internal intervening variables as the cause of behavior.

1.2 Psychological Research Methods

Because psychology is defined as a science, psychologists must engage in the scientific method to gather data, propose, test, and potentially revise hypotheses based on data. Psychological research involves using both descriptive and experimental research methodologies to gather data. Some common descriptive research procedures include case studies, surveys/questionnaires, and correlations.

1.2.1 Descriptive Research Methods

Case studies are in-depth observations and/or interviews for an extended period of time with one or a few individuals that display a specific behavior of interest. Case studies are frequently used in clinical psychology to gather data about rare psychopathological behaviors. Surveys and questionnaires are other types of descriptive research tool that can be used to quickly gather data about a particular topic or phenomenon. For example, if we wanted to gather data about health behaviors, we could simply ask individuals what they ate, how much they smoked, etc. This would be more efficient than watching and recording each of their meals, or each cigarette smoked (i.e., case study). We might also be interested in whether cigarette smoking is associated with healthy food consumption. In this case, we would use questionnaire data (amount of cigarettes smoked and amount of healthy food consumed) to calculate a correlation between the two variables. If these two variables are positively correlated, then as individuals smoke more, they typically consume more healthy food. By contrast, a negative correlation would imply that individuals that smoke more typically consume less healthy foods. While correlations provide information about general relationships, they do not provide information about specific causal relationships between the two variables. Causal relationships between variables can only be established through experimental methods.

1.2.2 Experimental Research Methods

Experimental psychological research focuses on establishing cause–effect relationships between variables by systematically manipulating one variable to determine its effect on another variable. The manipulated variable is called the independent variable, whereas the variable affected by the manipulation is called the dependent variable. The three main types of experimental methods used by psychologists are randomized control trials (RCTs), single-case experimental designs, and quasi-experimental studies. As described below, the type of experimental method used is primarily a function of the type of behavior under study.

RCTs consist of randomly assigning each participant to either a control group or an experimental group. Participants in the control group either do not come in contact with the independent variable or are provided with something that is not intended to change their behavior (i.e., placebo). Participants in the experimental group(s) receive the independent variable. Because random assignment equates participant characteristics before the experiment, any significant difference in the dependent variable between the control and experimental groups should be a function of the independent variable. For example, researchers interested in the effect of attention on childhood tantrums may randomly assign children and their parents to either an experimental (attention withheld) or control (no restrictions on attention) group. Tantrum frequency would be assessed via a standardized measure both before and after the experimental variable (attention) is manipulated.

Another way to show causality without random assignment involves using single-case (small n) experimental designs (e.g., Barlow et al. 2009; Iversen 2013). Each participant serves as both a control and experimental participant by repeatedly measuring behavior (i.e., dependent variable) with and without the independent variable present. For example, in three consecutive weeks, we could measure tantrum behavior when attention is withheld, without any constraints on attention, and again when attention is withheld for a child. If tantrum behavior reliably changes when attention is withheld, and changes back after constraints on attention are relaxed for that child, then we can infer a causal relationship between attention and childhood tantrums.

However, not all variables can be systematically manipulated, either for logistic or ethical reasons. For example, it would be unethical to potentially increase a person's chances of having cancer if you were interested in testing the relationship between cell phone use and brain cancer. In this case, quasi-experimental methods could be used to examine differences in cell phone use in people that do and do not have brain cancer. Unlike RCTs, there is no participant randomization. Therefore, statements about causality are typically weaker for quasi-experimental methods, relative to RCTs and single-case designs.

2 Behavior Analysis

2.1 Overview of Behavior Analysis

Behavior analysis is a research field in psychology for which prediction and control of behavior is the main research subject. Researchers employing the behavior analytic approach examine the factors critical for behavior change and maintenance. Based on a functional analysis between environment and behavior, researchers seek to find the causes of behavior within a given environment.

The field of behavior analysis can be further subdivided into two branches, the experimental analysis of behavior and applied behavior analysis. In the former, fundamental laws and principles that control behavior are primarily examined in the laboratory using different species, such as humans, monkeys, rats, or pigeons. Applied behavior analysis is characterized by the application of these fundamental behavioral laws and principles to practical social problems, such as increasing functionality for people with developmental disabilities or increasing efficiency in the workplace through organizational behavior management. For procedures and interventions developed in applied behavior analysis, emphasis is placed on whether these procedures and interventions have social validity, which refers to the social appropriateness of the procedures and the social significance of the results (Kennedy 1992; Winett et al. 1991).

In psychology, the term "learning" is often defined as a measurable change in behavior due to experience with the environment. Therefore, behavior analysis addresses a wide range of behavioral phenomena involved in learning. Thus far, two fundamental types of learning have been studied: respondent conditioning and operant conditioning.

Respondent conditioning was first systematically examined by the Russian physiologist Pavlov (1927). In respondent conditioning, behavior change is governed by antecedent stimuli (i.e., what happens before the behavior). Pavlov was interested in the salivary reflex of dogs and showed that when a piece of meat was put into a dog's mouth, the dog always salivated. That is, due to the salivary reflex, the dog did not have to learn the relationship between meat and salivation. Next, Pavlov repeatedly rang a bell before each presentation of meat. It should be noted that the sound of the bell is a neutral stimulus which initially does not elicit salivation for dogs. Eventually, after pairing the bell and meat several times, the sound of the bell alone came to elicit salivation. The salivation produced by the bell alone is considered to be the learned behavior, as the dog did not salivate to the sound of the bell prior to the pairing of the bell and meat.

In operant conditioning, what happens after the behavior is primarily responsible for behavior change. That is, the future likelihood of a behavior increases or decreases based on the consequences produced by that behavior. This process is called operant conditioning. Behavior analysis has centered on the prediction and control of operant behavior produced through this type of conditioning.

2.2 *Basic Principles of Operant Conditioning*

2.2.1 Reinforcement and Punishment

In operant conditioning, increasing the future likelihood of a behavior as a function of a consequence is known as reinforcement. There are two forms of reinforcement: positive and negative. The term "positive" refers to the addition of a stimulus as a consequence of the operant behavior. For example, imagine a child receiving allowance money from their parents only after helping with the household chores. If the child's helping behavior increases in frequency, then this procedure is an example of positive reinforcement. The term "negative" refers to the removal or elimination of a stimulus as a consequence of the operant behavior. For example, imagine that a person has a painful toothache. Receiving dental treatment will eliminate the toothache. If the person is more likely to go to the dentist the next time they have a toothache, then this type of reinforcement is called negative reinforcement.

Punishment produces the opposite effect on behavior relative to reinforcement. That is, punishment decreases the likelihood of behavior. As with reinforcement, there are two forms of punishment: positive and negative. Positive punishment refers to a decrease in behavior when a stimulus is added as a consequence. Negative punishment refers to a decrease in behavior when a stimulus is removed or eliminated as a consequence. Children usually decrease the frequency of misbehaving when their parents scold them for the misbehavior (positive punishment). However, parents could also reduce misbehavior by cutting off their allowance (negative punishment) contingent on misbehavior. Figure 1 shows the relation between the increase or decrease in behavior and the presentation or removal of stimulus.

Like a snack or allowance for a child, a stimulus that functions to increase response frequency is called a reinforcer. A primary reinforcer (also called an unconditioned reinforcer) is a stimulus that innately increases any response. Examples of primary reinforcers include food, water, or sexual stimulation. A secondary or conditioned

		Stimulus	
		Present	Withdraw
Behavior	Increase	Positive Reinforcement	Negative Reinforcement
	Decrease	Positive Punishment	Negative Punishment

Fig. 1 The relationship between the increase or decrease in behavior and the presentation or removal of a stimulus

reinforcer starts as a neutral stimulus (a stimulus which does not increase behavior as a consequence) and acquires reinforcing strength by being paired with already established reinforcers. Verbal praise such as saying "good job" and smiles are examples of conditioned reinforcers. A conditioned reinforcer that can be exchanged for various unconditioned and/or other conditioned reinforcers is known as a generalized conditioned reinforcer. Money is an example of a generalized conditioned reinforcer, because money can be exchanged for a wide variety of reinforcing goods and services.

Like scolding a child, a stimulus that functions to decrease response frequency is called a punisher. Punishers can also be unconditioned or conditioned. The pain caused by a whip is an example of an unconditioned punisher, while being scolded is an example of a conditioned punisher.

2.2.2 Discriminative Stimuli and the Contingency of Reinforcement

Although operant behavior is mainly governed by consequences, the stimuli preceding the operant behavior also have an effect on the occurrence of that behavior. Unlike respondent behavior, an antecedent stimulus does not elicit behavior. Instead, these antecedent stimuli provide information about what consequences may follow the emitted behavior. These stimuli occurring prior to the operant behavior are called discriminative stimuli. For example, the walk signal at an intersection generally corresponds to the time when it is safe to walk across the intersection. However, an individual may cross at any time, whether the walk signal is on or not. The walk signal simply signals when the frequency of crossing is the safest.

Thus, the relationship between an antecedent stimulus (i.e., discriminative stimulus), operant behavior, and consequence (i.e., a reinforcer or punisher) is important for understanding why a given behavior occurs. This relationship is called the three-term contingency of reinforcement and is the most fundamental principle for behavior analysis.

2.2.3 Schedules of Reinforcement

A reinforcement schedule is a rule that describes when a consequence will be likely to follow a given behavior. When every occurrence of a behavior is followed by a reinforcer, a continuous reinforcement (CRF) schedule is in effect. However, in many instances, a reinforcer is not delivered after every response. A partial or intermittent reinforcement schedule is the general term used for this type of schedule. Moreover, extinction is a procedure defined as the removal or withdrawal of the reinforcer for a previously reinforced response. As a result of extinction, the frequency of the response gradually declines and eventually ceases to occur (i.e., extinguishes).

In one type of intermittent reinforcement schedule, known as an interval schedule, reinforcement is contingent on the first response after a certain period of time elapses. Interval schedules can be classified as either fixed interval (FI) or variable interval (VI) reinforcement schedules. During FI schedules, the interval before reinforcement is available is always the same fixed amount of time. For example, during an FI 10 s schedule, the first response an organism makes after 10 s elapses will result in a reinforcer. During a VI schedule, the interval is represented by an average amount of time. For example, during a VI 10 s schedule, reinforcement for the first response may occur after 3 s, 8 s, or 19 s have elapsed. On average, reinforcement is available for the first response after 10 s has elapsed. A time schedule is similar to an interval schedule except that no response is required for reinforcer delivery. Time schedules can be classified as either fixed-time (FT) or variable-time (VT) schedules. During FT schedules, reinforcement is delivered automatically after a fixed amount of time has passed. During VT schedules, the time between reinforcement deliveries is variable.

Another type of intermittent reinforcement schedule is a ratio schedule, in which reinforcement is contingent on the number of responses. Like interval schedules, there are two subtypes of ratio schedule: fixed ratio (FR) and variable ratio (VR) schedules. The difference between these two subtypes is whether the number of responses required for reinforcement is predictable or not. For example, during an FR 10 schedule, a reinforcer is delivered after every 10 responses. During a VR 10 schedule, a reinforcer is delivered after 10 responses, on average.

These four schedules (FI, VI, FR, and VR) are considered the basic schedules of reinforcement. Organisms show stereotypic behavior patterns when responding to each basic schedule. These patterns can be shown on a cumulative record, which plots time on the horizontal (x) axis and cumulative responses on the vertical (y) axis. Figure 2 illustrates a cumulative record with each of the four basic schedules. Each time a response occurs, the line increases one step upward. A dashed line (i.e., oblique pip) represents reinforcer delivery. The number of response per unit time is represented as response rate. In a cumulative record, response rates are expressed as the slope. The higher the response rate, the steeper the slope. Likewise, the lower the response rate, the shallower the slope. FI schedules are characterized by a pause after reinforcer delivery, and then a gradual response rate increase until the next reinforcer delivery. This FI schedule pattern is called "scalloped" because the shape of cumulative response curve resembles the edge of a scallop. During a VI schedule, organisms produce moderate but stable response rates. During FR schedules,

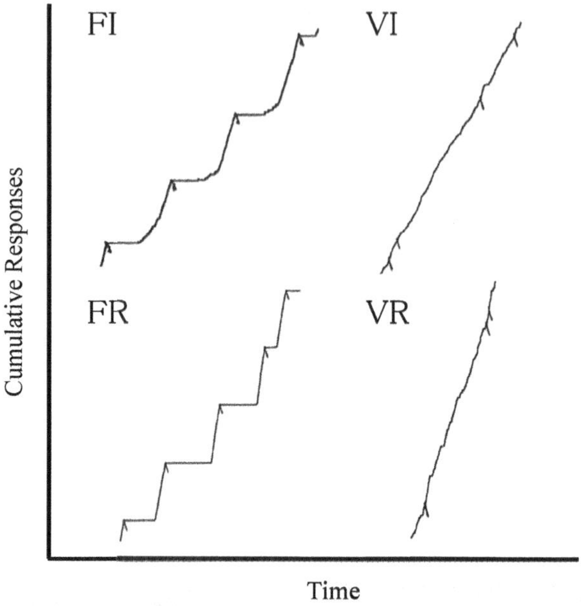

Fig. 2 Cumulative records for four basic reinforcement schedules: fixed interval 4 min, variable interval 3 min, fixed ratio 120, variable ratio 360 (based on Ferster and Skinner 1957)

organisms make a post-reinforcement pause after the reinforcer is delivered, which produces a stepwise (i.e., break and run) pattern for the cumulative response curve. Finally, during VR schedules, organisms produce high steady response rates without post-reinforcement pauses.

Two or more basic schedules can also be combined, which is then called a compound schedule. One of the most important compound schedules is a concurrent schedule, in which two reinforcement schedules are simultaneously available. Concurrent schedules are used to measure preference in choice behavior. Other compound schedules successively present organisms each basic schedule (that is, one reinforcement schedule is presented at a time). There are four main types of these compound schedules: multiple, mixed, chained, and tandem schedules. In a multiple schedule, the discriminative stimulus (e.g., color) is different between each basic reinforcement schedule, and a reinforcer is delivered for completing each basic reinforcement schedule. A mixed schedule is the same as a multiple schedule except that each reinforcement schedule is signaled by the same discriminative stimulus. During a chained schedule, different discriminative stimuli also represent each basic schedule. However, the reinforcer is delivered only after organisms complete the response requirement for the last basic schedule. Each basic schedule comprising a chained schedule is referred to as a link. For example, if a chained schedule consists of two basic schedules, the first schedule is called the initial link and the second schedule is the terminal link. Finally, a tandem schedule is the same as a chained schedule except that each of the basic schedules is not signaled by a different discriminative stimulus.

2.2.4 Animal Experiments in the Laboratory

During operant conditioning research, especially in the experimental analysis of behavior, animal subjects, such as rats and pigeons, are often used. This is because environmental variables can be more easily controlled, and their behavior is simpler than that of humans (Mazur 2016). Prior to most operant conditioning experiment, the animals' body weight is decreased to approximately 80–85% of free-feeding weight through food restriction. This food restriction makes it possible for food to be a reliable reinforcer during the experiment. During the experiments, animals are placed in an enclosed box, which is known as an operant chamber. In the operant chamber, animals are reinforced for responding in many different ways. Rats can press a lever which may result in a food pellet as a reinforcer. Pigeons can peck at an illuminated disk to activate a grain feeder for a short period of time. Figure 3 represents a typical operant chamber for pigeons. A circular disk mounted on the front panel can be illuminated white, red, or green, which functions as the discriminative stimulus. During choice procedures, more than one illuminated disk can be provided. Using these apparatus, animal reinforcement schedule performance during operant conditioning can be reliably and validly examined. Figure 4 shows a representative result from a laboratory experiment using animal subjects in which an ABAB design (a type of single-case design) was used (Hammond 1980). During an ABAB design, conditions A and B are presented successively and alternated to each subject. Baseline responding is measured during the A condition, whereas the effect of the independent variable on behavior is measured during the B condition. Baseline training (A condition) continues until steady-state responding is established. After a stability criterion (e.g., little variability or absence of systematic trends across trials) is met, the independent variable is presented during the B condition. The second A and B conditions are repeated to make sure that the initial results can be replicated, and causation between the independent and dependent variable can be inferred. In Fig. 4, the mean response rates of lever pressing for 10 rats are shown, indicating that the contingency between responding and reinforcer delivery is needed to maintain moderate responding.

2.2.5 Representative Experimental Variables for Operant Conditioning

As described above, response rate is expressed as the number of responses per unit time. This is typically an important dependent variable during operant conditioning experiments. The proportion of responses to one option, relative to another (also called preference), is also often used as a dependent variable in choice experiments. Latency, the time that elapses from stimulus onset to response, is often used as a dependent variable in applied settings.

Reinforcement rate, the number of reinforcers presented during a unit of time, is a typical independent variable during operant conditioning experiments. Additionally, the delay to reinforcer delivery, the amount of reinforcement per delivery, and the

Fig. 3 An operant chamber for pigeons. During an experiment, pigeons are placed in the operant chamber. A plastic disk, generally referred to as a "key", is located in the upper part of the front panel. Pigeons are trained to peck the key that can be illuminated with different colored lights. Reinforcers are delivered through a grain feeder which is shown in the lower part of the front panel. Pigeons can earn access to a food hopper filled with grains (i.e., the reinforcer) for a few seconds for pecking the illuminated keys

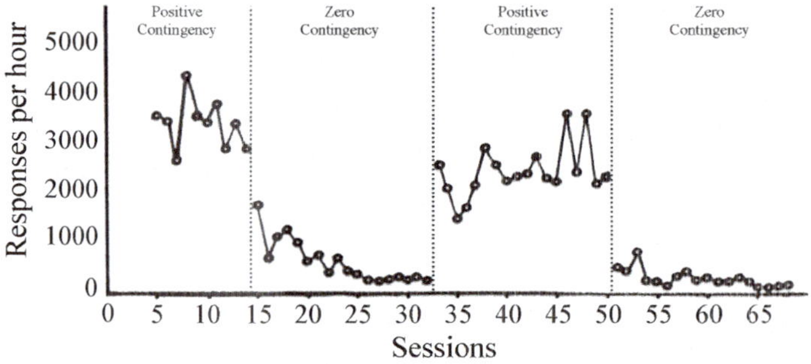

Fig. 4 Representative data from a laboratory experiment using animal subjects. The mean response rates for 10 rats' lever presses when either positive or zero contingencies were successively arranged (Reproduced from Hammond 1980)

probability of reinforcement per response are also often controlled for during operant conditioning experiments.

The time between two responses, known as the inter-response time (IRT), is also an important experimental variable which can be both a dependent and independent variable. IRTs are operants, and thus, a modifiable behavior. For example, short IRTs can be reinforced, increasing their probability in the future. As a result, high response rates are observed. This procedure is called a differential reinforcement of high rates (DRH) schedule. On the other hand, if long IRTs are reinforced, the probability of long IRTs will increase in the future. Consequently, low response rates are observed.

This is a differential reinforcement of low rates (DRL) schedule. Furthermore, since IRTs reflect a moment-to-moment property of behavior, IRTs can also be used to account for behavioral phenomena from a molecular point of view.

2.3 Choice

Using an experimental framework and principles described above, various types of behavior analytic research have been conducted. Historically, choice behavior has been one of the major research topics in behavior analysis (see Mazur and Fantino 2014, for a review). Concurrent reinforcement schedules are typically used during choice research. As a result of this research, a consistent pattern of behavior allocation has been described. This pattern is now known as the matching law.

2.3.1 The Matching Law

Using concurrent VI VI reinforcement schedules (two VI reinforcement schedules available at the same time), Herrnstein (1961, 1970) found that relative response rates for one response alternative were proportional (i.e., matched) to the relative reinforcement rates on that same alternative. The mathematical expression of the matching law is as follows:

$$\frac{B_1}{B_1 + B_2} = \frac{R_1}{R_1 + R_2} \tag{1}$$

In this equation, B_1 and B_2 represent the number of responses for alternative 1 and 2. R_1 and R_2 represent the number of reinforcers obtained for alternatives 1 and 2. Thus, the matching law allows us to predict an organism's behavioral allocation in a choice situation by examining the allocation of reinforcement in that situation.

However, subsequent research suggests that there are some cases in which behavior allocation deviates from the matching law's predictions. Baum (1974, 1979) proposed a generalized matching equation which can account for some of these systematic deviations from matching. The generalized version of the matching law is as follows:

$$\frac{B_1}{B_2} = b\left(\frac{R_1}{R_2}\right)^a \tag{2}$$

In Eq. 2, the number of responses and reinforcers for each alternative is represented in the form of a ratio. Moreover, by adding the coefficient b and the exponent a, Eq. 2 can describe two typical deviations from matching. Coefficient b represents bias and exponent a represents sensitivity to the reinforcement ratio. When $b = 1$ and $a = 1$, Eq. 2 becomes the simple ratio formula that is algebraically equivalent to Eq. 1.

Bias is indicated by a deviation in coefficient b from 1 and is produced by factors unknown to the experimenter, usually related to the subject and/or experimental conditions. For example, if a subject has a preference or aversion for one of the choice alternatives based on location or color independent of reinforcement schedule, response bias for that alternative may be observed.

In terms of sensitivity to the reinforcement ratio, values "$0 \leq a < 1$" represent undermatching, whereas values "$a > 1$" represent overmatching. Undermatching indicates a shift in the response ratio toward indifference, relative to the reinforcement ratio arranged by the experimenter. That is, the organism responds relatively less to the more favorable alternative than predicted by the reinforcement ratio. Undermatching is typically observed when it is difficult for the subject to discriminate between the different response alternatives. Overmatching indicates that response ratio changes are greater than the arranged reinforcement ratio. That is, the organism responds relatively more to the more favorable alternative than predicted by the reinforcement ratio. Overmatching is typically observed when switching between alternatives requires a large amount of effort on the organism's part. There are other instances which have resulted in dramatic departures from matching. These are treated as instances of irrational choice in the next part of this chapter.

Moreover, Rachlin et al. (1980) indicated that Eq. (2) can also apply to situations where reinforcers for choice alternative are qualitatively different, such as food and water (i.e., complementary goods). In this case, as reinforcer rates for one alternative increase, response rates for that alternative decrease. This phenomenon is called antimatching, which is expressed as values "$a < 0$". Rachlin et al. (1981) showed that in various studies using food and water as reinforcers, a was about -10, suggesting that a could be thought of as an index of goods substitutability.

2.3.2 Graphical Representation for a Choice Procedure

Before explaining the details of irrational choice, we will briefly describe a graphical representation of the choice procedures discussed in this chapter. Figure 5 shows the basic elements for this graphical representation. Each element is distinguished by shape, line type (solid or dotted), line width, and the contrasting density of the lines (see additional details in the caption for Fig. 5). Figure 6 shows a typical concurrent reinforcement schedule in which VI 60 s and VI 30 s schedules are arranged as each choice alternative.

Although concurrent schedules are a standard procedure for measuring preference, it is debatable whether a pure preference measurement can be achieved when different types of reinforcement schedules are operating during each alternative. Reinforcement schedules require the organism to respond according to the property of the schedule (e.g., high response rate for a VR schedule). If the same type of schedule is used for both concurrent schedule alternatives, the response characteristics will be relatively counterbalanced. However, if different schedules are used for each alternative (e.g., FI and VR), it may not be clear whether any response rate difference between schedules is due to the schedule requirements or preference between the

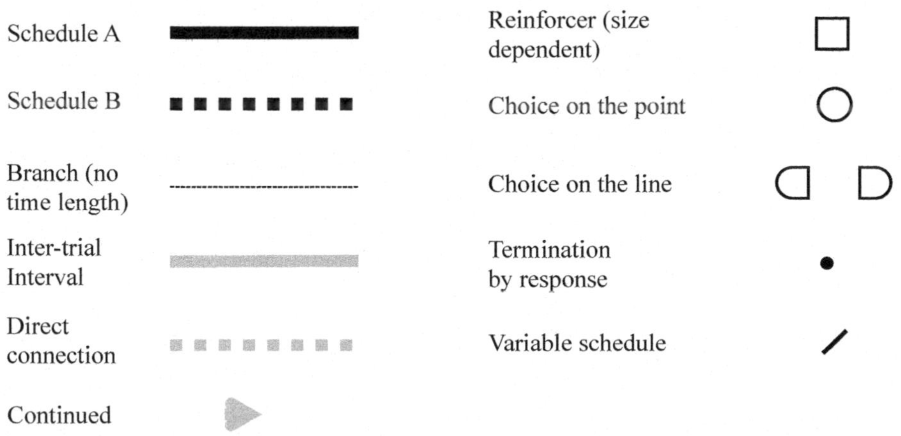

Fig. 5 Basic elements for a graphical representation Schedule A and Schedule B: when two choice alternatives need to be clearly distinguished, solid or dotted lines are used. Inter-trial interval: the choice trial is often repeated several times during operant choice experiments, and the interval between choice trials is called the inter-trial interval. Reinforcer (size dependent): when reinforcer amounts (i.e., the number of reinforcers) are different, the square varies in size. Choice on the line: organisms make a choice on the segment surrounded by the semicircle. Variable: a diagonal line overlaps with a horizontal line when the value of the reinforcement schedule varies, such as a VI schedule

Fig. 6 An example of concurrent schedules

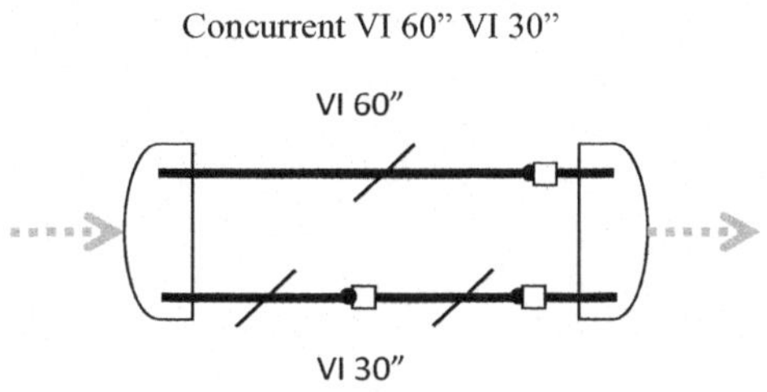

two schedules. Thus, the reinforcement schedules directly influence response rates and can obscure pure preference measurements.

One way to overcome this response rate problem is to use a concurrent-chain schedule (see Fig. 7). First, the initial links for each chained schedule are presented as concurrent schedules. For both alternatives (i.e., initial links of the two chain schedules), the same schedules are typically used. The relative number of responses during the concurrent schedules is a putative preference measure. During the terminal link of each chained schedule, the reinforcement schedules differ. Completing the schedule requirement for one alternative during the concurrent schedule results in the corresponding terminal-link schedule in the chained schedule, while the other (not completed) alternative becomes inactive. By responding during the corresponding terminal-link schedule, subjects earn a primary reinforcer such as food. After terminal-link reinforcement, the initial links reappear, and the next trial begins. Dur-

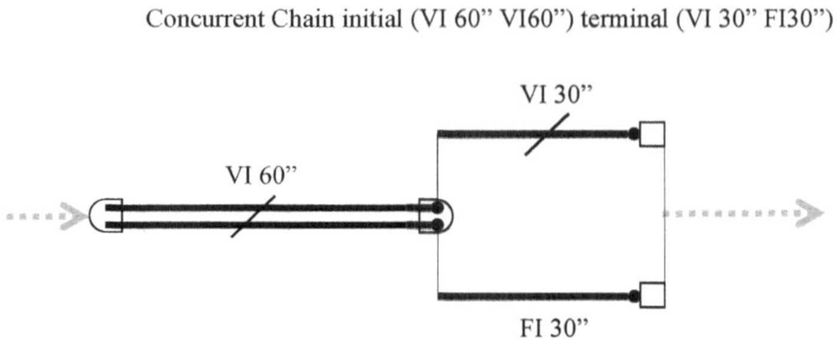

Fig. 7 An example of concurrent-chain schedules

ing the concurrent-chain schedule, the terminal-link stimulus acquires conditioned reinforcer strength through the presentation of primary reinforcers during the terminal link. Therefore, preference during the initial link reflects the relative value of terminal-link stimulus (i.e., conditioned reinforcers) (Fantino and Romanowich 2007; Williams 1988).

Figure 7 shows an example of the concurrent-chain schedules with VI 30 s and FI 30 s schedules arranged during the mutually exclusive terminal links. Identical VI 60 s schedules serve as a preference measure during the initial links. Therefore, if the organism prefers the VI 30 s terminal-link schedule, the corresponding VI 60 s initial-link schedule should have relatively more responses than the VI 60 s initial-link schedule corresponding to the FI 30 s schedule. This example describes measuring choice between VI and FI schedules with same reinforcement rates. Previous research (e.g., Fantino 1967; Herrnstein 1964) showed that subjects exhibit greater preference for a VI schedule over an FI schedule even though equal reinforcement rates were arranged for both schedules. This phenomenon showed preference for an alternative which delivered reinforcers at varying, irregular intervals and is also an example of a deviation from matching.

By using concurrent-chain schedules, we can obtain a clearer preference measure by isolating the terminal-link schedules and eliminating any response rate effects. However, it has been shown that the degree of preference in the concurrent-chain schedule is also influenced by the relative duration of the initial-link and terminal-link schedules (Fantino 1969; Grace 1994; Grace et al. 2006; Romanowich et al. 2017; Squires and Fantino 1971). For example, as initial-link length increases, preference for the terminal-link correlated with higher reinforcement rates decreases (i.e., initial-link effect). Similarly, as terminal-link length increases, preference for richer terminal-link decreases (i.e., terminal-link effect). Different theories have been proposed to explain these effects by expanding the generalized matching law (Eq. 2). Delay reduction theory (Fantino et al. 1993) and the contextual choice model (Grace 1994) are examples of these expanded matching law theories.

3 Rationality

3.1 Rationality in Economics

Although the definition of "rationality" varies across different research areas, rationality is typically defined as adherence to a normative model or theory in economics (Hardman 2009). The traditional normative economic theory is known as the expected utility theory, first postulated by Daniel Bernoulli in 1738. In economics, utility is defined as the total sum of satisfaction that an individual receives from consuming a good or service. Expected utility theory assumes that an individual chooses rationally in order to maximize the expected utility obtained from alternatives under conditions of uncertainty.

Thus, expected utility theory is a normative theory that explains how to make optimal decisions under uncertainty (e.g., Lea 1994; Vriend 1996). In fact, expected utility theory has proven useful for explaining choice behavior in situations such as gambling and lotteries. However, organisms do not always act optimally, and expected utility theory violations, such as the Allais paradox, may be more the norm than the exception, as described below.

Moreover, in many economic theories, including expected utility theory, "homo economicus" or "economic man" are assumed to be rational human beings. For example, homo economicus pursues their goals using the shortest and easiest path, without biased judgments or emotional considerations. However, organisms living in the real world have worries, doubts, and sometimes make biased judgements. Similar to violations for expected utility theory, deviations from an ideal model of homo economicus have been described as an "anomaly". However, these anomalies have proven so reliable that the field of behavioral economics, which began with prospect theory proposed by Kahneman and Tversky (1979), has blossomed over the past 40 years. Unlike expected utility theory, prospect theory is a descriptive theory and focuses on the process of irrational decision-making with an eye toward behavior in real-world settings. Therefore, the research themes in behavioral economics have been a great source of irrational choice.

3.2 Rationality in Behavior Analysis

Research about choice behavior has also evolved over the past 40 years in the field of behavior analysis (see Sect. 2.3), although somewhat separately from the development of decision-making research in economics or other psychological fields, such as social and cognitive psychology. Unlike economic research, behavior analytic choice research focuses on the fundamental mechanisms underlying choice, and not on concepts of irrationality. As previously noted, reinforcement is an important concept for the prediction and control of operant behavior. Thus, reinforcement is also an important factor controlling choice behavior. The generalized matching law represented in Eq. 2 describes how the relative reinforcement rate is proportional to relative rates of emitted behavior. Subsequently, other reinforcement parameters, such as reinforcement amount and delay, have been shown to influence preference in choice procedures (Davison and McCarthy 1988; Williams 1988). As a result of these findings, the right side of Eq. 2 has been expanded to include these reinforcement parameters:

$$\frac{B_1}{B_2} = b\left(\frac{R_1}{R_2}\right)^a \left(\frac{A_1}{A_2}\right)^c \left(\frac{D_2}{D_1}\right)^d \tag{3}$$

In this equation, A represents the reinforcer amount, D represents the reinforcer delay, and c and d represent the sensitivity to the amount and delay ratios, respectively. Equation 3 is considered to be a comprehensive model for choice behavior.

However, one criticism of the matching equation is that it only describes *how* organisms allocate their behavior but does not explain *why* organisms show matching behavior. To overcome this shortcoming, some theories have been proposed such as momentary maximizing (Shimp 1966), molar maximizing (Rachlin et al. 1976), and melioration (Herrnstein and Vaughan 1980). Above all, the concept of maximization also holds an important position in explaining the matching phenomenon, as is the case with expected utility maximization in economics. Momentary maximizing theory suggests that organisms maximize reinforcers according to moment-to-moment schedule contingencies. That is, subjects tend to choose the alternative which has the higher probability of reinforcement at each moment in time. By contrast, molar maximization theory explains matching behavior as organisms allocating their behavior to maximize overall reinforcement rate during a wider time period (e.g., entire experimental session). Thus, both momentary and molar maximizing theories postulate that matching behavior emerges as a byproduct of the maximization processes, but through different reinforcement rate sensitivities by the organism. Molar maximization theory is closely related to economics. In fact, Rachlin et al. (1981) noted that the idea of molar maximization is borrowed from economics. Molar maximization has also been proposed as an alternative to the reinforcement principle and matching theory. Thus, molar maximization is a normative theory for behavior analysis, like expected utility theory for economics.

However, just like prospect theory has shown inconsistencies between expected utility theory and economic behavior, behavior analytic research has often shown that organisms choice behavior is not always consistent with the prediction of molar maximization theory (e.g., Mazur 1981; Vaughan 1981). Currently, molar maximization theory is not universally supported as a normative theory for behavior analysis. Nonetheless, the reinforcement principle and derivatives of the matching law (Eq. 3) remain as fundamental choice behavior laws for behavior analysis. In fact, the history of the experimental analysis of behavior has been filled with research about how reinforcement's effect should be measured, and what effect reinforcement has on an organisms' behavior. Therefore, we make a provisional assumption that these theories regarding reinforcement and choice are normative theories in behavior analysis.

The following sections describe examples of irrational choice situations in which a large amount of behavior analysis research has focused. These include (1) self-control, (2) suboptimal choice, and (3) the segmentation effect. Before discussing the details of these situations, we must operationally define irrational choice. In these situations, we use the term "irrational choice" in the following two cases: (A) subjects prefer the alternative with a lower objective reinforcer rate/amount to the one with a higher objective reinforcer rate/amount in a choice situation (i.e., subjects do not maximize reinforcement), or (B) subjects show a strong preference for one of the alternatives even though both alternatives have an equal objective reinforcer rate/amount. Self-control and suboptimal choice are described by case (A), whereas the segmentation effect is described by case (B).

4 Self-control

We begin with self-control because both behavioral economic and behavior analysis researchers have substantially contributed to the existing scientific literature. This is perhaps one of the few scientific themes where these two areas have profitably cooperated and worked together.

4.1 Experimental Paradigm for Self-control

Behavior analytic researchers treat self-control as a choice situation between a sooner and smaller alternative (abbreviated SS) and a later and larger alternative (abbreviated LL) (Green et al. 1981; Rachlin and Green 1972). For example, a hungry individual may be faced with a choice between immediate access to junk food (i.e., SS), versus preparing their own nutritious and healthy meal (i.e., LL). The junk food is immediately available, but provides minimal nourishment, whereas the healthy meal takes longer to prepare, but leads to better overall health. In everyday language, we might call the individual who constantly selects the SS option "impulsive", whereas constantly selecting the LL option shows "self-control".

The experimental paradigm for testing self-control/impulsivity is depicted in Fig. 8. Time runs from left to right, and an individual must choose at the choice point (open circle) between two mutually exclusive alternatives. The SS alternative is represented by a short line ending with a small rectangle depicting reinforcer magnitude. The LL alternative has a longer delay line and ends with a larger rectangle. Notice that the gray inter-trial interval line begins when the small reinforcer ends and ends when the large reinforcer ends. This procedure equates the total length of each trial whether the subject chooses the SS or LL alternative. The subject then experiences the next choice point after the inter-trial interval ends.

We can imagine other examples of SS versus LL alternatives, such as reading comics versus reading textbooks just before a term exam; eating sweet desserts

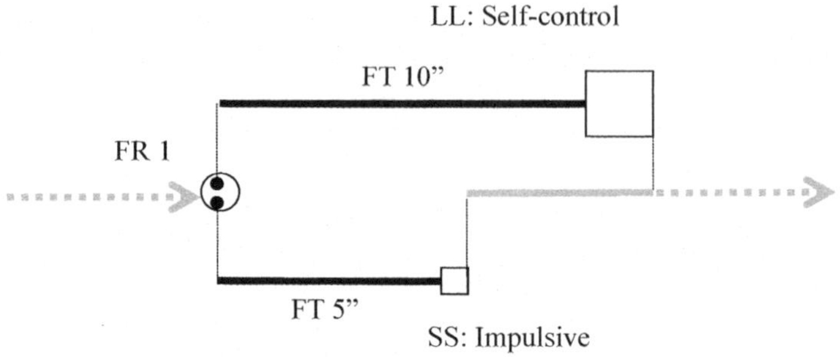

Fig. 8 The experimental paradigm for self-control

and gaining weight versus not eating sweets and maintaining a healthy weight, and smoking/drinking versus abstaining from smoking/drinking, all from this simple paradigm. However, because of the inter-trial interval that equates overall trial time, individuals cannot maximize reinforcement during a daily session if they exclusively select the SS alternative. Even so, many individuals prefer the SS alternative to the LL alternative. From the operational definition mentioned above, this clearly demonstrates irrational behavior in terms of case (A). Although the SS/LL choice procedure described above is a representative method for examining self-control, it should be noted that there exist other experimental procedures for self-control such as the primrose path (Kudadjie-Gyamfi and Rachlin 1996) and token reinforcement (Hackenberg 2009).

4.2 Delay Discounting

A theoretical framework to explain why some individuals choose the SS alternative more frequently than the LL alternative is known as delay discounting. First, longer delays to a potential reinforcer make that reinforcer less valuable. For example, if given a choice between a computer that is very responsive to input versus one that takes more time to register a keystroke, almost everyone will choose the former, especially when a term paper is due the next morning. However, sensitivity to the delay differs between individuals and organisms. Thus, for humans, choice questionnaires using paper and pencil tasks or computers are typically used to assess delay sensitivity (see Critchfield and Kollins 2001; Odum 2011 for details). For nonhuman animal subjects, an adjusting delay choice procedure has been developed (see Mazur 1987 for details).

For either humans or nonhuman organisms, these choices can be plotted on a graph, with the delay to rewards on the horizontal (x) axis and subjective rewards value on the vertical (y) axis (see Fig. 9). Usually, the resulting curve is negatively sloped. The obtained data for subjective reward value (y-axis) can then be fitted to a theoretical model. The two most common models used are exponential and

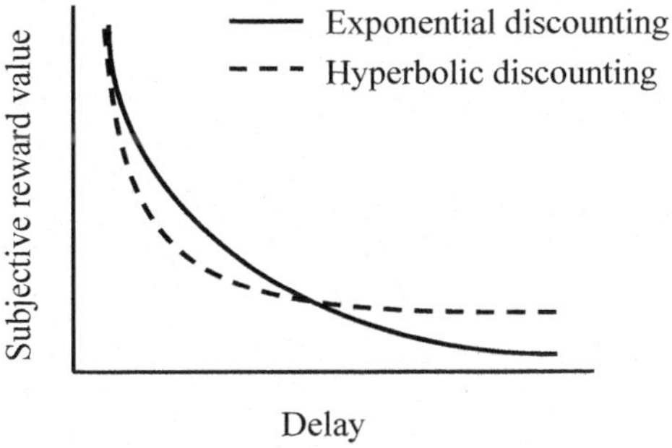

Fig. 9 The delay discounting function

hyperbolic functions. Figure 9 illustrates these two types of discounting functions. Exponential functions have been traditionally used in economics to describe delay discounting. More recently, hyperbolic functions have been shown to provide a better fit for delay discounting data, relative to exponential functions (Johnson and Bickel 2002; Madden et al. 2003; Mazur and Biondi 2009). A mathematical description of a hyperbolic function is shown below:

$$V = \frac{A}{(1 + kD)} \tag{4}$$

where V represents the subjective reward value, A represents reward amount, k represents the degree (or rate) of discounting, and D represents reward delay. The parameter k, known as the discounting rate, is determined on an individual basis. Larger k values indicate a greater sensitivity to delay (i.e., higher impulsivity) expressed as a steeper discounting function graphically. Figure 10 shows two examples of hypothetical hyperbolic discounting functions. The closed circles show an individual with a greater delay sensitivity, which results in a steeper curve. The open squares show an individual with relatively less delay sensitivity, which results in a shallower curve. In both cases, the k values for each hyperbolic discounting curve can be calculated based on nonlinear regression.

Because k represents an individual's delay sensitivity or impulsivity, various factors affecting k have been explored. For example, the relationship between k and other personal factors, such as income (Green et al. 1996), age (Green et al. 1994b), culture (Du et al. 2002), addiction (Bickel et al. 1999; Petry 2001; Petry and Casarella 1999), and others have been examined. In addition, aspects of the reinforcer such as type (Odum and Rainaud 2003), inflation (Ostaszewski et al. 1998), and magnitude (Green et al. 1997) also exert an influence on the value of k.

The hyperbolic function in Eq. 4 not only provides a good fit for delay discounting data but also predicts a differential sensitivity for short and long delays. That is, as can be seen in Fig. 9, the slope of the hyperbolic function is steeper during the short delays, and then somewhat shallower during the long delays. This indicates that reward value sharply decreases, even at short delays, but remains relatively constant

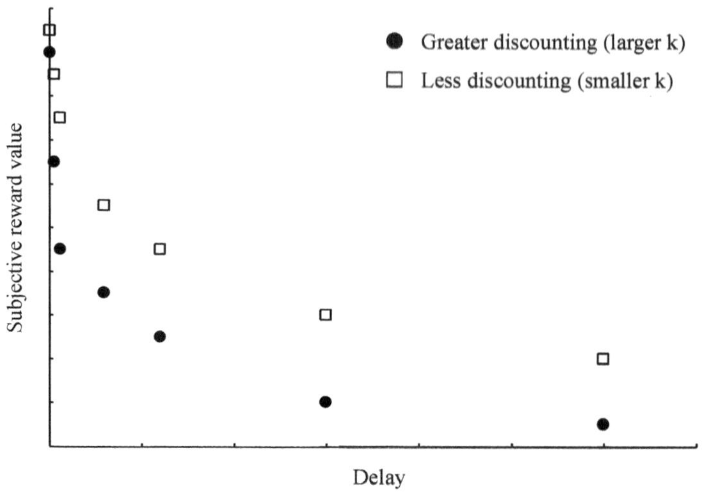

Fig. 10 Hypothetical delay discounting data demonstrating two examples of hyperbolic discounting functions

at longer delays. By contrast, in exponential functions, the decreasing slope of the reward value is constant across the full range of delays.

4.3 Preference Reversal

The differential sensitivity for short and long delays predicted by the hyperbolic function allows us to explain a phenomenon called preference reversal. Preference reversal[1] refers to the finding that when delays are relatively long for both alternatives, organisms typically prefer the LL alternative. However, when the delays are shortened, organisms will switch to the SS alternative (Ainslie and Herrnstein 1981; Green et al. 1981; Rachlin and Green 1972). For example, you may set your alarm clock the night before to get up early and exercise (LL choice). However, in the morning when the alarm sounds, you hit the "snooze" button repeatedly to sleep in (SS choice). Initially, you made an LL response by setting the alarm when both getting up early to exercise and more sleep were temporally distant. However, when faced with the immediate choice of waking up and exercising, and sleeping in, your preference had reversed to the SS alternative.

Preference reversal is predicted by the hyperbolic function's differing change in value as a function of delay. When two alternatives are temporally distant, organisms

[1]It is important to note that preference reversal mentioned in this section is different from the one typically examined in behavioral economics, which describes a divergence between the preference for objects (e.g., lotteries) and the monetary evaluation for those objects (for a review, see Seidl 2002).

make self-control choices, as delay to reward does not affect value as strongly (i.e., the value for both alternatives is already low). However, for relatively immediate choices, organisms make impulsive choices, as the delay to reward is more strongly affecting value. By contrast, exponential functions do not predict preference reversal because the function predicts the same discounting rates throughout all delays. Exponential functions predict that if organisms show preference for one alternate with a certain delay, then that preference will not change if the overall delay is either increased or decreased for both alternatives. Thus, assuming hyperbolic discounting helps to predict one irrational aspect of an organisms' choice behavior in this self-control situation.

However, researchers can also take advantage of preference reversals to increase organisms' self-control choices. One way of doing this is to use the precommitment technique (Ariely and Wertenbroch 2002; Strotz 1955; Thaler and Shefrin 1981). In the precommitment technique, once organisms show self-control for a temporally distant choice, the choice becomes locked in and unchangeable. That is, an organism cannot shift their choice from the LL to the SS alternative. For example, dieting individuals are encouraged to quit buying unhealthy snacks. When they are at home and get hungry, their most immediate option is to eat the healthy food available at home. Going out to get unhealthy snacks may take too much time, devaluing that option. Another frequently cited example of the precommitment technique is the story of the hero Odysseus in Greek mythology. He commanded his crew to tie him to the mast of a ship before encountering the Siren's songs, so that he was already physically unable to give into the Siren's temptations when in their immediate presence.

The precommitment technique has also been effective in increasing nonhuman animal's self-control choices. Rachlin and Green (1972) and Green et al. (1981) showed that pigeons would successfully choose the precommitment alternatives when both rewards were temporally delayed. Figure 11 depicts the Rachlin and

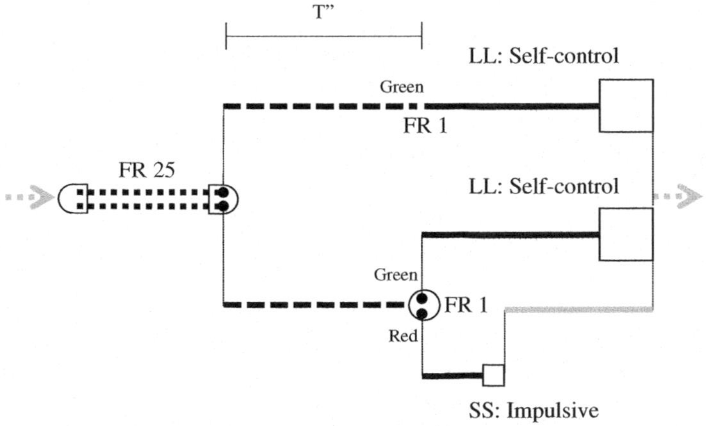

Fig. 11 Self-control procedure conducted by Green et al. (1981)

Green (1972) procedure where the terminal links in a concurrent chains schedules were composed of either LL-only alternative (top) versus a choice between the SS and LL alternatives (bottom). In this procedure, the interval between the end of initial link and the onset of terminal link (T sec) was manipulated. As expected, when this interval was relatively short, pigeons mostly selected the choice between the SS and LL alternatives, and subsequently chose the SS alternative. However, as the interval increased, the percentages for the LL-only alternative gradually increased. These same results have also been obtained using human subjects (Green et al. 1994a).

5 Suboptimal Choice

Equation 3 predicts that organisms will show a preference for the alternative with a higher reinforcement value. However, contrary to this prediction, there is research showing that organisms often choose a more unreliable alternative, relative to a more reliable alternative in the terminal link of concurrent-chain schedules. Preference for the more unreliable alternative does not lead to the maximization of reinforcement, and therefore is another example of irrational choice. Such a paradoxical preference is called "suboptimal choice" and has been extensively studied. Suboptimal choice was first demonstrated by Kendall (1974). Dunn and Spetch and their colleagues have examined the factors that govern this phenomenon since the late 1980s. Furthermore, Zentall and his colleagues have also worked diligently to address this phenomenon since the late 1990s from a comparative cognitive approach, rather than a behavior analytic approach.

5.1 The Study of Kendall (1974)

If organisms are given a choice between an alternative that always leads to food reinforcement after a delay, and an alternative that either leads to food reinforcement after the same delay, or blackout with equal probability, organisms usually prefer the former to the latter (e.g., Mazur 1989). However, if these same alternatives are arranged in the terminal link of a concurrent-chain schedule and signaled with different stimuli, suboptimal choice appears, whereby organisms prefer the less probable food reinforcement.

Kendall (1974) first reported this suboptimal choice behavior with pigeons in a concurrent-chain procedure. In his procedure shown in Fig. 12, choosing one alternative in the initial link leads to a white signal to appear representing entry into the corresponding terminal link. After a delay, the pigeon received food reinforcement on 100% of those trials. By contrast, when subjects choose the other alternative, they were then shown one of two different colors (red or green) with equal (50%) probability. The green-colored option leads to food reinforcement 100% of the time. However, the red-colored option leads to no reinforcement. Thus, for these alterna-

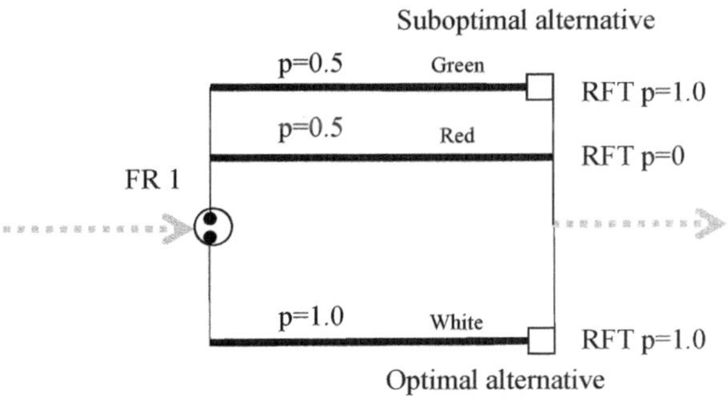

Fig. 12 Suboptimal choice procedure by Kendall (1974)

tives, food reinforcement only occurred on 50% of the trials. Correspondingly, the alternative that produced 100% reinforcement was defined as the optimal alternative, and the alternative that produced 50% reinforcement was the suboptimal alternative. Intuitively, many people would think that the subjects should always choose the optimal alternative. But, surprisingly, Kendall (1974) observed a preference for the suboptimal alternative. This finding has been repeatedly replicated in many experiments and expanded on by other researchers (Dunn and Spetch 1990; Fantino et al. 1979; Mazur 1996; Pisklak et al. 2015; Spetch et al. 1990; Spetch and Dunn 1987; Spetch et al. 1994; see McDevitt et al. 2016 for a review).

5.2 Studies by Zentall and Colleagues

Subsequent experiments by Zentall and his colleagues have broadened the scope of the suboptimal choice paradigm even further (Laude et al. 2014b; Gipson et al. 2009; Roper and Zentall 1999; Stagner and Zentall 2010; Zentall et al. 2015; Zentall and Stagner 2011a, b; see Zentall 2016 for a review). They refined the basic procedure and examined various factors affecting preference for the suboptimal alternative. For example, Stagner and Zentall (2010) examined whether suboptimal choice preferences can be observed even when the probability of reinforcement in the suboptimal alternative decreases from 50 to 20%. As shown in Fig. 13, subjects choosing the suboptimal alternative are presented with a red signal 20% of the time or a green signal 80% of the time. The subject receive reinforcement 100% of the time during the red signal and never receive reinforcement during the green signal. Therefore, subjects choosing the suboptimal alternative receive reinforcement during approximately 20% of the trials. When subjects choose the optimal alternative, they are presented with either a blue or yellow signal, each 50% of the time. Both the blue and yellow signals are followed by a reinforcer 50% of the time. Therefore, the subject receives reinforcement on 50% of the trials during the optimal alternative. Similar to Kendall (1974), the suboptimal alternative is consistently preferred even though

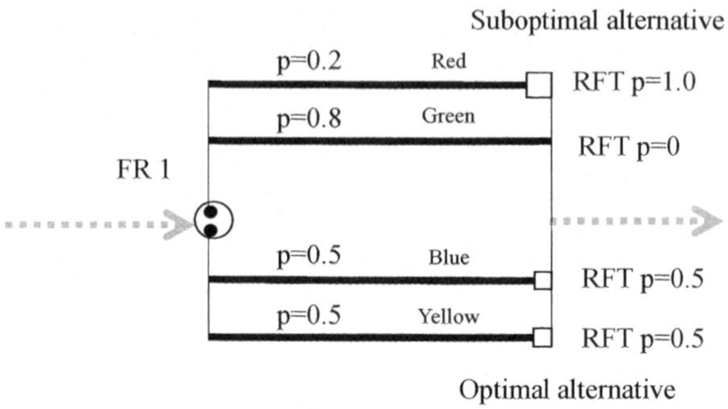

Fig. 13 Suboptimal choice procedure by Stagner and Zentall (2010)

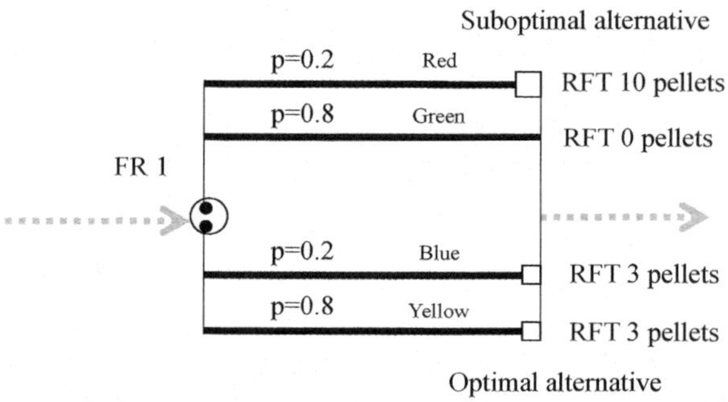

Fig. 14 Suboptimal choice procedure by Zentall and Stagner (2011a)

the suboptimal alternative produces fewer trials ending in reinforcement compared to the optimal alternative.

Zentall and Stagner (2011a) have also examined whether pigeons' suboptimal preference can be observed by manipulating food amount instead of food probability (see Fig. 14). Subjects choosing the suboptimal alternative are presented with a red signal 20% of the time, or a green signal 80% of the time. The subject receives 10 food pellets during the red signal, and no food reinforcement during the green signal. Thus, in the suboptimal alternative, subject receives on average two food pellets. Subjects choosing the optimal alternative are presented with a blue signal 20% of the time, or yellow signal 80% of the time. Both the blue and yellow signals are followed by three food pellets, resulting in an average of three food pellets during the optimal alternative. Again, average reinforcement amount delivered for the optimal alternative was greater than that of the suboptimal alternative. However, the suboptimal alternative was consistently preferred.

Why do subject consistently show preference for the suboptimal alternative? Both McDevitt et al (2016) and Zentall (2016) attributed this suboptimal preference to the value of the signal correlated with a 100% chance of receiving food reinforcement. That is, the signal for food on the suboptimal alternative acquires a relatively higher value than expected because it occurs in a context of uncertainty about the outcome.

5.3 Suboptimal Choice and Other Behavioral Phenomena

Zentall and his colleagues have also examined the relationship of choice to other behavioral phenomena such as gambling and delay discounting. For example, Molet et al. (2012) pointed out that the suboptimal choice task used by Zentall and Stagner (2011a) is similar to human gambling situations. The signal associated with a lower probability but higher payoff (i.e., 10 pellets on 20% of the trials) in the suboptimal alternative is analogous to a jackpot in a slot machine. In both cases, organisms appear to overvalue the large payoff trials and undervalue the no reinforcement or loss trials.

Molet et al. (2012) used undergraduate students to examine whether humans also show suboptimal choice preferences. They designed a suboptimal choice task for humans similar to that used by Zentall and Stagner (2011a). In addition, they also asked participants whether they had any gambling experience. They were then able to compare the results between these two groups: the gambling experience group and the no gambling experience group. Results showed that participants that had prior gambling experience were significantly more likely to show a suboptimal choice preference, relative to participants without prior gambling experience. These findings suggest that gamblers have a higher tendency to fall into suboptimal choice patterns.

Based on the above results, Laude et al. (2014a) continued investigating the association between the degree of suboptimal choice preference and delay discounting. Significant correlations exist between problem gambling and impulsivity measured through a delay discounting task (Alessi and Petry 2003; Dixon et al. 2003; Petry 2001; Petry and Casarella 1999). Thus, there may also be significant correlations between suboptimal choice and impulsivity. Laude et al. (2014a) used pigeons as subjects to independently measure the degree of suboptimal choice preference and impulsivity in the delay discounting task. They found that pigeons making more impulsive choices also showed a greater degree of suboptimal choice preference. From these results, Laude et al. (2014a) concluded that the theoretical construct of impulsivity may be involved in both the suboptimal choice task and delay discounting, the latter of which has already been shown to be a good predictor of problem gambling.

6 The Segmentation Effect

The last case of irrational choice is a phenomenon called the segmentation effect. This pattern of irrational choice has also been examined with a concurrent-chain procedure. Unlike self-control (see Sect. 4) or suboptimal choice (see Sect. 5), the reinforcement rates or magnitudes for the two alternatives are the same. The only difference is in what the subject experiences during the terminal links. Figure 15 shows the procedure used by Duncan and Fantino (1972) in the initial segmentation effect study. Pigeons' responses produced reinforcement through either an FI 60 s

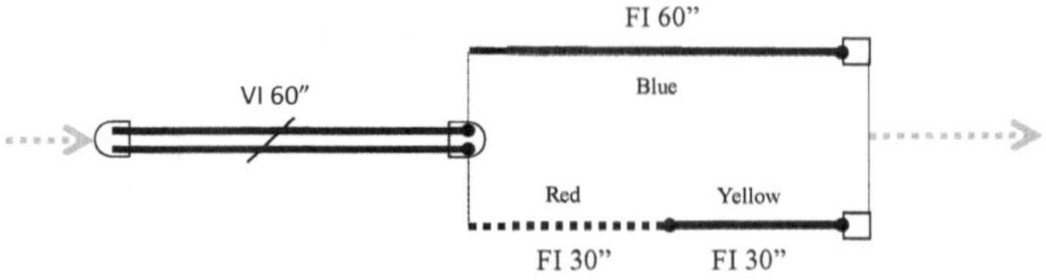

Fig. 15 The procedure by Duncan and Fantino (1972)

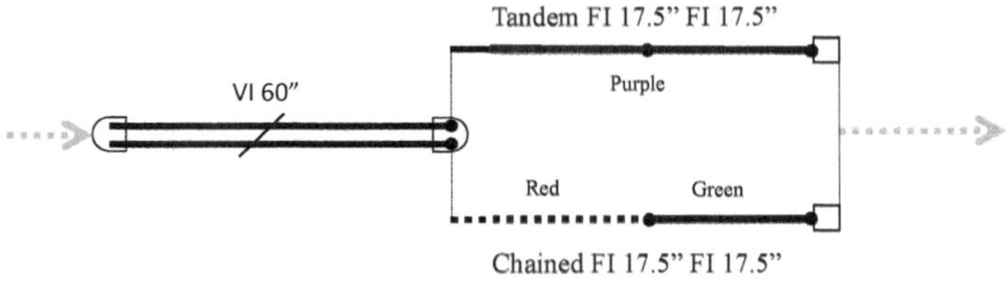

Fig. 16 The procedure by Leung and Winton (1985)

schedule or through a chained FI 30 s FI 30 s schedule. Thus, the terminal-link schedules were either unsegmented for a simple (FI) schedule or segmented for the chained (FI FI) schedule. The total time to reinforcement was equal for both terminal-link alternatives. However, subjects clearly preferred the unsegmented schedule, relative to the segmented schedule.

Leung and Winton (1985) examined the segmentation effect in greater detail with procedural variations, including a replication of Duncan and Fantino's (1972) original procedure. Figure 16 illustrates one of these procedural variations. Here, a chained FI FI schedule produced food reinforcement in one terminal link, whereas a tandem FI FI schedule produced food reinforcement in the other terminal link. Each FI schedule was signaled by a different color in the chained schedule, whereas the tandem schedules were signaled by the same color. In both cases, subjects obtained reinforcement after completing two consecutive FI schedules, which were identical in total time to reinforcement. However, like Duncan and Fantino (1972), subjects preferred the tandem schedules (unsegmented) relative to the chained (segmented) schedules. Similar findings have been demonstrated with monkeys (Takahashi 1993) and humans (Leung 1989, 1993). However, it should be noted that while these species also showed a preference for the unsegmented schedules, the extent of this preference was weaker compared to pigeons.

Other variations of the segmentation effect have also been found. For example, Fig. 17 shows two mutually exclusive alternatives. For one alternative, the first interval lasts 5 s and is signaled by a green light, which is then followed by a 2 s interval signaled by a red light. The other alternative simply reverses the order of the intervals while keeping the light colors constant (green = 5 s; red = 2 s). Like the segmentation effect, the total time to reinforcement is equal for both alternatives. The third author of this chapter has demonstrated that pigeons show a consistent preference for the

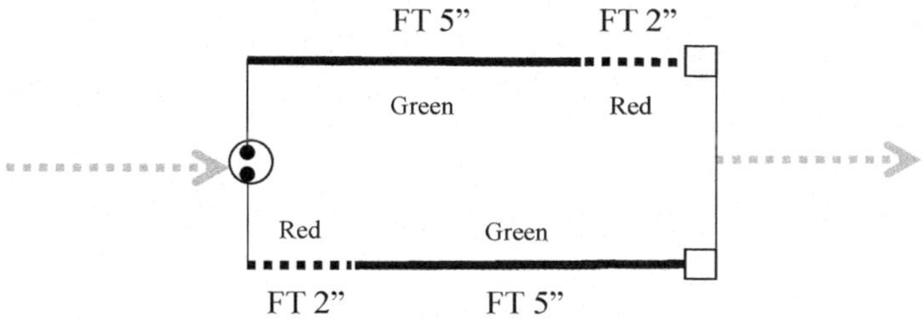

Fig. 17 A transposing effect example

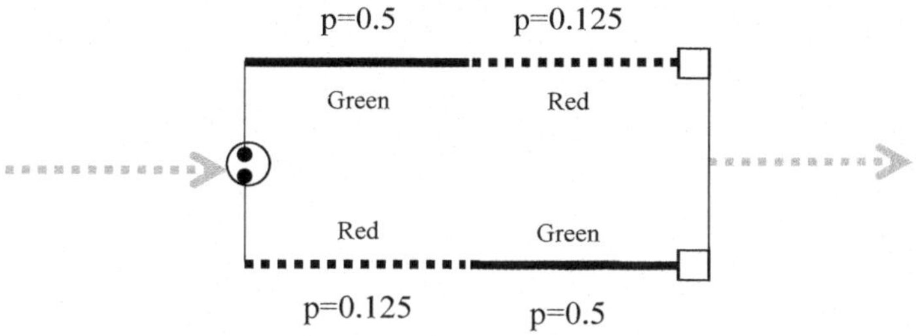

Fig. 18 A compound lottery example

option that begins with a 5 s (longer) interval followed by a 2 s (shorter) interval. He named this phenomenon "the transposing effect" to describe this type of preference bias.

A compound lottery is like the transposing effect but manipulates order of probabilistic outcomes instead of time in each outcome. Like the previous examples, each alternative is composed of two stages (see Fig. 18). For the top alternative, subjects move from one stage to the next with a 0.5 probability and then obtain reinforcement with a 0.125 probability. The bottom alternative is the same as the top, except the order of probability for each stage has been reversed. Budescu and Fischer (2001) found that humans showed a strong preference for the alternative which changes from a high to a low probability (the top option in Fig. 18). However, this chapter's third author has tried to replicate these results with rats, but without clear results.

In sum, these three phenomena, the segmentation effect, the transposing effect, and the compound lottery, have two common features: identical outcomes (either time to reinforcement, magnitude, or probability) and different experiences during each alternative. One way to decrease this irrational preference is to devalue the preferred alternative. For example, increasing the reinforcement delay and increasing the effort needed to obtain the preferred alternative are two ways of devaluing an alternative. Duncan and Fantino (1972) found that when the time to reinforcement for the simple FI schedule was sufficiently longer than that for the chained schedule, preference eventually reversed toward the chained schedule. Thus, by devaluing one of the alternatives, the choice procedure will approximate "the self-control" or "the suboptimal choice" situation that we began with, which contained both optimal

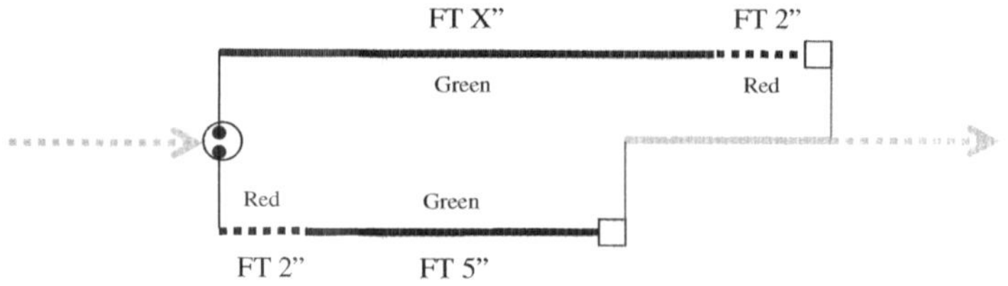

Fig. 19 An example of devaluation during the transposing effect

and nonoptimal alternatives. Figure 19 shows an example for devaluing the preferred alternative with the transposing effect. That is, devaluing the FT Xs FT 2 s alternative can be achieved by increasing the duration for the FT Xs schedule.

7 Discussion

In this chapter, we discussed irrational choice from a behavior analytic perspective. In the first half of the chapter, we explained the fundamental research methods in psychology, with an emphasis on experimental methodology. We then briefly discussed the theoretical orientation of behavior analysis. In the last half of the chapter, we discussed irrational choice issues by providing rationality definitions from economics and behavior analysis. Lastly, we explored three instances of irrational choice studied by behavior analysts: self-control, suboptimal choice, and the segmentation effect.

In the following discussion, we first focus on the possibility of mutual exchange between behavior analysis and some subfields of economics. We then discuss issues surrounding irrational choice that have included both behavior analysis and economic perspectives, such as irrational choice in behavioral ecology and the rational reasons for irrational choice. Finally, we discuss a common theme among the examples of irrational choice provided within this chapter from a behavior analytic perspective.

7.1 The Possibility for Mutual Exchange

We primarily chose irrational choice as a topic for this chapter because there are many interesting examples from psychology experiments, and we feel that it is a theme for which behavioral economics and behavioral analysis can successfully collaborate with each other. The possibility of a successful collaboration is partly due to the accumulation of evidence against rational and normative theories of choice in both fields. In this chapter, we have shown some examples of deviations from normative theories in behavior analysis. Additionally, as described earlier in behavioral economics, the irrationality of decision-making itself was the main research subject.

Comparing these deviations from both fields makes it possible to broaden the scope of irrational choice research. Although the purpose of studying irrational processes has not always been identical for both fields, we believe collaborative research will offer several benefits for both fields. For example, if a finding from one research field is reexamined and replicated in the other field from a different perspective, the generality of that research finding will become clearer. Fantino (1998a, b) pointed out that behavior analytic techniques and principles can be applied to study research topics in behavioral economics. Furthermore, he suggested that research from a behavior analytic perspective can complement research in behavioral economics.

Furthermore, comparing quantitative descriptions of irrational behavior is also an important issue to be addressed in the future. Several quantitative functions have been invented to describe behavioral or economic phenomenon in both fields. The discounting functions in self-control research (see Sect. 4) illustrate how research may progress by comparing different functions from both fields. In the self-control paradigm, exponential functions originated in behavioral economics, whereas hyperbolic functions in behavior analysis were proposed to describe discounting phenomena. Much of the discussion centered around which function better described the data (e.g., Laibson 1997; Mazur and Biondi 2009; McKerchar et al. 2009). Although less research has focused on this comparison recently, it is undeniable that self-control research has advanced through these discussions and idea exchanges.

Next, we compare behavior analysis and experimental economics. There are also common principles that link experimental economics and behavior analysis. One common principle is the "experiment" as a means of testing hypotheses. As described earlier, most experimental designs in psychology use group comparisons, based on RCTs and related quasi-experimental methodology. Group comparisons are a good way to examine cause-and-effect relationships, but they also have drawbacks such as requiring a large participant sample and taking a long time to assess the effects of an independent variable on the dependent measure (Clay 2010; Kazdin 2010). The single-case experimental designs used in many of the experiments of the second half of this chapter can also demonstrate cause-and-effect relationships, while minimizing the problems that group comparisons have. Because behavior analytic research focuses on examining and modifying organisms' ongoing behavior, single-case experimental designs allow researchers to introduce and remove independent variables flexibly and promptly. Experimental economics may also profit from single-case experimental designs used in behavior analysis, by comparing the effects of these methods with those already used in economics. RCTs have already been used in some fields of economics (e.g., Barrett and Carter 2010). Therefore, adding single-case experimental designs to experimental economists "toolbox" may move both fields forward and establish closer methodological links.

Conversely, experimental methodology used by economists may also be incorporated into mainstream experimental psychology. Besides studies in social psychology such as group polarization (Stoner 1968) and groupthink (Janis 1971), most experimental psychology studies focus on the behavior of the individual organism. Group comparisons are used as a psychological research method because it gives a researcher a more efficient means for detecting independent variable effects. However, the individual behavior is still the main topic of interest for psychologists. On the other hand, experimental economics often deal with group behavior and focus on explaining interactions between people (Levine 2012). Thus, experimental psychology could also profit by incorporating the methodology used by experimental economists when exploring groups and interactions between individuals and groups.

7.2 *Irrational Choice in Behavioral Ecology*

There is at least one irrational choice research area, behavioral ecology, which has profited from both economists and behavior analysts. Behavioral ecology is the study of the ecological and evolutionary causes of animal behavior based on natural selection, and the adaptive value of the behavior when an animal fits its environment. In behavioral ecology, there also exists a normative theory, known as optimal foraging theory (Stephens and Krebs 1986). This theory describes how animals behave when searching for food. Because searching for food requires energy, animals are continually faced with choices about which foraging behavior is better for maximizing energy. In the short term, energy efficacy needs to be maximized. However, inclusive fitness needs to be maximized in the long term (Bateson 2010). When animals maximize inclusive fitness, their behavior can be described as optimal or rational.

In behavioral ecology, several examples of irrational choice originating in behavioral economics have been studied using animal subjects. For example, Bateson et al. (2003) examined the decoy effect (e.g., Huber et al. 1982) using rufous hummingbirds, and Dawkins and Brockman (1980) examined the sunk cost effect (e.g., Arkes and Blumer 1985) using digger wasps. However, it should be noted that these studies emphasized the possibility that these behaviors could be considered as a rational strategy from a natural selection perspective and not simply the irrationality of an animal's foraging behavior. For example, Dawkins and Brockman (1980) showed that the fighting behavior between a pair of female wasps over a nest was seemingly in line with the sunk cost effect. However, if we assume that wasps have limited information about nests and future resources, their fighting behavior can be considered a rational survival strategy (i.e., evolutionarily stable strategy). That is, although these animal behaviors appeared to be irrational from a normative point of view, they can also be interpreted as rational for maximizing energy consumption or increasing inclusive fitness. Further studies by economists and behavior analysts should strongly consider such evolutionary survival strategies when attempting to explain seemingly irrational behavior patterns.

7.3 *Rationality in Hyperbolic Discounting*

We may be able to also apply an evolutionary interpretation for the examples discussed in this chapter. For example, one of the most distinctive features of hyperbolic discounting is the different rates of discounting found between short and long delays (see Sect. 4.2), which leads to preference reversal. This high discounting rate during very short delays, in particular, is viewed as an instance of irrational choice. However, neuroeconomists (e.g., Glimcher and Fehr 2014) have recently begun to examine the relationship between decision-making and brain function, particularly from an evolutionary perspective similar to behavioral ecology. This research may be able to provide more convincing evidence for a link between choice and evolutionary explanations. For example, McClure et al. (2004) showed that discounting during short and long delays are differentially engaging separate brain areas (see also Tanaka et al. 2004). In this procedure, participants were required to make decisions about intertemporal choice in which SS and LL alternatives were presented. Brain activity during the intertemporal choices was measured by fMRI and showed that the brain areas involved in emotion (i.e., cerebral limbic system) were activated when choice alternatives either contained short-term gains or when participants chose those short-term gains. Furthermore, brain areas involved in advanced cognitive processing (i.e., lateral division of the frontal cortex and parietal lobe) were activated for all intertemporal choices, irrespective of delay length. From an evolutionary perspective, the emotion-based brain areas were formed phylogenetically in the distant past, while the cognitive processing-based brain areas are relatively more recent.

Organisms that possessed these distinct brain areas that correspond with short and long delays might have been better able to adjust to changing environmental conditions using either (or both) areas, depending on the prevailing circumstances. That is, environments in which resources quickly decrease (i.e., a disaster) demand that organisms quickly cope with these changes by activating the emotional/impulsive brain area, if they are to survive. From this perspective, the existence of rapid discounting for short delays does not appear to be so irrational. Similar explanations can be applied for human's strong preference for fat and sugar. Because fat and sugar have been critical nutrients for the survival of the human species, these nutrients have evolved to become a powerful appetitive stimulus. However, when access to foods that contain fat and sugar is no longer constrained, this adaptation is no longer adaptive and is now part of what is causing the worldwide obesity epidemic. More generally, the impulsive brain areas were more adaptive when humans frequently encountered resource fluctuation, and as a result, had shorter life expectancies. Today, such impulsivity may not be as adaptive for a relatively stable environment, in a species that lives for a relatively long time.

7.4 Irrationality Controlled by Molecular Contingencies

From a behavior analytic perspective, the theme of reinforcement contingency unites the examples of irrational choice described in this chapter. However, there are two ways of looking at reinforcement contingencies, either from a molar or molecular viewpoint. The molar view hypothesizes that overall reinforcement rates (value) control behavior. The molecular view hypothesizes that moment-to-moment changes in reinforcement rate (value) control behavior. In terms of the matching theory described earlier (see Sect. 2.3.1), much discussion has focused on which contingency controls matching behavior (Baum 2002, 2004). For irrational choice, it has been suggested that molecular, not molar contingencies play a more important role. For example, during hyperbolic discounting, shorter delays exert a relatively stronger influence on discounting. A series of studies on suboptimal choice showed that the local (i.e., molecular) conditioned reinforcers for one alternative that predict reinforcers 100% of the time during the uncertain condition had a relatively more powerful effect on preference than those in the certain condition (see Sect. 5.1). Takahashi (1997) has pointed out that the segmentation effect may also be controlled by molecular contingencies. That is, the segmentation effect is observed when organisms are sensitive to local contingencies in which stimulus change is not directly correlated with overall reinforcement rates. It is still unclear why molecular contingencies exert such a strong influence during these irrational choice procedures, and further examination is needed to determine the causal mechanisms of irrational choice. One way to do this would be through the use of measures that reflect moment-to-moment behavioral or environmental change, such as the distribution of IRTs (see Sect. 2.2.5) or local changes of reinforcement rates.

As described in this chapter, irrational choice is a research theme that is currently being examined from psychological, economic, and ecological points of view. However, future irrational choice research will require a multidisciplinary approach to find a comprehensive explanation for this type of behavior (cf. Green and Kagel 1987). We have discussed a variety of issues that each discipline should address in the near future. Examining these issues will allow for a more interdisciplinary and integrated research approach to irrational choice.

References

Ainslie, G., & Herrnstein, R. J. (1981). Preference reversal and delayed reinforcement. *Animal Learning & Behavior, 9,* 476–482.

Alessi, S. M., & Petry, N. M. (2003). Pathological gambling severity is associated with impulsivity in a delay discounting procedure. *Behavioural Processes, 64,* 345–354.

Ariely, D., & Wertenbroch, K. (2002). Procrastination, deadlines, and performance: Self-control by precommitment. *Psychological Science, 13,* 219–224.

Arkes, H. R., & Blumer, C. (1985). The psychology of sunk cost. *Organizational Behavior and Human Decision Processes, 35,* 124–140.

Barlow, D. H., Nock, M. K., & Hersen, M. (2009). *Single case experimental designs: Strategies for studying behavior change* (3rd ed.). Boston, MA: Allyn and Bacon.

Barrett, C. B., & Carter, M. R. (2010). The power and pitfalls of experiments in development economics: Some non-random reflections. *Applied Economic Perspectives and Policy, 32,* 515–548.

Bateson, M. (2010). Rational choice behavior: Definitions and evidence. In M. D. Breed & J. Moore (Eds.), *Encyclopedia of animal behavior* (Vol. 3, pp. 13–19). Oxford, UK: Academic Press.

Bateson, M., Healy, S. D., & Hurly, T. A. (2003). Context-dependent foraging decisions in rufous hummingbirds. *Proceedings of the Royal Society of London B: Biological Sciences, 270,* 1271–1276.

Baum, W. M. (1974). On two types of deviation from the matching law: Bias and undermatching. *Journal of the Experimental Analysis of Behavior, 22,* 231–242.
Baum, W. M. (1979). Matching, undermatching, and overmatching in studies of choice. *Journal of the Experimental Analysis of Behavior, 32,* 269–281.
Baum, W. M. (2002). From molecular to molar: A paradigm shift in behavior analysis. *Journal of the Experimental Analysis of Behavior, 78,* 95–116.
Baum, W. M. (2004). Molar and molecular views of choice. *Behavioural Processes, 66,* 349–359.
Bickel, W. K., Odum, A. L., & Madden, G. J. (1999). Impulsivity and cigarette smoking: delay discounting in current, never, and ex-smokers. *Psychopharmacology (Berl), 146,* 447–454.
Budescu, D. V., & Fischer, I. (2001). The same but different: An empirical investigation of the reducibility principle. *Journal of Behavioral Decision Making, 14,* 187–206.
Clay, R. A. (2010). More than one way to measure. *Monitor on Psychology, 41,* 52.
Critchfield, T. S., & Kollins, S. H. (2001). Temporal discounting: Basic research and the analysis of socially important behavior. *Journal of Applied Behavior Analysis, 34,* 101–122.
Davison, M., & McCarthy, D. (1988). *The matching law: A research review*. Hillsdale, NJ: Erlbaum.
Dawkins, R., & Brockmann, H. J. (1980). Do digger wasps commit the Concorde fallacy? *Animal Behaviour, 28,* 892–896.
Dixon, M. R., Marley, J., & Jacobs, E. A. (2003). Delay discounting by pathological gamblers. *Journal of Applied Behavior Analysis, 36,* 449–458.
Du, W., Green, L., & Myerson, J. (2002). Cross-cultural comparisons of discounting delayed and probabilistic rewards. *The Psychological Record, 52,* 479–492.
Duncan, B., & Fantino, E. (1972). The psychological distance to reward. *Journal of the Experimental Analysis of Behavior, 18,* 23–34.
Dunn, R., & Spetch, M. L. (1990). Choice with uncertain outcomes: Conditioned reinforcement effects. *Journal of the Experimental Analysis of Behavior, 53,* 201–218.
Fantino, E. (1967). Preference for mixed- versus fixed-ratio schedules. *Journal of the Experimental Analysis of Behavior, 10,* 35–43.
Fantino, E. (1969). Choice and rate of reinforcement. *Journal of the Experimental Analysis of Behavior, 12,* 723–730.
Fantino, E. (1998a). Behavior analysis and decision making. *Journal of the Experimental Analysis of Behavior, 69,* 355–364.
Fantino, E. (1998b). Judgment and decision making: Behavioral approaches. *The Behavior Analyst, 21,* 203–218.
Fantino, E., Dunn, R., & Meck, W. (1979). Percentage reinforcement and choice. *Journal of the Experimental Analysis of Behavior, 32,* 335–340.
Fantino, E., Preston, R. A., & Dunn, R. (1993). Delay-reduction: Current status. *Journal of the Experimental Analysis of Behavior, 60,* 159–169.
Fantino, E., & Romanowich, P. (2007). The effect of conditioned reinforcement rate on choice: A review. *Journal of the Experimental Analysis of Behavior, 87,* 409–421.
Ferster, C. B., & Skinner, B. F. (1957). *Schedules of reinforcement*. New York: Appleton-Century-Crofts.
Gipson, C. D., Alessandri, J. J., Miller, H. C., & Zentall, T. R. (2009). Preference for 50% reinforcement over 75% reinforcement by pigeons. *Learning & Behavior, 37,* 289–298.
Glimcher, P. W., & Fehr, E. (Eds.). (2014). *Neuroeconomics: Decision making and the brain* (2nd ed.). New York: Academic Press.
Grace, R. C. (1994). A contextual model of concurrent-chains choice. *Journal of the Experimental Analysis of Behavior, 61,* 113–129.
Grace, R. C., Berg, M. E., & Kyonka, E. G. (2006). Choice and timing in concurrent chains: Effects of initial-link duration. *Behavioural Processes, 71,* 188–200.
Green, L., Fisher, E. B., Perlow, S., & Sherman, L. (1981). Preference reversal and self control: Choice as a function of reward amount and delay. *Behaviour Analysis Letters, 1,* 43–51.
Green, L., Fristoe, N., & Myerson, J. (1994a). Temporal discounting and preference reversals in choice between delayed outcomes. *Psychonomic Bulletin & Review, 1,* 383–389.

Green, L., Fry, A. F., & Myerson, J. (1994b). Discounting of delayed rewards: A life-span comparison. *Psychological Science, 5*, 33–36.

Green, L., & Kagel, J. H. (Eds.). (1987). *Advances in behavioral economics* (Vol. 1). Norwood, NJ: Ablex.

Green, L., Myerson, J., Lichtman, D., Rosen, S., & Fry, A. (1996). Temporal discounting in choice between delayed rewards: The role of age and income. *Psychology and Aging, 11*, 79–84.

Green, L., Myerson, J., & McFadden, E. (1997). Rate of temporal discounting decreases with amount of reward. *Memory & cognition, 25*, 715–723.

Hackenberg, T. D. (2009). Token reinforcement: A review and analysis. *Journal of the Experimental Analysis of Behavior, 91*, 257–286.

Hammond, L. J. (1980). The effect of contingency upon the appetitive conditioning of free-operant behavior. *Journal of the Experimental Analysis of Behavior, 34*, 297–304.

Hardman, D. (2009). *Judgment and decision making: Psychological perspectives*. Hoboken, NJ: Wiley.

Herrnstein, R. J. (1961). Relative and absolute strength of response as a function of frequency of reinforcement. *Journal of the Experimental Analysis of Behavior, 4*, 267–272.

Herrnstein, R. J. (1964). Aperiodicity as a factor in choice. *Journal of the Experimental Analysis of Behavior, 7*, 179–182.

Herrnstein, R. J. (1970). On the law of effect. *Journal of the Experimental Analysis of Behavior, 13*, 243–266.

Herrnstein, R. J., & Vaughan, W. (1980). Melioration and behavioral allocation. In J. E. R. Staddon (Ed.), *Limits to action: The allocation of individual behavior* (pp. 143–176). New York: Academic Press.

Huber, J., Payne, J. W., & Puto, C. (1982). Adding asymmetrically dominated alternatives: Violations of regularity and the similarity hypothesis. *Journal of Consumer Research, 9*, 90–98.

Iversen, I. H. (2013). Single-case research methods: An overview. In G. J. Madden (Ed.), *APA handbook of behavior analysis* (Vol. 1, pp. 3–32)., Methods and principles Washington, DC: American Psychological Association.

Janis, I. L. (1971). Groupthink. *Psychology today, 5*, 43–46.

Johnson, M. W., & Bickel, W. K. (2002). Within-subject comparison of real and hypothetical money rewards in delay discounting. *Journal of the Experimental Analysis of Behavior, 77*, 129–146.

Kahneman, D., & Tversky, A. (1979). Prospect theory: An analysis of decision under risk. *Econometrica, 47*, 263–291.

Kazdin, A. E. (2010). *Single-case research designs: Methods for clinical and applied settings* (2nd ed.). New York: Oxford University Press.

Kendall, S. B. (1974). Preference for intermittent reinforcement. *Journal of the Experimental Analysis of Behavior, 21*, 463–473.

Kennedy, C. H. (1992). Trends in the measurement of social validity. *The Behavior Analyst, 15*, 147–156.

Kudadjie-Gyamfi, E., & Rachlin, H. (1996). Temporal patterning in choice among delayed outcomes. *Organizational Behavior and Human Decision Processes, 65*, 61–67.

Laibson, D. (1997). Golden eggs and hyperbolic discounting. *Quarterly Journal of Economics, 112*, 443–477.

Laude, J. R., Beckmann, J. S., Daniels, C. W., & Zentall, T. R. (2014a). Impulsivity affects suboptimal gambling-like choice by pigeons. *Journal of Experimental Psychology: Animal Learning and Cognition, 40*, 2–11.

Laude, J. R., Stagner, J. P., & Zentall, T. R. (2014b). Suboptimal choice by pigeons may result from the diminishing effect of nonreinforcement. *Journal of Experimental Psychology: Animal Learning and Cognition, 40*, 12–21.

Lea, S. E. G. (1994). Rationality: The Formalist View. In H. Brandstätter & W. Güth (Eds.), *Essays on Economic Psychology* (pp. 71–89). Berlin, Heidelberg: Springer.

Leung, J. P. (1989). Psychological distance to reward: A human replication. *Journal of the Experimental Analysis of Behavior, 51*, 343–352.

Leung, J. P. (1993). Psychological distance to reward: Segmentation of aperiodic schedules of reinforcement. *Journal of the Experimental Analysis of Behavior, 59,* 401–410.

Leung, J. P., & Winton, A. S. (1985). Preference for unsegmented interreinforcement intervals in concurrent chains. *Journal of the Experimental Analysis of Behavior, 44,* 89–101.

Levine, D. K. (2012). *Is behavioral economics doomed? The ordinary versus the extraordinary.* Cambridge, England: Open Book Publishers.

Madden, G. J., Begotka, A. M., Raiff, B. R., & Kastern, L. L. (2003). Delay discounting of real and hypothetical rewards. *Experimental & Clinical Psychopharmacology, 11,* 139–145.

Mazur, J. E. (1981). Optimization theory fails to predict performance of pigeons in a two-response situation. *Science, 214,* 823–825.

Mazur, J. E. (1987). An adjusting procedure for studying delayed reinforcement. In M. L. Commons, J. E. Mazur, J. A. Nevin, & H. Rachlin (Eds.), *Quantitative analyses of behavior* (Vol. 5, pp. 55–73)., The effect of delay and intervening events on reinforcement value Hillsdale, NJ: Erlbaum.

Mazur, J. E. (1989). Theories of probabilistic reinforcement. *Journal of the Experimental Analysis of Behavior, 51,* 87–99.

Mazur, J. E. (1996). Choice with certain and uncertain reinforcers in an adjusting-delay procedure. *Journal of the Experimental Analysis of Behavior, 66,* 63–73.

Mazur, H. E. (2016). *Learning & behavior* (8th ed.). Englewood Cliffs, NJ: Prentice-Hall.

Mazur, J. E., & Biondi, D. R. (2009). Delay-amount tradeoffs in choices by pigeons and rats: Hyperbolic versus exponential discounting. *Journal of the Experimental Analysis of Behavior, 91,* 197–211.

Mazur, J. E., & Fantino, E. (2014). Choice. In F. K. McSweeney & E. S. Murphy (Eds.), *The Wiley Blackwell handbook of operant and classical conditioning* (pp. 195–220). New York: Wiley.

McClure, S. M., Laibson, D. I., Loewenstein, G., & Cohen, J. D. (2004). Separate neural systems value immediate and delayed monetary rewards. *Science, 306,* 503–507.

McDevitt, M. A., Dunn, R. M., Spetch, M. L., & Ludvig, E. A. (2016). When good news leads to bad choices. *Journal of the Experimental Analysis of Behavior, 105,* 23–40.

McKerchar, T. L., Green, L., Myerson, J., Pickford, T. S., Hill, J. C., & Stout, S. C. (2009). A comparison of four models of delay discounting in humans. *Behavioural Processes, 81,* 256–259.

Molet, M., Miller, H. C., Laude, J. R., Kirk, C., Manning, B., & Zentall, T. R. (2012). Decision making by humans in a behavioral task: Do humans, like pigeons, show suboptimal choice? *Learning & Behavior, 40,* 439–447.

Odum, A. L. (2011). Delay discounting: I'm ak, you're ak. *Journal of the Experimental Analysis of Behavior, 96,* 427–439.

Odum, A. L., & Rainaud, C. P. (2003). Discounting of delayed hypothetical money, alcohol, and food. *Behavioural Processes, 64,* 305–313.

Ostaszewski, P., Green, L., & Myerson, J. (1998). Effects of inflation on the subjective value of delayed and probabilistic rewards. *Psychonomic Bulletin & Review, 5,* 324–333.

Pavlov, I. P. (1927). *Conditioned reflexes: An investigation of the physiological activity of the cerebral cortex* (G. V. Anrep, Trans. & Ed.). London, England: Oxford University Press (Original work published 1927).

Petry, N. M. (2001). Substance abuse, pathological gambling, and impulsiveness. *Drug and Alcohol Dependence, 63,* 29–38.

Petry, N. M., & Casarella, T. (1999). Excessive discounting of delayed rewards in substance abusers with gambling problems. *Drug and Alcohol Dependence, 56,* 25–32.

Pisklak, J. M., McDevitt, M. A., Dunn, R. M., & Spetch, M. L. (2015). When good pigeons make bad decisions: Choice with probabilistic delays and outcomes. *Journal of the Experimental Analysis of Behavior, 104,* 241–251.

Rachlin, H., Battalio, R., Kagel, J., & Green, L. (1981). Maximization theory in behavioral psychology. *Behavioral and Brain Sciences, 4,* 371–388.

Rachlin, H., & Green, L. (1972). Commitment, choice and self-control. *Journal of the Experimental Analysis of Behavior, 17,* 15–22.

Rachlin, H., Green, L., Kagel, J. H., & Battalio, R. C. (1976). Economic demand theory and psychological studies of choice. In G. H. Bower (Ed.), *The psychology of learning and motivation* (Vol. 10, pp. 129–154). New York: Academic Press.
Rachlin, H., Kagel, J. H., & Battalio, R. C. (1980). Substitutability in time allocation. *Psychological Review, 87,* 355–374.
Romanowich, P., Cozine, A., & Worthen, D. L. (2017). Effects of reinforcement context on initial link responding in concurrent chain reinforcement schedules. *Psychological Record, 67,* 43–50.
Roper, K. L., & Zentall, T. R. (1999). Observing behavior in pigeons: The effect of reinforcement probability and response cost using a symmetrical choice procedure. *Learning and Motivation, 30,* 201–220.
Seidl, C. (2002). Preference reversal. *Journal of Economic Surveys, 16,* 621–655.
Shimp, C. P. (1966). Probabilistically reinforced choice behavior in pigeons. *Journal of the Experimental Analysis of Behavior, 9,* 443–455.
Spetch, M. L., Belke, T. W., Barnet, R. C., Dunn, R., & Pierce, W. D. (1990). Suboptimal choice in a percentage-reinforcement procedure: Effects of signal condition and terminal-link length. *Journal of the Experimental Analysis of Behavior, 53,* 219–234.
Spetch, M. L., & Dunn, R. (1987). Choice between reliable and unreliable outcomes: Mixed percentage-reinforcement in concurrent chains. *Journal of the Experimental Analysis of Behavior, 47,* 57–72.
Spetch, M. L., Mondloch, M. V., Belke, T. W., & Dunn, R. (1994). Determinants of pigeons' choice between certain and probabilistic outcomes. *Animal Learning & Behavior, 22,* 239–251.
Squires, N., & Fantino, E. (1971). A model for choice in simple concurrent and concurrent-chains schedules. *Journal of the Experimental Analysis of Behavior, 15,* 27–38.
Stagner, J. P., & Zentall, T. R. (2010). Suboptimal choice behavior by pigeons. *Psychonomic Bulletin & Review, 17,* 412–416.
Stephens, D. W., & Krebs, J. R. (1986). *Foraging theory*. Princeton, NJ: Princeton University Press.
Stoner, J. A. F. (1968). Risky and cautious shifts in group decisions: The influence of widely held values. *Journal of Experimental Social Psychology, 4,* 442–459.
Strotz, R. H. (1955). Myopia and inconsistency in dynamic utility maximization. *The Review of Economic Studies, 23,* 165–180.
Takahashi, M. (1993). Psychological distance to reward in monkeys. *Behavioural Processes, 30,* 299–308.
Takahashi, M. (1997). Recent developments in the study of choice behavior: Towards a comparative study of decision making. *Japanese Journal of Behavior Analysis, 11,* 9–28.
Tanaka, S. C., Doya, K., Okada, G., Ueda, K., Okamoto, Y., & Yamawaki, S. (2004). Prediction of immediate and future rewards differentially recruits cortico-basal ganglia loops. *Nature Neuroscience, 7,* 887–893.
Thaler, R. H., & Shefrin, H. M. (1981). An economic theory of self-control. *Journal of Political Economy, 89,* 392–406.
Vaughan, W. (1981). Melioration, matching, and maximization. *Journal of the Experimental Analysis of Behavior, 36,* 141–149.
Vriend, N. J. (1996). Rational behavior and economic theory. *Journal of Economic Behavior & Organization, 29,* 263–285.
Williams, B. A. (1988). Reinforcement, choice, and response strength. In R. C. Atkinson, R. J. Herrnstein, G. Lindzey, & R. D. Luce (Eds.), *Stevens' handbook of experimental psychology: Vol. 2. Learning and Cognition* (2nd ed., pp. 167–244). New York: Wiley.
Winett, R. A., Moore, J. F., & Anderson, E. S. (1991). Extending the concept of social validity: Behavior analysis for disease prevention and health promotion. *Journal of Applied Behavior Analysis, 24,* 215–230.
Zentall, T. R. (2016). Resolving the paradox of suboptimal choice. *Journal of Experimental Psychology: Animal Learning and Cognition, 42,* 1–14.

Zentall, T. R., Laude, J. R., Stagner, J. P., & Smith, A. P. (2015). Suboptimal choice by pigeons: Evidence that the value of the conditioned reinforcer rather than its frequency determines choice. *The Psychological Record, 65,* 223–229.
Zentall, T. R., & Stagner, J. (2011a). Maladaptive choice behaviour by pigeons: An animal analogue and possible mechanism for gambling (sub-optimal human decision-making behaviour). *Proceedings of the Royal Society of London B: Biological Sciences, 278,* 1203–1208.
Zentall, T. R., & Stagner, J. P. (2011b). Sub-optimal choice by pigeons: Failure to support the Allais paradox. *Learning and Motivation, 42,* 245–254.

Evolutionary Psychology and Economic Game Experiments

Yohsuke Ohtsubo and Hiroki Tanaka

1 Introduction

Evolutionary psychology is a discipline devoted to understanding the human mind under a unifying meta-theoretical framework—the theory of *natural selection* (e.g., Barkow et al. 1992; Buss 2015; Pinker 1997). From this perspective, the human mind is a collection of information-processing systems that are each designed to solve a specific adaptive problem (e.g., foraging, mating). Natural selection is a process whereby more adaptive traits (i.e., advantageous in survival and reproduction) increase while maladaptive traits decrease. For example, humans have a taste for fatty foods. Fatty foods, such as meats, were probably the best source of calories in ancestral environments. Therefore, it is not difficult to imagine that those who preferred energy-rich fatty foods were more likely to survive than those who did not. Consequently, individuals with these tastes became common by natural selection.

If natural selection shaped the design of human mind, which comprises cognition, emotions, and behaviors, we might expect people to behave so as to maximize their fitness (i.e., survival and reproduction) under environmental constraints. Replacing fitness with utility, the above proposition of evolutionary psychology is quite similar to the assumption of neoclassical economics (i.e., the maximization of utility). Indeed, evolutionary biologists use a branch of game theory (i.e., evolutionary game theory; Maynard Smith 1982) to build models of animal social behaviors, such as cooperation and signaling. Moreover, evolutionary psychologists use evolutionary game theory as a reasoning tool, and they often use economic games, such as the Prisoner's Dilemma game, public goods game, trust game, ultimatum game, and

Y. Ohtsubo (✉)
Kobe University, Kobe, Japan
e-mail: yohtsubo@lit.kobe-u.ac.jp

H. Tanaka
Brain Science Institute, Tamagawa University, Machida, Japan
e-mail: htanaka@lab.tamagawa.ac.jp

T. Kawagoe and H. Takizawa (eds.), *Diversity of Experimental Methods in Economics*,
https://doi.org/10.1007/978-981-13-6065-7_6

dictator game, to test their predictions. Despite similarities in their reasoning and experimental tools, however, experimental economists and evolutionary psychologists might disagree in their predictions. This is because evolutionary psychologists do not assume that people rely on rational deliberations while playing these games.

In this chapter, we first explain why evolutionary psychologists assume that people can behave in an adaptive manner without rational deliberation (Sect. 2). We then consider how experiments employing economic games inform or do not inform evolutionary psychology. In Sect. 3, we examine the case where the results of economic game experiments are relatively uninformative—that is when different evolutionary models yield the same behavioral prediction. In Sects. 4 and 5, we examine cases where economic game experiments are informative—that is, when people's behavior systematically deviates from a prediction based on an evolutionary game model (Sect. 4), and when different evolutionary models yield different behavioral predictions (Sect. 5).

2 How Can Human Behaviors Be Adaptive Without Rational Deliberation?

2.1 Altruistic Behavior and Kin Selection

Altruistic behavior is defined as a behavior that reduces the actor's own fitness while increasing someone else's fitness. In biology, altruistic behavior and cooperation are often used interchangeably. As cooperation in the one-shot Prisoner's Dilemma game is puzzling for experimental economists, the presence of altruistic behavior is puzzling for evolutionary biologists (Alcock 2013). A biological example of altruistic behavior is emitting alarm calls to warn conspecific members of the presence of a predator. On the one hand, the individual emitting the alarm calls suffers the increased risk of predation because of the conspicuousness of the call. On the other hand, his/her alarm call enhances conspecific members' fitness (i.e., it increases their chance of being able to safely run away from the approaching predator). Emitting an alarm call not only reduces the caller's absolute fitness but also makes the caller relatively disadvantageous in competition with others. Therefore, it appears to run counter to the logic of natural selection, which favors individuals with greater fitness.

Hamilton (1964a, b) advanced the first evolutionary explanation of altruistic behavior. He showed that altruistic behavior directed at kin is evolvable if the cost of the altruistic behavior for the actor is canceled out by the benefit for the recipient. Suppose that you can give your full sibling a benefit of b by incurring a cost of c. The relatedness (r) between full siblings is 0.5.[1] Therefore, from the gene's point

[1] Relatedness is often understood as the chance that two individuals share a particular gene by common descent. However, it is more accurately defined as a regression coefficient—the degree to which the actor's genotype predicts the recipient's genotype. If r is positive and high, an individual with an altruistic allele (A) is likely to help other individuals with A (see McElreath and Boyd 2007).

of view, if $0.5 \times b$ (the sibling's benefit weighted by relatedness) is greater than c, net benefit $0.5 \times b$ (the indirect fitness effect) minus c (the direct fitness effect) is positive. Hamilton called this *inclusive fitness* (i.e., the sum of indirect and direct fitness effects), and his thesis, *kin selection* theory, posits that natural selection favors traits that maximize inclusive fitness. This is easily generalizable to other values of r such that altruistic behavior is evolvable when $rb > c$ (Hamilton's rule) holds.

Renowned anthropologist Sahlins (1977) criticized kin selection by pointing out that the concept of fractions tends not to be part of the languages of people in traditional societies. Yet Hamilton's rule includes a decimal number, r, as its critical element. For example, the relatedness between an aunt and her nephew (her full sibling's son) is 0.25. Hamilton's rule appears to predict that an aunt is willing to help her nephew when and only when his benefit multiplied by 0.25 exceeds her cost. Sahlins considered that it would be impossible for people without the concept of fractions to behave in accordance with this prediction. Therefore, Sahlins rejected kin selection theory.

Dawkins (1979) took up Sahlins' criticism as a common misunderstanding of kin selection. According to Dawkins, Sahlins' critique would be akin to arguing that spiders must be equipped with sophisticated mathematical abilities because the designs of their webs are mathematically complex. Yet unconscious "rules of thumb" enable spiders to weave their webs. Dawkins (1979) further wrote, "The machinery that automatically and unconsciously builds webs must have evolved by natural selection" (p. 11).

2.2 Kin Recognition and Kin-Directed Altruism

Although Dawkins' counterargument is compelling, we would like to complement it with some concrete examples to clarify how unconscious "rules of thumb," to use Dawkins' term, work in the context of kin selection. Although species are not capable of reading other conspecifics' genomes directly, many species can distinguish kin from nonkin, and they treat them differently (e.g., Holmes and Sherman 1982; Mateo 2003). Two important mechanisms of kin recognition are *prior association* and *phenotype matching*. Prior association refers to discrimination based on familiarity. Animals learn phenotypes of genetically close individuals, such as parents and siblings, during early development. They later treat familiar individuals more favorably than unfamiliar individuals. Phenotype matching refers to discrimination based on similarity. Animals compare unknown individuals' phenotypes with their own or genetically close individuals' phenotype. If they see phenotypic similarity (e.g., someone looks similar to their parent; someone smells like themselves), they will treat an unknown individual as kin.

Since relatedness is not probability, it can take a negative value. Negative relatedness implies that each individual with A interacts with individuals without the gene (nonkin) more frequently than by chance.

Believe or not, both prior association and phenotype matching seem to operate in humans. Lieberman et al. (2007) found that two prior association cues predicted sibling-directed altruistic behavior/intent. For example, in their study, participants indicated the number of favors they had performed for their siblings in the last month. In addition, they indicated their willingness to donate an organ to their sibling. Lieberman et al. found that such sibling-directed altruism could be predicted by whether participants had observed their mother caring for their sibling at birth. This cue is called maternal perinatal association (MPA). However, MPA is only available for older siblings—it is impossible for younger siblings to observe their mother taking care of older siblings at birth. Lieberman et al. found that in the absence of MPA, childhood coresidence duration (i.e., how long the participants resided in the same household with a particular sibling from the ages of 0 to 18) could serve as a substitute and predict kin-directed altruism.

Phenotype matching also seems to play an important role in human kin-directed altruism. A study conducted in a traditional society in Senegal explored whether father–child phenotypic similarities would predict paternal investment in child rearing (Alvergne et al. 2009). The researchers focused on the father–child relationship because it is not necessarily certain, unlike the mother–child relationship. In other words, in any mammalian species, females are always certain that they are genetically related to the babies they deliver, whereas males are less certain; their partner might deliver a baby sired by someone else. This is called paternity uncertainty. Owing to the presence of paternity uncertainty, it is expected that males utilize some kinship cues to decide whether to invest their resources in supposed offspring. The researchers photographed the faces of fathers and their children. They also collected T-shirts worn by the fathers and children. They then had third-party judges rate the resemblance of each father–child pair in terms of their faces and body odors. Furthermore, mothers and fathers reported the level of paternal investment in each of their children. For example, mothers reported the amount of time that fathers had spent with a child and levels of father–child attachment. After controlling for the effects of potentially confounding variables (e.g., the number of children the couple has, child's sex), both resemblance cues predicted paternal investment.

2.3 Role of Emotions in Adaptive Behaviors

In these examples, neither siblings nor fathers are consciously aware of the logic of kin selection, let alone the relatedness with the target of their altruistic behaviors. They unconsciously respond to adaptive cues (i.e., familiarity and similarity) that are correlated with genetic relatedness. As a result, they behave more altruistically toward someone who is likely to be their kin. This "unconscious" process implies that rational deliberation is not necessary for organisms to preferentially direct altruistic behaviors to their kin. However, the evolutionary arguments do not preclude all subjective experiences from this process. In fact, emotional reactions seem to be the essential driver of kin-directed altruistic behaviors.

Korchmaros and Kenny (2006) asked their participants to imagine that their relatives were in immediate need of assistance. Participants reported their willingness to help relatives with different levels of relatedness. In addition, participants reported their emotional closeness to each relative as well as their past experiences with each relative (e.g., whether they had lived in the same household). They found that relatedness was correlated with prior association cues (e.g., the amount of interaction) and phenotype matching cues (i.e., perceived similarity). The effects of these kin recognition cues on willingness to help (i.e., altruistic intent) were mediated by emotional closeness. Therefore, this result suggests that the presence of kin recognition cues fosters emotional closeness (subjective feeling) to targets, and the enhanced emotional closeness motivates altruistic behaviors (see Hames 2016, for a review).

It is interesting to note that the two aforementioned association cues (MPA and coresidence duration) can also serve for the purpose of incest avoidance (Lieberman et al. 2007). Those who observed a close perinatal association between their younger opposite-sex sibling and their mother reported a stronger sense of disgust about imagining sexual relations with the sibling. Coresidence duration (if MPA is not available) also predicts sexual disgust. Such sexual disgust strongly drives people to avoid having sexual relationships with their genetic siblings. As MPA and coresidence duration enhanced emotional closeness, which leads to kin-directed altruism, the same prior association cues trigger an emotional mechanism (disgust) that, in turn, makes people behave in an adaptive manner (not having sex with their siblings).

2.4 *Errors Are Inevitable*

Although kin recognition cues, such as MPA, coresidence duration, and phenotypic resemblance, are correlated with relatedness, they are not perfect predictors of relatedness. Accordingly, systematic errors may result from such cues. For example, people might feel disproportionately high levels of emotional closeness to others whom they resemble and behave more altruistically toward them. In fact, DeBruine (2004) found that people found images of faces resembling their own more attractive than dissimilar faces. Moreover, DeBruine (2002) manipulated the resemblance of partners playing the trust game. Participants put more trust in partners whose faces resembled their own. These results imply that although facial resemblance is often a reliable cue for detecting kin, it sometimes misguides behavior. That is, people might treat someone who happens to be physically similar to themselves more favorably than they should. This type of error is inevitable because facial resemblance is only probabilistically associated with relatedness. Although errors occasionally occur, organisms are better off by relying on such probabilistic cues than by using nothing. In other words, if people consistently use facial resemblance to decide whether to help others, they will be more likely to help genetic kin in the long run.

The same error might be caused by prior association. Bevc and Silverman (2000) surveyed people who reported having sexual intercourse with a sibling. These people were divided into two groups—those who reported procreative sexual activity with a sibling and those who reported any other sexual activity with a sibling. The researchers also surveyed a control group consisting of people who had not had sexual relations with a sibling. Respondents were asked whether they and their sibling had been separately reared for longer than a year. Those who had engaged in procreative sexual activity with a sibling were more likely to report childhood separation (31.5%) than those who had engaged in other types of sexual activity (2.9%) and those who had had no sexual activity with a sibling (3.8%).

The presence of these errors (i.e., overly altruistic to similar but unrelated others, having sexual interest in separately reared siblings) is inevitable when we rely on probabilistic, thus imperfect, cues. Moreover, the presence of these errors clearly suggests that we are not aware of evolutionary logic, such as kin selection, and not following logic based on rational deliberation.

2.5 Kin Selection and the Evolution of Unconditional Cooperation

Although we emphasized the role of kin recognition in the previous subsections, kin recognition is not necessary for kin-directed altruistic behavior to evolve. Suppose that social organisms are unlikely to move far away from their birthplaces (i.e., their dispersal is limited). In such "viscous" populations, each individual tends to be surrounded by his/her close relatives (Hamilton 1964a, b). In such viscous populations, even randomly encountered individuals are highly likely to be close kin. Accordingly, there is no need for altruistic individuals to discriminate kin from nonkin, and thus kin selection predicts the evolution of unconditional altruism. Imagine, for example, that biologists experimentally had genetically unrelated individuals of such species encounter each other. As this species would not use any kinship recognition cues, individuals might immediately start cooperating with each other. It is unlikely that anyone would consider this species rational. Nevertheless, for this species, their nondiscriminatory altruism is adaptive in their ecological environments.

We do not claim that viscosity literally applies to the evolution of human altruism. Instead, we would like to underscore that even kin selection theory, which includes the gradient of relatedness as an important theoretical basis, sometimes predicts the evolution of unconditional cooperation (i.e., cooperating with anyone without paying any attention to the relatedness with the target). This is not confined to kin selection. If evolutionarily relevant environments remained unchanged for a long period of time and favored a certain behavior, natural selection might have fixated the behavior in the species.

2.6 Summary

We used kin selection to illustrate some characteristics of evolutionary hypotheses. First, evolutionary hypotheses do not presume the rationality of people. Instead, people behave adaptively by responding to certain cues, which were relevant to fitness in ancestral environments. Second, which cues people use is an empirical question. Without empirical evidence, we are not certain whether people use MPA and coresidence duration or rely on only one of them. Third, although reliance on cues obviates the necessity of rational deliberation in performing adaptive behaviors, it does not imply that no subjective experiences are involved in these processes. In fact, emotions seem to mediate the processes between the perception of cues and execution of adaptive behaviors. Fourth, the reliance of cues makes some systematic errors unavoidable. Fifth, if ancestral environments were highly unitary and stable (e.g., individuals were always surrounded by close relatives), the evolutionary logic predicts the evolution of unconditional behaviors that rely on no cues at all.

Empirical studies are typically informative for determining the validity of evolutionary hypotheses. However, if different evolutionary game models make the same behavioral prediction, economic game experiments may not be informative. In the next section, we argue that although cooperation in anonymous one-shot games is an interesting phenomenon, which economic game experiments have revealed, the observed behavior itself is not informative in determining evolutionary forces that allowed such an apparently maladaptive behavior to spread in the human population.

3 Evolution of "Other-Regarding" Preferences?

3.1 Strong Reciprocity as an Explanation of Human Cooperation

After Hamilton (1964a, b) proposed the theory of kin selection, several authors noticed its limitations and proposed other models of cooperation. Trivers (1971), for example, highlighted the importance of reciprocity and argued that it enables the evolution of cooperation between different species, which kin selection cannot explain. Trivers' thesis, known as *reciprocal altruism*, explains cooperation between individuals in stable relationships regardless of whether cooperation is likely to benefit genetically related individuals or not. For example, the tit-for-tat strategy (TFT), which cooperates in the initial round and then mimics the partner's previous behavior (either cooperation or defection), is an adaptive strategy in enduring reciprocal relationships (Axelrod and Hamilton 1981; see also the next section for further discussion about TFT and dyadic cooperation). Although kin selection and reciprocal altruism explain a wide range of altruistic behaviors/cooperation observed in many species, human cooperation does not seem to be amenable to these explanations (e.g., Fehr and Fischbacher 2004; Gintis 2000). This is because humans cooperate in large groups consisting of genetically unrelated individuals. Cooperative units in traditional societies (e.g., bands in hunter–gatherer societies) comprise a few dozen people, and thus TFT-like strategies, which are effective in stable dyadic relationships, are not necessarily effective. Moreover, owing to their members' (especially women's) frequent intergroup migrations, relatedness within such groups is estimated to be not high enough to allow for the evolution of kin-based cooperation.

To overcome the limitations of traditional biological models of the evolution of cooperation, a collaborative team of economists and evolutionary biologists/anthropologists proposed *strong reciprocity* to explain the evolution of large-scale cooperation in human societies (Bowles and Gintis 2011; Fehr and Fischbacher 2004; Gintis 2000; Gintis et al. 2003; Gintis et al. 2008). According to the proponents of strong reciprocity, the traditional conceptualization of reciprocity (e.g., reciprocity based on TFT) is fragile because its stability critically depends on the prospect of benefits accruing from future interactions. Such a prospect precipitates in the face of serious adversity, such as war and famine, and prospect-based cooperation easily breaks down (Ginits 2000). Instead, the proponents of strong reciprocity argue that people are equipped with *social preferences* (or *other-regarding preferences*)—that is, "a concern for the well-being of others and a desire to uphold ethical norms" (Bowles and Gintis 2011, p. 10). In the context of strong reciprocity, social preferences drive people to cooperate unconditionally (regardless of the prospect of reciprocal benefits) and punish norm violators.

3.2 Evolution of Strong Reciprocity

Gintis (2000) presented a group selection model of strong reciprocity, which presumes that groups that can maintain cooperation in times of adversity outcompete groups that cannot. Gintis pointed out that although strong reciprocators, who unconditionally cooperate with the group and punish noncooperators, tend to be worse off within their own group, but can be better off in between-groups competition under certain conditions. For example, suppose that the group risks extinction (i.e., non-strong reciprocators are tempted to defect). If strong reciprocators can impose a great cost on noncooperators with a relatively cheap cost to themselves, the group can maintain cooperation and increase its chances of survival. The presence of punishment per se might, thus reduce within-group fitness differences by compelling other members to cooperate in the interest of the group. Cultural learning or conformism also reduces within-group fitness differences and increases the relative importance of the between-groups fitness differences. More importantly, this within-group uniformity reduces the cost of punishment as well—only a minority of group members would behave uncooperatively in cooperative groups (see also Boyd et al. 2003).

Such a cultural group selection model of strong reciprocity is consistent with standard evolutionary models in the sense that it assumes that fitness-enhancing traits increase their frequency.[2] In addition, strong reciprocity does not assume rationality as a driving force behind cooperation. The presence of other-regarding preferences implies that people are predisposed to cooperate with other group members. The group setting might activate other-regarding preferences, or other-regarding choices may be a default strategy. In any case, other-regarding preferences cannot be reduced to rational deliberation—people simply prefer seeing increases in others' well-being. Bowles and Gintis (2011) also acknowledged the importance of social emotions. They argued that within-group cooperation might be facilitated by, for example, shame. In addition, moral anger promotes costly punishment (Fehr and Fischbacher 2004).

3.3 *Other-Regarding Preferences*

Strong reciprocity consists of two separate components: (i) unconditional cooperativeness (altruism) toward community members and (ii) a punitive tendency directed at norm violators. In this section, to clarify how economic game experiments inform evolutionary models of human behavior (or fail to do so), we focus on the first component. Unconditional cooperation is conceived as a product of genuinely other-regarding preferences, which motivate people to increase others' well-being for its own sake. However, it is difficult to find convincing evidence of the presence of other-regarding preferences. Even if participants choose cooperation in the anonymous one-shot Prisoner's Dilemma game or give a substantial amount of money in the anonymous one-short dictator game, it is possible to interpret that these results are due to participants' confusion (Andreoni 1995). Therefore, experiments showing the presence of other-regarding preferences must eliminate the possibility of participants' confusion.

Bowles and Gintis (2011) did not consider that confusion explains cooperation in anonymous one-shot games because behavioral manifestations of other-regarding preferences seem to follow the rule of utility maximization. Readers might be perplexed by this thesis (i.e., other-regarding preferences follow the rule of utility maximization). Therefore, let us first explain their understanding of some optimizing models. Although Bowles and Gintis (2011) explicitly denied that optimizing models accurately describe underlying psychological processes of human decision-making, they still considered optimizing models as useful tools for capturing and analyz-

[2] In fact, West et al. (2011) maintained that the model of strong reciprocity is a variant of the limited dispersal model of kin selection (recall that the limited dispersal model can explain the evolution of unconditional cooperation). The proponents of strong reciprocity seem to notice the mathematical equivalence (e.g., Bowles and Gintis 2011). However, they also seem to interpret that strong reciprocity cannot be accounted for by kin selection because strong reciprocators do not rely on any kinship cues in deciding whether to cooperate. However, as is obvious from the fact that the limited dispersal model is involved in kin selection, evolutionary biologists do not consider that the applicability of kin selection hinges on organisms' use of kinship cues. Such different conceptualizations of kin selection seem to be a major cause of controversy between the proponents of strong reciprocity and standard evolutionary biologists.

ing human decision-making: "Optimizing models are commonly used to describe behavior not because they mimic the cognitive processes of the actors, which they rarely do, but because they capture important influences on individual behavior in a succinct and analytically tractable way" (Bowles and Gintis, p. 9).

Bowles and Gintis (2011) further argued that having social preferences does not imply irrationality. If social preferences appear irrational, it is because rationality is mistakenly equated with the pursuit of self-interest. Instead, people's altruistic behaviors can be rational given the presence of social preferences. They referred to Andreoni and Miller's (2002) study, in which the researchers employed a variant of the dictator game to examine whether social preferences adhered to a standard principle in economics. In their experiment, participants assigned to the allocator role decided how many tokens they would transfer to the recipient. In the standard dictator game, each token has a value of 1 point for both players. Andreoni and Miller varied the values of each token across the two players. For some games, the token was more valuable for the allocator, while for other games, it was more valuable for the recipient. Their results evinced rationality behind social preferences—most of participants' allocation decisions exhibited transitivity. More importantly, some participants consistently behaved as a utilitarian: They gave more to the recipient, when the token was more valuable for the recipient and gave less when the token was more valuable for themselves. Bowles and Gintis (2011) concluded that this result finely illustrates that people care about others' well-being as well as their own and take both into account in making social decisions. Most importantly, this pattern cannot be explained by confusion.

3.4 Mismatch Hypothesis

Hagen and Hammerstein (2006), however, argued that the apparent evidence of other-regarding preferences was due to "mistakes." According to them, anonymous one-shot interactions did not occur in our ancestral environments. Therefore, the human mind is not designed to deal with anonymous one-shot interactions, which only exist in modernized societies and experimental laboratories. Hagen and Hammerstein noticed two variants of the mismatch hypothesis. First, people are simply confused; hence, apparent other-regarding behaviors are a product of the malfunctioning of our minds. Second, it is possible that people apply their default strategy (i.e., the strategy evolved for reputation building and maintenance in repeated interactions) to the artificial, experimental game situations.

Simple malfunctioning due to confusion may be unlikely, as Bowles and Gintis (2011) cited evidence against confusion. However, there is well-established evidence that people are concerned about their reputation, and this concern influences their behaviors in experimental game settings. For example, Bateson et al. (2006) examined the effect of an image of eyes on anonymous cooperation in a real-life setting—contributions to an honesty box placed in a university coffee room. The result indicated that university faculty and staff members contributed more to the honesty box when an image of eyes was printed on a payment instruction than when an image of flowers was printed on it. Clearly, the image of eyes cannot influence one's reputation. Therefore, this result cannot be attributed to participants' rational reputation-maintenance efforts. Although some criticisms exist against the watching-eyes effect (Northover et al. 2017, for a meta-analytic review), if we expand our scope to a broader range of studies, there is firm evidence that reputational concerns facilitate prosocial behaviors (e.g., Barclay and Willer 2007; Bereczkei et al. 2007; Jacquet et al. 2011; Yoeli et al. 2013).

Gintis et al. (2003) argued that people are acutely aware of the differences between one-shot interactions and repeated interactions. For example, they referred to evidence that the cooperation rate in the dyadic Prisoner's Dilemma game is generally higher when the game is repeated with the same partner than when it is a one-shot game. Although we consider this to be convincing evidence of the human ability to distinguish one-shot from repeated interactions, it is not decisive enough to support their claim: the cultural group selection model of strong reciprocity explains other-regarding behaviors observed in anonymous one-shot games. In fact, Delton et al. (2011) proposed a variant of the mismatch hypothesis that invokes the direct reciprocity context to explain the evolution of other-regarding behaviors in one-shot encounters. According to Delton et al., although there might have been one-shot encounters in human ancestral environments, it was not clear whether a particular encounter would ultimately be a one-time or repeated interaction. It is typically more costly to forfeit long-term benefits accruing from repeated interactions than to lose a small amount of cost to do a favor for a one-time partner. Therefore, Delton et al. argued that it was safer for our ancestors to assume that every interaction would be repeated and use strategies for repeated interactions as default strategies.

We close this section by pointing out that it is very difficult to decipher which is the *correct* evolutionary model to explain a particular behavior (or behavioral tendency). As we explained in the previous section, evolutionary models cannot single out the cues that organisms evolved to use. The models envisage adaptive problems that organisms must solve and demonstrate that particular behavior (or strategy) is useful for this goal. This is a functional explanation, or what is often called the *ultimate* explanation (Scott-Phillips et al. 2011). The question of which cue the organisms evolved to use is about mechanism underlying a particular behavior, and called as *proximate* explanation. Empirical studies are always informative for determining which cues organisms use. However, if different ultimate explanations agree that a particular strategy is adaptive, it is difficult to determine the function for which it evolved (because experiments simply show that organisms behave as the two models predict). However, if organisms behave differently in different contexts, it is easier to determine whether a particular strategy evolved to solve an adaptive problem in a particular context.

4 Can the Tit-for-Tat Strategy Explain Human Friendship?

In the case of strong reciprocity, the results of economic game experiments are not decisive regarding whether the cultural group selection model of strong reciprocity offers a valid explanation for human altruism. However, if we focus on more contextualized cooperation (e.g., friendship), the results of game experiments may be more informative. We can, for example, compare human cooperative behaviors within the target context (e.g., friendship) and some other contexts (e.g., interactions between strangers). In this section, taking this approach, we explore whether the standard model of dyadic cooperation (i.e., TFT-based reciprocity) can explain the evolution of human friendship.

4.1 Tit-for-Tat and the Evolution of Dyadic Cooperation

Compared to large-scale cooperation, evidence of cooperation within enduring dyadic relationships is more abundant in the animal kingdom (Seyfarth and Cheney 2011). Most cooperative relationships, however, occur within kin relationships, such as a mother–offspring relationship. Hence, they are possibly explained by kin selection. Nevertheless, cooperative relationships involving unrelated individuals are not uncommon, and some of them are not readily explained by kin selection. An alternative explanation for nonkin-based cooperation is reciprocal altruism (Trivers 1971).

Suppose that you play the Prisoner's Dilemma game with the same partner several times (the number of repetitions is unspecified in advance). If you cooperate, you will lose c, but your partner will receive b ($>c$). If you choose defection, both you and your partner will receive 0. The partner has the same choice. Therefore, both players will obtain the benefit of $b - c$ if both cooperate, whereas both players will receive 0 if both choose not to cooperate. If one player cooperates and the other player does not cooperate, the former (i.e., cooperator) will lose c, while the latter (i.e., noncooperator) will obtain b. Since the benefit of unilateral defection (b) is greater than the benefit of mutual cooperation ($b - c$) and the payoff of mutual defection (0) is still better than the payoff of being exploited ($-c$), defection is the dominant strategy in the one-shot Prisoner's Dilemma game. Then, what if the Prisoner's Dilemma game is iterated with the same partner? Whether some cooperative strategies could outcompete the uncooperative strategy in the iterated Prisoner's Dilemma remained unclear before Axelrod's (1984) seminal study.

Axelrod (1984) invited researchers in various disciplines to submit the strategy that they believed would outcompete other strategies in the iterated Prisoner's Dilemma game. Axelrod ran a tournament of the submitted strategies, and the simplest strategy (i.e., TFT) won. TFT cooperates in the initial round and mimics the partner's previous choice after the second round. The rule is simple: If you choose cooperation in this round, TFT will choose cooperation in the next round, and if you choose not to cooperate in this round, TFT will not cooperate in the next round. Axelrod listed three characteristics that made TFT the winning strategy in his tournament. First, TFT is nice in the sense that it does not mean choosing defection unless the partner provokes it by choosing defection. Second, TFT is retaliatory in the sense that it switches to defection if the partner chose defection in the previous round. Therefore, it does not allow uncooperative strategies to exploit its niceness too much. Third, TFT is forgiving in the sense that it immediately resumes cooperating with the former defector if he/she chooses cooperation again. The last two characteristics imply that TFT is an account-keeping strategy, which entails referring to the partner's past behavior to determine present behavior.

Although TFT is a backward-looking strategy, its evolutionary stability critically depends on the number of future interactions with the current partner, or the "shadow of the future," as Axelrod (1984) put it. Suppose that the probability of meeting the same partner again and playing the game is ω. If both you and your partner deploy the TFT strategy, you will keep earning the payoff of $b - c$ (i.e., the benefit accruing from the partner's cooperation minus the cost of your own cooperation) in each round until the game is terminated with a probability of $1 - \omega$. Hence, your expected payoff is $(b - c) + \omega(b - c) + \omega^2(b - c) \cdots = (b - c)/(1 - \omega)$. Suppose instead of that you use the unconditional defection strategy (ALLD) against TFT. You (an ALLD player) will simply continue choosing defection. Consequently, you will receive b in the initial round and keep earning 0 until the end of the game (because your partner, a TFT player, will never choose cooperation for your consistent defection). Thus, the expected payoff of ALLD is b. Accordingly, as far as $(b - c)/(1 - \omega) > b$, ALLD cannot invade a population of TFT players. This condition is rewritten as $\omega b > c$. Therefore, if the probability of another interaction is sufficiently high, TFT is evolutionarily stable against the invasion of a small number of ALLD players.

4.2 *What Psychological Mechanisms Does the Model Predict?*

As we saw in the previous section on strong reciprocity, whether people would use cues associated with the shadow of the future is not clear. Some scholars predict that people should not care about how long the future interactions will last because our ancestors rarely interacted with one-shot partners or because it was never certain that they would continue interacting with the same partner in the future (Delton et al. 2011; Hagen and Hammerstein 2006). Others, however, might argue that people should be able to switch their strategy depending on the perceived shadow of the future (e.g., Gintis 2000). In contrast, there is little ambiguity in predicting whether people would rely on a partner's past behaviors because the behavioral rules of TFT are backward-looking. Therefore, the model predicts that people would make their cooperation contingent on their partner's previous behavior.

In fact, an unconditional cooperative strategy (ALLC), which does not make use of a partner's past behaviors, is easily invaded by ALLD and is thus not evolutionarily stable. Suppose that ALLC meets ALLD; ALLD earns the payoff of $b/(1 - \omega)$, while ALLC loses the payoff of $c/(1 - \omega)$. Therefore, unlike TFT, ALLC has no means to defy exploitative strategies, such as ALLD. In other words, some retaliatory characteristic is necessary to deter exploitation by ALLD. Hence, undoubtedly, the TFT model is predicated on account-keeping (i.e., a tendency to keep track of favors given and received in a focal relationship) of the evolved psychological mechanism.

Are people, in fact, retaliatory like TFT? The answer to this question is an unreserved "yes" (see McCullough et al. 2012, for a review). TFT was submitted to Axelrod's tournament by Anatol Rapoport who had observed that many participants in his Prisoner's Dilemma experiments had behaved in a TFT-like manner and successfully solicited cooperation from their partners (Rapoport and Chammah 1965).[3] However, whether people exhibit retaliatory behaviors only when the shadow of the future is salient is unclear, as proponents of strong reciprocity argue that many people are inclined to punish unfair partners even in the anonymous one-shot ultimatum game (e.g., Gintis et al. 2003).

4.3 Does TFT Explain the Evolution of Human Friendship?

We now return to the central question of this section: Does TFT-based reciprocity explain the evolution of human friendship? The answer seems to be "no" in this case (Hruschka 2010; Silk 2003). As we noted, the critical characteristic of TFT is a concern for a partner's past behavior (or account-keeping). However, people tend not to be influenced by a friend's immediate behavior when determining whether to do a favor for the friend. Silk, for example, referred to the social psychological dichotomy of *communal relationships* (emotionally close relationships, including friendship) and less intimate *exchange relationships* (Clark and Mills 1979), and argued that contingency (especially short-term contingency) between a focal pair's behaviors (e.g., giving and receiving favors) is greater in exchange relationships than in communal relationships. Moreover, people expect friendship to be characterized by tolerance for short-term imbalances in giving and receiving. Therefore, when one receives a favor from one's partner, immediate returns in kind are perceived as a sign of psychological distance. In a laboratory experiment, participants behaved more favorably toward an experimental partner (i.e., a stranger) who had provided a small favor beforehand. However, when participants were paired with one of their real friends, the effect of a prior small favor disappeared; specifically, they treated a friend favorably regardless of the friend's preceding small favor (Boster et al. 1995).

[3] Although the notion of reciprocal altruism was originally developed in biology, the question of whether many instances of animal cooperation, in fact, require the notion of reciprocity (especially TFT-based reciprocity) is controversial (Dugatkin 1997; Silk 2003). A textbook example of reciprocity in biology is food-sharing among vampire bats: they regurgitate undigested blood in order to feed hungry roostmates (Wilkinson 1990). However, whether their food-sharing habit qualifies as an instance of reciprocity (and if so, to what extent) has yet to be firmly determined (Carter and Wilkinson 2013).

Xue and Silk (2012) conducted an experiment that incentivized careful monitoring of a partner's behavior, to test whether people would be less cautious in monitoring friends' behaviors than strangers' behaviors. Participants played the role of responder in a modified version of the ultimatum game, in which their partner (either a friend or a stranger) made a series of resource allocation decisions. Participants worked on an arithmetic task while the partners made the decisions. Each time the partner made a decision, it was signified by a beep to the participant. Participants' rewards were contingent on the performance on their own task as well as the partner's allocation decisions. Participants were allowed to reject their partner's proposal and forcibly take half of the total endowment that the partner allocated if and only if they correctly stated the number of decisions that the partner had made. However, to do so, they had to pay careful attention to the beeps they heard while completing the arithmetic task. Monitoring the number of beeps would necessarily hinder the performance on the arithmetic task. Xue and Silk revealed that participants were less accurate in identifying the number of beeps in the friend condition than in the stranger condition.

Notice that these studies not only evince that people are less interested in the cost–benefit balance in their friendships but also that they behave in a more TFT-like manner in interactions with strangers. Therefore, it can be said that people tend not to rely on TFT to maintain cooperation with their friends. This interpretation implies that the TFT model explains some part of human dyadic cooperation (e.g., the ability to form cooperative business-like relationships), but does not explain the evolution of friendship.

4.4 Less Concern About the Shadow of the Future in Friendship

If people are acutely responsive to the prospect of future interactions in a friendship, their relative disinterest in the short-term cost–benefit balance may be compensated by larger, long-term benefits (Delton et al. 2011). However, evidence indicates that people tend to incur higher costs to benefit their friends than strangers even when the prospect of future interaction is experimentally removed. Leider et al. (2009) had participants play the dictator game with multiple partners, whose social distances to the participants were systematically varied. The researchers also manipulated the anonymity of the allocators. In one condition, the partners were informed of their allocator's identity. In the other condition, the partners were not aware of their allocator's identity, although each participant knew who their partner was. Therefore, the participants in the latter condition had no reason to expect reciprocity from their current partner in the future. Leider et al. showed that participants' allocations were, in fact, influenced by the manipulation of the anonymity condition (i.e., whether recipients in the dictator game were informed of the allocator's identity). Nevertheless, participants allocated more money to socially close partners than socially distant partners even when their partner was unaware of their identity.

Disinterest in future reciprocation in a friendship seems implicit in our everyday understanding of friendship. Suppose that you are on the verge of bankruptcy—you may not be able to help your friends in the future. Some of your friends may still be willing to help you, while other friends will simply leave you. You may call the latter type of people fair-weather friends, and distinguish them from the former, true friends. This distinction implies that true friendship is characterized by a willingness to help even when one cannot expect future reciprocation. This led the founders of evolutionary psychology to propose an evolutionary paradox associated with human friendship—namely, the *banker's paradox* (Tooby and Cosmides 1996). They argued that "just when individuals need money most desperately, they are also the poorest credit risks and, therefore, the least likely to be selected to receive a loan" (p. 113). In a similar vein, they continued that "selection would seem to favor decision rules that caused others to desert you exactly when your need for help was greatest" (p. 132). Therefore, the paradox is that despite its ubiquity, human friendship does not seem to be evolvable.

4.5 Risk-Pooling in Uncertain Environments

The banker's paradox implies that people tend to help their friends when they are in dire need, regardless of the prospect of future reciprocation. Hruschka (2010) formally showed that such a need-based transfer system (i.e., you help your partner according to his/her current need, irrespective of the cost–benefit balance in the relationship or the prospect of future reciprocation) is evolvable in uncertain environments. In the traditional iterated Prisoner's Dilemma setting, both players simultaneously (or alternatively) decide whether to give a benefit to their partner. Implicit in this is that people become needy with some regularity: *A* is needy today, and *B* helps *A* today; *B* will be needy tomorrow, and *A* will help *B* tomorrow; and so on. Such regularity is not something we can expect in the real world. A might be needy today and be needy again in the near future, while *B* will stay safe for a relatively long period of time. Nevertheless, without a mutual support system, *B*, let alone *A*, may eventually die because no one will help them when they are in dire need. To cope with such unpredictable risks, *A* and *B* might form a committed friendship, within which they help each other when they are in need, ignoring the short-term imbalance of their exchanges and the prospect of future reciprocation. In other words, strict account-keeping is not an adaptive exchange rule if the ultimate purpose of partnership is risk-pooling.

Such a risk-pooling friendship (i.e., a need-based transfer system) is found in many traditional societies (Cronk et al. 2017). For example, Maasai herders have such a system called *osotua*, which means "umbilical cord" in their language. The *osotua* relationship is characterized by need-based transfers (Aktipis et al. 2011, 2016; Cronk 2007; Cronk et al. 2017). After losing their animals due to drought or other disasters, they ask their *osotua* partners (called *isotuatin*) for help. The requesters ask for help only when they are truly in need, and they do not exaggerate this need. The requested *isotuatin* give what they have been requested as far as they can afford it. Conducting agent-based simulations, Aktipis et al. (2011, 2016) have shown that the need-based transfer system increases the pair's survivability more so than other systems, such as the account-keeping transfer system, under which the requested parties help their partners only when the requesters have already paid back past debts. Aktipis et al. (2016) further demonstrated that without generosity, the need-based transfer would not be an efficient risk-pooling system.

Nevertheless, you might wonder why *osotua* or other need-based transfer systems would remain free from exploitation. If some free-riders began exploiting their generous partners, the system would eventually break down. Recall that populations of generous strategies, such as ALLC, are easily invaded by exploitable strategies, such as ALLD. Hruschka (2010) noted that the invasion of exploitative strategies becomes difficult if partner switches are costly. For example, if it is time-consuming to form a mutually reliable relationship, frequent partner switchers must survive a substantially long period of time without any reliable partners. In fact, according to Cronk's (2007) interviewees, people must undergo a period of gift giving and receiving to establish an *osotua* relationship (see also Cronk et al. 2017). Moreover, interviewees agreed that once established, *osotua* is eternal and cannot be destroyed. If community members share such norms, switching *osotua* partners is extremely costly (if not impossible). In addition, Cronk et al. (2017) noted that many need-based transfer systems in various societies entail strict norms of self-reliance. The coexistence of these institutional mechanisms appears to enable need-based transfer systems to persist.

4.6 Summary

In this section, we showed that economic game experiments are informative if they generate an expected pattern in one context but not in another context. Although a paradigmatic explanation for dyadic cooperation between genetically unrelated individuals is TFT-based reciprocity, the results of psychology experiments, including economic game experiments, suggest that people tend not to use TFT in friendship. This pattern is clear because people behave like TFT in a different context (i.e., interactions with strangers). However, this apparently puzzling pattern may be understandable if the ultimate function of friendship is risk-pooling via need-based transfers. Agent-based simulation studies have shown how the need-based transfer system works in a herd society (Maasai).[4] This is consistent with the basic frame-

[4]There is also some circumstantial evidence indicating that friendship is associated with need-based transfers. For example, people seem to be more attentive to their friends' needs. In a psychology experiment, when participants engaged in a joint task with their friends, they paid more attention to their partner's needs, whereas when they engaged in the same task with strangers, they paid attention to the partner's contribution, instead of needs (Clark 1984). Moreover, when friends fail to pay attention to their needs, people tend to perceive this as a sort of betrayal and as damaging to their relationship (Yamaguchi et al. 2015). There is also evidence on the flipside: When people

work of evolutionary psychology. Most people are unaware of the ultimate function of friendship (i.e., risk-pooling), and have never thought about the rationality behind their generosity toward friends. More importantly, unconscious cues and emotions seem to play a role in changing their exchange modes. The presence of a sense of intimacy or closeness makes people more generous toward a partner, while a lack of intimacy or closeness causes them to behave in a more TFT-like manner.

5 How People Maintain a Good Reputation

In this section, we argue that if there are two competing strategies predicted by different evolutionary models, economic game experiments are informative for determining which strategy people are more prone to use. As an illustrative case, we compare two strategies proposed to explain the reputation-based cooperation in human societies, *indirect reciprocity* (Alexander 1987).

5.1 Indirect Reciprocity and the Image Scoring Strategy

In Trivers' (1971) framework, cooperation occurs in closed dyads. Players help their partner, and the relation is directly reciprocal. However, as we already noted in Sect. 3.1, human cooperation is not restricted to kin and dyadic relationships. People occasionally help total strangers. You may have given directions to someone you do not know; you may have given a seat to an elderly person in a crowded train; you may have donated some of your money to save the lives of unknown people. Although the target of your altruistic behavior may not return any favor to you, you can still earn a good reputation by behaving altruistically. Moreover, when you are in need in the future, someone who recognizes your good reputation may help you. This reputation-based helping functions as follow: X helps Y (i.e., conferring a benefit of b to Y); X is helped by Z (not Y) at some later time. This is called indirect reciprocity, which was originally proposed by Alexander (1987), and later formalized by Nowak and Sigmund (1998a, b; see also Nowak and Sigmund 2005, for a review).

Nowak and Sigmund (1998a, b) formally showed that indirect reciprocity is evolvable if each player discriminates the targets of his/her helping behavior on the basis of each one's reputation. This strategy is called the image scoring strategy. In its simplest form, its only considers the current partner's last behavior. If X helped Y in the previous round, an image scoring player Z considers X a good person, and helps X. If X failed to help Y in the previous round, Z considers X a bad person, and

notice that someone (a stranger) is paying attention to their needs, they increase their intimacy and tend to behave more favorably toward the person (Ohtsubo et al. 2014; Ohtsubo and Yamaguchi 2017).

declines to help X. If image scoring players comprise an entire population, this will prevent the invasion of an exploitative strategy, such as ALLD.

Suppose that each player plays the role of either donor or recipient with a probability of 0.5 in each round. Every player's reputation is initially good. The interactions in the population are repeated with a probability of ω. The image scoring players earn b with a probability of 0.5 and incur c with a probability of 0.5, thus, the expected payoff in each round is $(b - c)/2$. Therefore, the expected net payoff of the image scoring players is $(b - c)/[2(1 - \omega)]$. If an ALLD player invades this population, he/she will keep earning b until he/she plays the donor role (as a donor, he/she does not help the partner, and after that, no one in the population will help him/her). Therefore, ALLD's expected benefit is $0.5b + 0.5^2\omega b + 0.5^3\omega^2 b + \cdots = b/(2 - \omega)$. Therefore, if $(b - c)/[2(1 - \omega)] > b/(2 - \omega)$ holds, ALLD cannot invade the population of image scoring. This condition can be written as $\omega > 2c/(b + c)$. If b is twice as large as c, this condition implies that ω only needs to be greater than 2/3 (or the interactions need to continue, on average, three times). Therefore, it can be said that the image scoring strategy is evolutionarily stable against ALLD under a wide range of conditions.[5]

5.2 Problem of the Image Scoring Strategy

Although the image scoring strategy does not allow ALLD to invade the population of the image scoring players, it is not evolutionarily stable against a second-order free-riding strategy (Leimar and Hammerstein 2001). To understand the second order free-rider problem in the context of indirect reciprocity, let us assume that there is a small probability that each player fails to follow his/her cooperative intent (e.g., Person X intends to give his/her seat to an elderly person, but someone else does so before X; X intends to encourage someone who has just broken up with his/her girl-/boyfriend, but X's words may hurt the person). The possibility of such implementation errors implies that image scoring players sometimes fail to cooperate. If X committed an error in a particular round, his/her next partner, Y, will perceive X as a bad player and refrain from helping X. The problem is that this hurts Y's reputation. Y earns a bad reputation for not helping X, and will not be helped in the next round. In a sense, a good reputation is a valuable asset in the indirect reciprocity context. Therefore, we can state that the image scoring players are punishers, who are willing to lose their good reputation to reduce bad players' payoffs (Hammerstein and Hagen 2005, Leimar and Hammerstein 2001). As in the case of strong reciprocity, non-punishers (i.e., unconditional cooperators) free-rides on punishers' policing effort and enjoy higher fitness than costly punishers.

---

[5]This argument may convey the impression that the critical condition for the evolution of indirect reciprocity is equivalent to the condition for the evolution of direct reciprocity (TFT-based reciprocity). However, in his review of five prominent rules of the evolution of cooperation, Nowak (2006) pointed out that the evolution of indirect reciprocity hinges on the cost of information acquisition. It is not evolvable unless the information about others' past behaviors is cheaply available.

Confirming that unconditional cooperators (or the players who only care for their own reputation) can easily invade a population of image scoring players, Leimar and Hammerstein (2001) introduced a slightly different reputation-assignment rule in their simulation: Not cooperating with a bad player can be justified and does not lead to a bad reputation. In other words, unlike the image scoring strategy, this strategy, the standing strategy (Sugden 1986), distinguishes justified defection (not cooperating with a bad player) from unjustified defection (not cooperating with a good player). If others follow this reputation-assignment rule, "not cooperating with a bad player" is no longer a costly punishment. It is not just a non-costly behavior, but beneficial for the "punishers"—they can avoid the costs of cooperation by refraining from cooperating with bad players. Therefore, Leimar and Hammerstein showed that the standing strategy can stabilize indirect reciprocity.

Ohtsuki and Iwasa (2004, 2006) generalized Leimar and Hammerstein's finding by conducting a comprehensive search of evolutionarily stable strategies in the indirect reciprocity context. They found that of 4096 strategies, only eight strategies, collectively called the *leading eight*, enabled the evolution of indirect reciprocity. In their analyses, more than eight strategies were stable against the invasion of ALLD; however, their cooperative equilibria easily broke down due to destructive reactions to justified defection. The image scoring strategy is one example. After ALLD acquires a bad reputation, no image scoring players cooperate with the ALLD player. Hence, every time ALLD is assigned to the role of recipient, one image scoring player temporarily loses his/her good reputation. As we noted, this initially justified defection produces a chain of defection (X refrains from cooperating with ALLD; Y refrains from cooperating with X; Z refrains from cooperating with Y; and ad infinitum). The number of such destructive chains increases as the ALLD player is assigned to the recipient role. Accordingly, due to the presence of even a single ALLD player, the cooperation rate of this population can decline substantially. According to Ohtsuki and Iwasa, only eight strategies, all of which distinguish justified defection from unjustified defection, are not only stable against the invasion of ALLD but are also capable of maintaining high levels of cooperation.

5.3 Do People Really Use the Standing Strategy?

Leimar and Hammerstein's (2001) simulation and Ohtsuki and Iwasa's (2004, 2006) mathematical analyses indicated that distinguishing justified defectors from unjustified defectors is crucial for the evolution of indirect reciprocity. In other words, the evolutionarily stable strategy in the indirect reciprocity context utilizes second-order information (i.e., the current partner's past partner's behavior) as well as first-order information (i.e., the current partner's past behavior). For example, suppose that X refrained from cooperating with Y, who refrained from cooperating with Z. If you play the image scoring strategy, you only look at X's behavior (i.e., first-order information). If you play the standing strategy, however, you must consider both X's and Y's behaviors (i.e., first- and second-order information).[6]

Milinski et al. (2001) explored whether people would actually utilize second-order information in the giving game, which was devised to investigate participants' strategies in the indirect reciprocity context (Wedekind and Milinski 2000). This multi-round game followed simple rules: In each round, participants were randomly assigned to either the donor or recipient role. The donor was asked to spend or not to spend his/her resource (c) to confer benefit (b) on his/her current partner (i.e., recipient). The donor was provided with information about the current partner's previous behavior. Wedekind and Milinski revealed that participants decided whether to give or not to give the resource on the basis of the partner's past behaviors (i.e., first-order information). When Milinski et al. (2001) provided second-order information in addition to first-order information in the giving game, participants rarely used the second-order information, and they decided whether to give mostly on the basis of first-order information.

Subsequent studies provided mixed evidence to support the standing strategy. Ule et al. (2009) categorized participants in terms of their behaviors in the experimental game. Ule et al. found that more participants used the image scoring strategy than the standing strategy. Therefore, Ule et al.'s participants were more likely to rely only on first-order information. More recently, Swakman et al. (2016) explicitly asked participants if they would like to check the second-order information. If explicitly asked, many participants examined the second-order information. Importantly, however, when participants had to pay a small amount of cost to check the second-order information, few of them utilized it.[7] Therefore, the empirical studies suggest that people are not inclined to utilize second-order information, and thus few people play the standing strategy.

5.4 The Intention Signaling Strategy as an Alternative

As we noted, the standing strategy, or the other strategies included in the leading eight, assumes that people utilize second-order information in determining whether the current partner's previous uncooperative behavior is justifiable or not. In other words, there is an assumption that real players—humans—are good at inferring someone's

[6]The explanation of second-order information is slightly inaccurate here. The standing strategy assigns a bad reputation to those who do not give a resource to a "good" player. Therefore, the second-order information is not simply Y's behavior; it is determined by Y's behavior and Z's *reputation* (not Z's behavior): Y's decision not to help Z is justified if Z's reputation is "bad," but is not justified if Z's reputation is "good." Nevertheless, in the experimental setting, it is difficult to accurately operationalize the second-order information. If the experimenter wishes to give this kind of information, it requires disclosing all past partners' behaviors from the outset of the experiment (assuming that all players start with a good reputation).

[7]This result is important given Nowak's (2006) model indicating that the evolution of indirect reciprocity crucially depends on the cost of information acquisition.

intentionality. People, in fact, utilize various types of circumstantial evidence, such as an actor's desires, beliefs, and other external constraints, to determine whether the actor *intentionally* performed a certain act (e.g., Malle and Knobe 1997). It may be true that such sophisticated theory-of-mind abilities make humans skillful mind-readers. In the indirect reciprocity context, however, the relevant information (i.e., second-order information) may be unavailable to the mind-readers. For example, even if you observe that X has publicly offended Y, you are not sure about X's intention: X may be simply a mean person, X might have been provoked by Y, or X might have tried to stop Y from offending someone else (Z). If second-order information was not always cheaply available in our ancestral environments, the human mind might not have evolved to readily use it.

Notice that the person who possesses the richest information about X's intention is X him-/herself. If X knows that whether other people will help him/her in the future depends on his/her current intention, it is wise for X to signal his/her current intention to others (especially if it is benign). Suppose that X does not spend his/her resource c to confer a benefit of b to Y. X saves the cost of c not because he/she is stingy but because he/she is aware of Y's bad reputation. To signal his/her non-malicious intent, X can conspicuously abandon c. This can serve as an honest signal of X's non-stingy intent because stingy defectors would make the "not help" decision in order to save c, and thus should not be willing to abandon c. Tanaka et al. (2016) called this strategy the intention signaling strategy (intSIG) and showed that it is stable against the invasion of ALLD. Moreover, if there is a small probability of implementation error, intSIG does not allow ALLC to invade the population.

Tanaka et al. (2016) then conducted a series of giving game experiments in which half of the participants were allowed to abandon their endowment c after deciding not to give it to their current partner (the signaling condition), and the other half provided second-order information along with first-order information (the standing condition). Whether participants are inclined to use second-order information was not clear in Tanaka et al.'s two experiments. In one experiment, participants helped justified defectors more than unjustified defectors, whereas in the other experiment, they did not distinguish the two types of defectors (they simply treated the previous cooperators more favorably than the previous defectors). In contrast, across the two experiments, participants assigned to the signaling condition clearly showed their inclination to use the signal option. Tanaka et al. divided participants' behaviors exhibiting defection into two types: If a participant refrained from giving the resource to a "bad" player, it was categorized as justified defection; if a participant refrained from giving it to a "good" player, it was categorized as unjustified defection, which was presumably caused by stinginess. In the two experiments, the signal option was more likely to be used after justified defection than after unjustified defection. Moreover, participants distinguished signalers from non-signalers. Even though signalers and non-signalers were indistinguishable in terms of their previous behavior (i.e., neither had given their resource to their partner), participants were more likely to give their resource to signalers than to non-signalers.

Tanaka et al. did not measure emotional reactions to the current partner in each round; thus, it is not possible to conclude that their participants were not driven by rational deliberation. Nevertheless, if participants consciously attempted to maintain their reputation, as we already discussed, it would have been easier for them to simply give their resources all the time. In the signaling condition, many participants did not choose this simpler strategy; rather, they chose not to give and subsequently abandoned the resource. Moreover, Tanaka et al.'s experiments at least suggest that people more readily employ intSIG than the standing strategy. The implication of this result is that in the indirect reciprocity context (where reputation matters), people try to signal their own intention instead of simply letting others to read it.

6 Conclusion

In this chapter, we first introduced the basic assumptions of evolutionary psychology. One such assumption is that adaptive strategies evolved via natural selection, and organisms are not necessarily aware of the functions of their strategies. In many cases, those strategies are driven by emotions (e.g., anger drives people to retaliation). Due to these assumptions, evolutionary psychologists and experimental economists may make different interpretations of the same results. If people adopt a strategy that is consistent with the predicted equilibrium, experimental economists may consider that they are rationally pursuing their self-interest, while evolutionary psychologists may suppose that people are equipped with a certain behavioral tendency shaped by natural selection.

Owing to this difference, evolutionary psychologists and experimental economists have different attitudes toward rational deliberation. For experimental economists, the involvement of rational deliberation in equilibrium supports their assumption that people rationally pursue their self-interest. For evolutionary psychologists, it could be a refutation of their thesis that people have an unconscious tendency to behave in a particular manner. This is why evolutionary psychologists are often concerned about underlying psychological mechanisms yielding particular behavioral responses. For this reason, evolutionary psychologists seek "rules of thumb" or probabilistic cues that make organisms adaptive (although such rules/cues sometimes lead them to commit systematic errors).

We argued, in this chapter, that behavioral responses per se may be informative or uninformative for evolutionary psychologists. Simply observing that people behave in a certain manner is sometimes uninformative. For example, as proponents of strong reciprocity emphasize (e.g., Bowles and Gintis 2011; Fehr and Fischbacher 2004; Gintis 2000), people often cooperate in anonymous one-shot games. This is considered to be strong counterevidence of rational deliberation (or a pursuit of self-interest). If their goal were to maximize self-interest, they should not cooperate in the absence of any possible reciprocation by the partner. However, as we noted, this is not decisive evidence of the cultural group selection model of strong reciprocity. There are alternative models and explanations, such as the mismatch hypothesis, that predicts the same result (i.e., cooperation in anonymous one-shot games). In this case, thus, the behavioral observation per se is not sufficiently informative.

However, if people behave differently under different conditions or use one strategy and not another, observing behaviors in economic game experiments is more informative. For example, people tend to behave in a TFT-like manner in anonymous Prisoner's Dilemma games. However, people do not use TFT in their friendships (e.g., do not appear to strictly keep track of the cost–benefit balance in the relationship), and tend to behave like unconditional cooperators. This suggests that psychological mechanisms underlying human friendship are not adapted to form TFT-based, well-balanced, exchange relationships. Instead, it is more likely that human friendships evolved for collectively managing unpredictable risks in our ancestral environments (e.g., Aktipis et al. 2011, 2016; Hruschka 2010).

When two competing models predict different strategies, economic game experiments are also informative. Two types of strategies allow for the evolution of indirect reciprocity: the standing strategy (or a set of strategies called the leading eight) and intSIG. The assumption underpinning the standing strategy is that in a reputation-assignment setting, observers determine whether an actor's intention was benign by taking second-order information into account. This is cognitively taxing, and the observers would incur some cognitive cost. The assumption underlying intSIG is that the actors, rather than the observers, would incur a signaling cost to honestly communicate their benign intention. A series of giving game experiments showed that people readily used the signaling option and interpreted other players' uses of the option as an indication of a benign intention. However, they were not necessarily utilizing second-order information to decide whether to cooperate with the current partner. These results indicate that intSIG is closer to our natural behavioral tendency in situations where a good reputation is of crucial importance.

Although we emphasized the role of emotions in Sect. 2.3, the studies we cited are not necessarily backed up by emotional evidence. As experimental economics is inclined toward cognitive explanations and evolutionary psychology is inclined toward emotional explanations, it seems to be more cross-fertilizing to separate the cognitive and emotional components underlying the observed behavioral tendencies. Even in the context of friendship, people in some societies seem to notice the function of their traditional risk-pooling systems (Cronk et al. 2017). Nevertheless, if they were not equipped with any (emotionally driven) behavioral tendencies, they might never have imagined behaving in a particular way. It would also be interesting to see how much such unconscious tendencies contribute to the formation of a particular institution in each society or community. Since both experimental economists and evolutionary psychologists work on similar models and share the same research tool, such cross-fertilization does not appear to be very difficult.

References

Aktipis, C. A., Cronk, L., & de Aguiar, R. (2011). Risk-pooling and herd survival: An agent-based model of a Maasai gift-giving system. *Human Ecology, 39,* 131–140. https://doi.org/10.1007/s10745-010-9364-9.

Aktipis, A., de Aguiar, R., Flaherty, A., Iyer, P., Sonkoi, D., & Cronk, L. (2016). Cooperation in an uncertain world: For the Maasai of East Africa, need-based transfers outperform account-keeping in volatile environments. *Human Ecology, 44,* 353–364. https://doi.org/10.1007/s10745-016-9823-z.

Alcock, J. (2013). *Animal behavior* (10th ed.). Sunderland, MA: Sinauer Associates.

Alexander, R. D. (1987). *The biology of moral systems*. New York, NY: Aldine de Gruyter.

Alvergne, A., Faurie, C., & Raymond, M. (2009). Father-offspring resemblance predicts paternal investment in humans. *Animal Behaviour, 78,* 61–69. https://doi.org/10.1016/j.anbehav.2009.03.019.

Andreoni, J. (1995). Cooperation in public-goods experiments: Kindness or confusion? *American Economic Review, 85,* 891–904.

Andreoni, J., & Miller, J. (2002). Giving according to GARP: An experimental test of the consistency of preferences for altruism. *Econometrica, 70,* 737–753. https://doi.org/10.1111/1468-0262.00302.

Axelrod, R. (1984). *The evolution of cooperation*. New York: Basic Books.

Axelrod, R., & Hamilton, W. D. (1981). The evolution of cooperation. *Science, 211,* 1390–1396. https://doi.org/10.2307/1685895.

Barclay, P., & Willer, R. (2007). Partner choice creates competitive altruism in humans. *Proceedings of the Royal Society B, 274,* 749–753. https://doi.org/10.1098/rspb.2006.0209.

Barkow, J. H., Cosmides, L., & Tooby, J. (Eds.). (1992). *The adapted mind: Evolutionary psychology and the generation of culture*. New York: Oxford University Press.

Bateson, M., Nettle, D., & Roberts, G. (2006). Cues of being watched enhance cooperation in a real-world setting. *Biology Letters, 2,* 412–414.

Bereczkei, T., Birkas, B., & Kerekes, Z. (2007). Public charity offer as a proximate factor of evolved reputation-building strategy: An experimental analysis of a real-life situation. *Evolution and Human Behavior, 28,* 277–284. https://doi.org/10.1016/j.evolhumbehav.2007.04.002.

Bevc, I., & Silverman, I. (2000). Early separation and sibling incest: A test of the revised Westermarck theory. *Evolution and Human Behavior, 21,* 151–161. https://doi.org/10.1016/S1090-5138(99)00041-0.

Boster, F. J., Rodríguez, J. I., Cruz, M. G., & Marshall, L. (1995). The relative effectiveness of a direct request and a pregiving message on friends and strangers. *Communication Research, 22,* 475–484. https://doi.org/10.1177/009365095022004005.

Bowles, S., & Gintis, H. (2011). *A cooperative species: Human reciprocity and its evolution*. Princeton, NH: Princeton University Press.

Boyd, R., Gintis, H., Bowles, S., & Richerson, P. J. (2003). The evolution of altruistic punishment. *Proceedings of the National Academy of Sciences of the U.S.A., 100,* 3531–3535. https://doi.org/10.1073/pnas.0630443100.

Buss, D. M. (2015). *Evolutionary psychology: The new science of the mind* (5th ed.). Oxon, U.K.: Routledge.

Carter, G., & Wilkinson, G. (2013). Does food sharing in vampire bats demonstrate reciprocity? *Communicative & Integrative Biology, 6,* e25783. https://doi.org/10.4161/cib.25783.

Clark, M. S. (1984). Record keeping in two types of relationships. *Journal of Personality and Social Psychology, 47,* 549–557. https://doi.org/10.1037/0022-3514.47.3.549.

Clark, M. S., & Mills, J. (1979). Interpersonal attraction in exchange and communal relationships. *Journal of Personality and Social Psychology, 37,* 12–24. https://doi.org/10.1037/0022-3514.37.1.12.

Cronk, L. (2007). The influence of cultural framing on play in the trust game: A Maasai example. *Evolution and Human Behavior, 28,* 352–358. https://doi.org/10.1016/j.evolhumbehav.2007.05.006.

Cronk, L., Berbesque, C., Conte, T., Gervais, M., Lyer, P., McCarthy, B., et al. (2017). *Managing risk through cooperation: Need-based transfers and risk pooling among the societies of the Human Generosity Project*. Unpublished manuscript at Rutgers University.

Dawkins, R. (1979). Twelve misunderstandings of kin selection. *Zeitschrift für Tierpsychologie, 51,* 184–200. https://doi.org/10.1111/j.1439-0310.1979.tb00682.x.

DeBruine, L. M. (2002). Facial resemblance enhances trust. *Proceedings of the Royal Society of London B, 269,* 1307–1312. https://doi.org/10.1098/rspb.2002.2034.

DeBruine, L. M. (2004). Facial resemblance increases the attractiveness of same-sex faces more than other-sex faces. *Proceedings of the Royal Society of London B, 271,* 2085–2090. https://doi.org/10.1098/rspb.2004.2824.

Delton, A. W., Krasnow, M. M., Cosmides, L., & Tooby, J. (2011). Evolution of direct reciprocity under uncertainty can explain human generosity in one-shot encounters. *Proceedings of the National Academy of Sciences of the U.S.A., 108,* 13335–13340. https://doi.org/10.1073/pnas.1102131108.

Dugatkin, L. A. (1997). *Cooperation among animals: An evolutionary perspective.* Oxford, U.K.: Oxford University Press.

Fehr, E., & Fischbacher, U. (2004). Social norms and human cooperation. *Trends in Cognitive Sciences, 8,* 185–190. https://doi.org/10.1016/j.tics.2004.02.007.

Gintis, H. (2000). Strong reciprocity and human sociality. *Journal of Theoretical Biology, 206,* 169–179. https://doi.org/10.1006/jtbi.2000.2111.

Gintis, H., Bowles, S., Boyd, R., & Fehr, E. (2003). Explaining altruistic behavior in humans. *Evolution and Human Behavior, 24,* 153–172. https://doi.org/10.1016/S1090-5138(02)00157-5.

Gintis, H., Henrich, J., Bowles, S., Boyd, R., & Fehr, E. (2008). Strong reciprocity and the roots of human morality. *Social Justice Research, 21,* 241–253. https://doi.org/10.1007/s11211-008-0067-y.

Hagen, E. H., & Hammerstein, P. (2006). Game theory and human evolution: A critique of some recent interpretations of experimental games. *Theoretical Population Biology, 69,* 339–348. https://doi.org/10.1016/j.tpb.2005.09.005.

Hames, R. (2016). Kin selection. In D. M. Buss (Ed.), *The handbook of evolutionary psychology* (2nd ed., pp. 505–553). Hoboken, NJ: Wiley.

Hamilton, W. D. (1964a). The genetical evolution of social behaviour. I. *Journal of Theoretical Biology, 7,* 1–16. https://doi.org/10.1016/0022-5193(64)90038-4.

Hamilton, W. D. (1964b). The genetical evolution of social behaviour. II. *Journal of Theoretical Biology, 7,* 17–52. https://doi.org/10.1016/0022-5193(64)90039-6.

Hammerstein, P., & Hagen, E. H. (2005). The second wave of evolutionary economics in biology. *Trends in Ecology & Evolution, 20,* 604–609. https://doi.org/10.1016/j.tree.2005.07.012.

Holmes, W. G., & Sherman, P. W. (1982). The ontogeny of kin recognition in two species of ground squirrels. *American Zoologist, 22,* 491–517. https://doi.org/10.1093/icb/22.3.491.

Hruschka, D. J. (2010). *Friendship: Development, ecology, and evolution of a relationship.* Berkeley, CA: University of California Press.

Jacquet, J., Hauert, C., Traulsen, A., & Milinski, M. (2011). Shame and honour drive cooperation. *Biology Letters, 7,* 899–901. https://doi.org/10.1098/rsbl.2011.0367.

Korchmaros, J. D., & Kenny, D. A. (2006). An evolutionary and close-relationship model of helping. *Journal of Social and Personal Relationships, 23,* 21–43. https://doi.org/10.1177/0265407506060176.

Leider, S., Möbius, M. M., Rosenblat, T., & Do, Q.-A. (2009). Directed altruism and enforced reciprocity in social networks. *Quarterly Journal of Economics, 124,* 1815–1851. https://doi.org/10.1162/qjec.2009.124.4.1815.

Leimar, O., & Hammerstein, P. (2001). Evolution of cooperation through indirect reciprocity. *Proceedings of the Royal Society B, 268,* 745–753. https://doi.org/10.1098/rspb.2000.1573.

Lieberman, D., Tooby, J., & Cosmides, L. (2007). The architecture of human kin detection. *Nature, 445,* 727–731. https://doi.org/10.1038/nature05510.

Malle, B. F., & Knobe, J. (1997). The folk concept of intentionality. *Journal of Experimental Social Psychology, 33,* 101–121. https://doi.org/10.1006/jesp.1996.1314.

Mateo, J. M. (2003). Kin recognition in ground squirrels and other rodents. *Journal of Mammalogy, 84,* 1163–1181. https://doi.org/10.1644/BLe-011.

Maynard Smith, J. (1982). *Evolution and the theory of games*. Cambridge, U.K.: Cambridge University Press.
McCullough, M. E., Kurzban, R., & Tabak, B. A. (2012). Cognitive systems for revenge and forgiveness. *Behavioral and Brain Sciences, 36,* 21–22. https://doi.org/10.1017/S0140525X12000386.
McElreath, R., & Boyd, R. (2007). *Mathematical models of social evolution: A guide for the perplexed*. Chicago, IL: University of Chicago Press.
Milinski, M., Semmann, D., Bakker, T. C. M., & Krambeck, H.-J. (2001). Cooperation through indirect reciprocity: Image scoring or standing strategy? *Proceedings of the Royal Society of London B, 268*, 2495–2501. https://doi.org/10.1098/rspb.2001.1809.
Northover, S. B., Pedersen, W. C., Cohen, A. B., & Andrews, P. W. (2017). Artificial surveillance cues do not increase generosity: Two meta-analyses. *Evolution and Human Behavior, 38,* 144–153. https://doi.org/10.1016/j.evolhumbehav.2016.07.001.
Nowak, M. A. (2006). Five rules for the evolution of cooperation. *Science, 314,* 1560–1563. https://doi.org/10.1126/science.1133755.
Nowak, M. A., & Sigmund, K. (1998a). The dynamics of indirect reciprocity. *Journal of Theoretical Biology, 194,* 561–574. https://doi.org/10.1006/jtbi.1998.0775.
Nowak, M. A., & Sigmund, K. (1998b). Evolution of indirect reciprocity by image scoring. *Nature, 393,* 573–577. https://doi.org/10.1038/31225.
Nowak, M. A., & Sigmund, K. (2005). Evolution of indirect reciprocity. *Nature, 437,* 1291–1298. https://doi.org/10.1038/nature04131.
Ohtsubo, Y., Matsumura, A., Noda, C., Sawa, E., Yagi, A., & Yamaguchi, M. (2014). It's the attention that counts: Interpersonal attention fosters intimacy and social exchange. *Evolution and Human Behavior, 35,* 237–244. https://doi.org/10.1016/j.evolhumbehav.2014.02.004.
Ohtsubo, Y., & Yamaguchi, C. (2017). People are more generous to a partner who pays attention to them. *Evolutionary Psychology, 15*(1). https://doi.org/10.1177/1474704916687310.
Ohtsuki, H., & Iwasa, Y. (2004). How should we define goodness?—Reputation dynamics in indirect reciprocity. *Journal of Theoretical Biology, 231,* 107–120. https://doi.org/10.1016/j.jtbi.2004.06.005.
Ohtsuki, H., & Iwasa, Y. (2006). The leading eight: Social norms that can maintain cooperation by indirect reciprocity. *Journal of Theoretical Biology, 239,* 435–444. https://doi.org/10.1016/j.jtbi.2005.08.008.
Pinker, S. (1997). *How the mind works*. New York: Norton.
Rapoport, A., & Chammah, A. M. (1965). *Prisoner's dilemma: A study in conflict and cooperation*. Ann Abor, MI: University of Michigan Press.
Sahlins, M. (1977). *The use and abuse of biology*. Ann Arbor, MI: University of Michigan Press.
Scott-Phillips, T. C., Dickins, T. E., & West, S. A. (2011). Evolutionary theory and the ultimate-proximate distinction in the human behavioral sciences. *Perspectives on Psychological Science, 6,* 38–47. https://doi.org/10.1177/1745691610393528.
Seyfarth, R. M., & Cheney, D. L. (2012). The evolutionary origins of friendship. *Annual Review of Psychology, 63*, 153–177. https://doi.org/10.1146/annurev-psych-120710-100337
Silk, J. B. (2003). Cooperation without counting: The puzzle of friendship. In P. Hammerstein (Ed.), *Genetic and cultural evolution of cooperation* (pp. 37–54). Cambridge, MA: MIT Press.
Sugden, R. (1986). *The economics of rights, co-operation and welfare*. Oxford, UK: Blackwell.
Swakman, V., Molleman, L., Ule, A., & Egas, M. (2016). Reputation-based cooperation: Empirical evidence for behavioral strategies. *Evolution and Human Behavior, 37,* 230–235. https://doi.org/10.1016/j.evolhumbehav.2015.12.001.
Tanaka, H., Ohtsuki, H., & Ohtsubo, Y. (2016). The price of being seen to be just: An intention signalling strategy for indirect reciprocity. *Proceedings of the Royal Society B*, 20160694. https://doi.org/10.1098/rspb.2016.0694.
Tooby, J., & Cosmides, L. (1996). Friendship and the Banker's paradox: Other pathways to the evolution of adaptations for altruism. *Proceedings of the British Academy, 88,* 119–143.
Trivers, R. L. (1971). The evolution of reciprocal altruism. *Quarterly Review of Biology, 46,* 35–57.

Ule, A., Schram, A., Riedl, A., & Cason, T. N. (2009). Indirect punishment and generosity toward strangers. *Science, 326,* 1701–1704. https://doi.org/10.1126/science.1178883.

Wedekind, C., & Milinski, M. (2000). Cooperation through image scoring in humans. *Science, 288,* 850–852. https://doi.org/10.1126/science.288.5467.850.

West, S. A., El Mouden, C., & Gardner, A. (2011). Sixteen common misconceptions about the evolution of cooperation in humans. *Evolution and Human Behavior, 32,* 231–262. https://doi.org/10.1016/j.evolhumbehav.2010.08.001.

Wilkinson, G. S. (1990). Food sharing in vampire bats. *Scientific American, 262,* 76–82. https://doi.org/10.1038/scientificamerican0290-76.

Xue, M., & Silk, J. B. (2012). The role of tracking and tolerance in relationship among friends. *Evolution and Human Behavior, 33,* 17–25. https://doi.org/10.1016/j.evolhumbehav.2011.04.004.

Yamaguchi, M., Smith, A., & Ohtsubo, Y. (2015). Commitment signals in friendship and romantic relationships. *Evolution and Human Behavior, 36,* 467–474. https://doi.org/10.1016/j.evolhumbehav.2015.05.002.

Yoeli, E., Hoffman, M., Rand, D. G., & Nowak, M. A. (2013). Powering up with indirect reciprocity in a large-scale field experiment. *Proceedings of the National Academy of Sciences of the U.S.A., 110,* 10424–10429. https://doi.org/10.1073/pnas.1301210110.

Part II
Critical Viewpoints

Reconsidering Induced Value Theory

Toshiji Kawagoe

1 Introduction

Why we should pay real monetary rewards to subjects in the laboratory experiment? This question is often raised not only by researchers of different disciplines such as psychology but also by our fellow economics researchers who are not so familiar with experimental methods.

But an answer to that question seems to be not always homogenous. Someone might simply think that cash payment in proportion with the points earned in an experiment is mandate for preparing a research article submitted to any academic journal. For example, a top-ranked journal such as *Econometrica* provides a detailed instruction about submitting experimental research article[1]. Among its checklist, it contains an instruction of description for payment method as follows.

> Suggested information to provide for the review process:
>
> ...
>
> 5. Subject payments, including whether artificial currency was used, the exchange rate, show up fees, average earnings, lotteries, and/or grades.

In other journals, though not sometimes so explicit in its submissions guidelines, payment method used and the amount paid is usually asked by the reviewers.

Or, someone might think that paying in cash in proportion with a subject's performance in an experiment makes the experiment "realistic," and allows to induce honest responses from subjects in the task.

[1] https://www.econometricsociety.org/publications/econometrica/information-authors/instructions-submitting-articles#experimental.

T. Kawagoe (✉)
Future University Hakodate, Hokkaido, Japan
e-mail: kawaoe@fun.ac.jp

T. Kawagoe and H. Takizawa (eds.), *Diversity of Experimental Methods in Economics*,
https://doi.org/10.1007/978-981-13-6065-7_7

But Vernon Smith, a pioneer of experimental economics, has made clear about why we should pay rewards. He was the person who stated that payment to subjects was essential in experimental research in the following reason.

> Control over preferences is the most significant element distinguishing laboratory experiments from other methods of economic inquiry. In such experiments, it is of the greatest importance that one be able to state that, as between two experiments, individual values (or derivative concepts such as demand or supply) either do or do not differ in a specified way. This control can be exercised by using a reward structure and a property right system to induce prescribed monetary value on (abstract) outcomes. (Smith 1982; p. 931)

Then, he proposed *induced value theory* in his influential papers (Smith 1976, 1982). Based on the mechanism design approach, he demonstrated that payment to the subjects was necessary to induce *preferences* from subjects. Moreover, by choosing appropriate exchange rate from points earned by subject in the experiment to cash rewards, an experimenter can *control* subject's preference, i.e., can induce any utility function as the experimenter would like to realize in the experiment. In other words, without any payment, the experimenter is not confident that he/she has any control over the subject's preference. For example, if he designed an experiment to test a theory assuming risk neutrality in the laboratory without making any payment to subjects according to induced value theory, the assumption of risk neutrality might be violated in reality (usually subjects are risk averse).

Though induced value theory soon became the standard methodology in economics, there were many controversies over experimental methods between experimental economists and psychologists/behavioral economists. One of the hottest topics was, of course, about payments to subjects. Experimental economists criticized psychologists/behavioral economists, as they frequently conducted experiments without any real payments, i.e., they simply asked subjects to think about hypothetical rewards and paid the same amount of money for all the subjects, regardless of their choices. Experimental economists criticized that as payments are not proportional to actual performances in the experiment, subjects' choices were not reliable because subjects' preferences are not controlled.

Since then, though the number of psychologists/behavioral economists accepting induced value theory is increasing, a controversy over payment methods still continues up to now. It is evident from, for example, Peter Wakker's document about justifying *random payment system* (Wakker 2007).

With random payment system, typically, a part of subjects are randomly chosen to pay and the paid amount is based on the points earned from a part of tasks randomly selected. Random payment system is used by many psychologists/behavioral economists (of course, the users are not limited to them.). One of the merits of random payment system is avoiding wealth (income) effect, which is explained later. But the main reason for adopting it might be reducing the total amount to pay. Actually, expected payment gets relatively smaller. So, the experimental economists are sometimes critical to random payment system, though evidence doesn't show any demerit about it, according to Wakker (2007). Wakker mentioned the debates over whether random payment system is a valid incentive system, and concluded that it was a valid method by referring several articles for the system.

> Unfortunately, experimental economics referees who emphasize the importance of real incentives but who do not know the field of experimental individual choice well, will again and again open up the debate of this incentive system…My experience at this moment of writing, January 2007, is that still more than half of the referees of economics journals open up this debate. (Wakker 2007)

Then, he concluded as follows.

> Remember that the random-lottery incentive system is the only real incentive system for individual choice known today that can avoid the income effect. Without it, real incentives for individual choice are no longer well possible. (Wakker 2007)

Recently, an extreme form of random payment system appears, that is, *one and only one* subject is chosen to pay and the paid amount is based on the points earned in *one and only one* of the tasks randomly selected. Is this still an appropriate payment system? That question led me to start to study the current status of research on payment methods in economic experiment.

The main discussion about payment systems will be given in Sect. 3. Before that, I will briefly summarize the characteristics of experimental methods in economics and differentiate among experimental economists and psychologists/behavioral economists in Sect. 2. Section 4 proposes a practical solution for answering criticisms against various payment systems and concludes.

2 Methodology of Economic Experiment

2.1 Objective of Economic Experiment

The heart of *induced value theory*, introduced by Smith (1976, 1982), that is fundamental of experimental economics methodology, is to achieve *experimental control over subject's preference* by means of reward medium, typically monetary payment.

One of the naïve criticisms raised against induced value theory is that it makes the economic experiment meaningless: if subjects' preferences are perfectly controlled, then their behaviors perfectly coincide with the theoretical prediction. Thus, there is no need to run the experiment.

For replying to this kind of criticism, reviewing the basic structure of economic model is useful. Here, we assume an experiment of individual decision-making such as asking risk preference or time preference. To generalize it to a game-theoretic situation where subjects interact with each other is easy but for the sake of notational simplicity, we mainly discuss by using individual decision-making experiment.

Then, the basic structure of an economic model is as follows.

$$x_i = f_i(u_i, e_i).$$

Here, x_i is the subject i's choice or *action*. If the number of subjects in an experiment is n, $X = \{x_1, \ldots, x_n\}$ is called an action profile. Denote $P(x_i)$ as the subject's *payoff* with this choice x_i. For example, in risky choice problem, $P(x_i)$ is a lottery that the subject receives as an outcome of his/her choice. Thus, P is the payoff function mapping from the subject's action to payoff value. $P(X) = (P(x_1), \ldots, P(x_n))$ is called *payoff profile.*

u_i is *utility function* of the subject i, defined over payoff profile $P(X)$. In traditional, neoclassical economics, the following *self-interested* utility function is usually assumed:

$$u_i(P(X)) = u_i(P(x_i)),$$

that is, subject only cares about his/her own payoff. Of course, even though every subject is self-interested, the functional forms of their utility functions may be different from each other.

e_i is the set of constraints or *environment* that the subject i faces. In traditional, neoclassical economics, budget constraint, and informational constraint are typically included in e_i.

f_i is the subject i's principle of decision-making (solution concept in game theory). In traditional, neoclassical economics, it is usually assumed that f_i is utility maximization:

$$f_i^*(u_i, e_i) = \arg\max_x u_i(P(x)), \qquad \text{subject to } x \in e_i.$$

For a naïve subject, random choice may be his/her principle of decision-making.[2]

Then, using this model, let us consider first how a theoretical economist in traditional, neoclassical school explains the subject's behavior in an experiment.

The theoretical economist in traditional, neoclassical school assumes that the subject's principle of decision-making is *utility maximization* ($f_i^* = f_j^*$ for any i, j). He also assumes that utility function is *self-interested* one for any subject and their utility functions are the same as the representative agent model assumes. Thus, if subjects' behaviors are different, the theoretical economist in traditional, neoclassical school explains that such difference occurs due to the difference between environments among subjects.

But experimental environment e_i can relatively easily be controlled in the laboratory (for example, by giving the same amount of budget and information to subjects). Utility function u_i can also be controlled according to induced value theory by paying real monetary rewards in proportion with the subject's performance. Then, if environment e_i and utility function u_i are well controlled in the laboratory, the subject's

[2]Sometimes, people may confuse the difference between utility functions with the difference between principles of decision-making. Such people mistakenly suppose that a player with self-interested utility function chooses a particular action A (e.g., defection in Prisoner's dilemma) and a player with altruistic utility function chooses another action B (e.g., cooperation in Prisoner's dilemma). But even if a player has self-interested utility function, he may choose cooperation in Prisoner's dilemma because his principle of decision-making is random choice. So, the distinction between utility function and principle of decision-making is important.

behavior cannot be different according to the model of the theoretical economist in traditional, neoclassical school. Thus, naïve criticism against induced value theory seems to apply.

But in reality, the subjects' behaviors are different even though environment e_i and utility function u_i are well controlled in the laboratory. What's wrong in the above argument? The answer is that it missed the fact that the subjects' principles of decision-making is not observable and cannot be controllable. If so, given e_i and u_i, only sources of difference in the subject's behavior must be in the subjects' principles of decision-making f_i.

Thus, the objective of the economic experiment is to find out the difference in principles of decision-making f_i between subjects by controlling environment e_i and utility function u_i. It is clear that such kind of experiment never be meaningless unlike naïve critics blames.

But, in reality, constraints that subjects face might be not limited to budget and informational constraints. Income level, investment carrier, gender, family structure, religious, cultural and social environments, etc., might also constraint a subject's behavior. Then, not only principle of decision-making f_i but also environment e_i might be different between subjects. If this is the case, difference in behaviors between subjects are indeterminate. In philosophy of science terminology, *the Duhem–Quine problem* matters.

Thus, the experimenter should try to identify and control further constraints that have been ignored but might affect the subject's behavior, for example, if gender difference matters, conducting further experiment by separating men from women subjects. Nevertheless, the real world is too complex that it might be the case that further constraint to be controlled would be found even though the experimenter had carefully controlled known constraints. This way, the experimenter expands the set of environment e_i up to the point that no further constraint to be controlled would be found. At that moment, finally, the experiment provides a legitimate test to identify solely principle of decision-making f_i. (But in practice, this ideal situation would never be attained because of time and budget constraints for the experimenter.)

Of course, during isolating environmental factors that might affect the subject's behavior, the principle of decision-making f_i so far accepted would be refined or be replaced with a new one. Anyway, identifying the principle of decision-making f_i is an ultimate objective that economic experiment tries to achieve.

2.2 *On Different Schools of Behavioral Economics*

As for traditional, neoclassical economics, their theories are usually regarded as the first approximations toward reality. Over 100 years have passed since modern economics is founded, economists, at last, start to move toward the second approximation by behavioral economics.

Behavioral economics incorporates many psychological insights into economic modeling. One of the well-accepted models for individual decision-making is *prospect theory* by Kahneman and Tversky (1979). Then, in what sense, prospect theory is new?

One may think that it uses only a different kind of utility function u_i (as well as probability weighting function) and the principle of decision-making f_i that prospect theory uses is still utility maximization. We will clarify it more formally.

First, expected utility theory (EUT) developed by von Neumann and Morgenstern (1944) and Savage (1954) is a fundamental model of individual decision-making in traditional, neoclassical economics. In this model, with utility function $u_i(x_j)$ over a prize x_j from lottery L and a linear probability function $p(x_j)$, expected utility function $E = \sum_j p(x_j)u_i(x_j)$ is constructed.

Next, in prospect theory, with value function $v_i(u_i(x_j))$ over a utility function $u_i(x_j)$ of prize x_j from lottery L, which is assumed as asymmetric between gain and loss outcomes, and a nonlinear, distorted weighting function $w_i(p(x_j))$ of probability, which evaluates a probability *more* than its face value when the probability is relatively small and *less* than its face value when the probability is relatively large, expected utility function $E' = \sum_j v_i(u_i(x_j))w_i(p(x_j))$ is constructed.

Even though expected utility functions E and E' are different, it is assumed that an individual tries to maximize its expected utility function. So, it can be thought that both traditional, neoclassical economics and behavioral economics follow the same principle of decision-making f_i, that is, utility maximization.

Then, if the subject's expected utility function is controlled with a certain experimental procedure (for example, Berg et al. (1986)'s method using a lottery as experimental payment), an experimenter could identify the subject's principle of decision-making in the laboratory, as explained in the previous subsection.

But one can think it otherwise. As both EUT and prospect theory assumes that an individual anyway tries to maximize his expected utility function, *principle of decision-making f_i should be fixed as utility maximization*. Therefore, the difference of subject's behavior in the experiment is due to the difference of utility function. Thus, in the given utility maximizing principle of decision-making f_i, identifying utility function in the experiment is the main focus for behavioral economists.

The same argument can also apply to the case of social preference model. Instead of self-interested utility function, social preference (or, other-regarding preference) such as altruism, inequality aversion, and reciprocity can be a candidate to explain the subject's behavior in the experiment. In this case, even if a subject has a certain social preference, it is assumed that he may try to maximize his utility function reflecting his social preference.

Behavioral economists following such kind of approach might be called "new school" of behavioral economics, as "old school" of behavioral economics takes a different approach.

For Kahneman and Tversky (1979), one of the pioneers of "old school," prospect theory was not merely using different utility functions from EUT. They actually thought that the prospect theory contained different principles of decision-making, such as framing effect.

Herbert Simon also proposed a boundedly rational model of decision-making. In his model, utility maximization was criticized and *satisficing* was proposed as an alternative principle of decision-making. Some researchers including Simon stress difference in principle of decision-making f_i, and proposed many boundedly rational models (recent models are such as quantal response equilibrium (QRE) and level-k model).

Then, why "old school" lost its popularity in economics? The probable answer is traditional, neoclassical economist's criticism that boundedly rational behavior can be explained as utility maximization by incorporating computational and cognitive constraints into economic models.

For example, satisficing can be explained by time constraint that a player faces. He could find out an action maximizing his utility function with sufficiently long time, but as he doesn't have enough thinking time in reality, he ends up with satisficing behavior. Or, as he may not have enough short-term memory, he cannot count up every contingency in a decision situation in short time. Anyway, taking these constraints into account in the set of environment e_i, the subject's behavior can be viewed as utility maximization. Thus, difference in behaviors between subjects are attributed to environments including different cognitive abilities and computational resources.

"New school" of behavioral economics is dominant in economics literature now. But "old school" still survives, as the recent success of QRE and level-k models to explain the subject's behavior in the laboratory is shown.

Thus, we have totally three approaches in conducting experimental research in the laboratory. In traditional, neoclassical economist's approach, difference in behaviors between subjects are explained by difference of the set of environment e_i. In "new school" of behavioral economist's approach, difference in behaviors between subjects is explained by different utility function u_i; Finally, in "old school" of behavioral economist's approach, difference in behaviors between subjects are explained by different principles of decision-making f_i.

From the discussion here, it is clear that for both traditional, neoclassical economist's and "old school" of behavioral economist's approaches, controlling subject's preference is vital for conducting a well-controlled, meaningful experiment. But for "new school" of behavioral economist, it is not the case. For their ultimate research, the objective is not to *control* utility function (preference) but to *identify* it. So, there is no reason for them to adopt induced value theory.

3 Pros and Cons with Payment Systems in the Experiment

3.1 Motivation

To achieve experimental control over subject's preference, monetary rewards paid in accordance with induced value theory is indispensable for both traditional, neoclassical economist's and "old school" of behavioral economist's approaches, as demonstrated in the previous section.

In fact, induced value theory is one of the fundamentals in experimental methodology in economics. Smith (1976, 1982) postulated it by using mechanism design framework. If the payment in the experiment satisfies several reasonable premises, salience, dominance, etc., experimental control over the subject's preference is achieved.

Then, payment in the economic experiment is usually done as follows. Each subject participated in an experiment is asked to perform several tasks in a session. Then, total points earned during the session by the subject are paid. In other words, points earned in all the tasks are paid. This is sometimes called "all-pay system." Basically, the experimental economists think that all-pay system is the gold standard of payment system which satisfies the premises of induced value theory.

By the way, mainly due to budget constraint for experimenters, it is also usual that points earned in only selected tasks are paid. In this case, tasks to be paid are randomly selected. This is called "random payment system."

Random payment system is widely used in individual decision-making and games with repeated interaction. The advantage of random payment system is robustness to the wealth effect. With all-pay system, if subjects accumulated a sufficient amount of rewards in the middle of the experiment, they might lose interest in later tasks. This is wealth effect. By using random payment system, it is considered that subjects should concentrate on every task because they don't know in advance which task will be selected for the payment.

Recently, an extreme form of random payment system appears in the laboratory experiment. When subjects participate in an experiment with several tasks, *one and only one* of the participants is chosen, and then *one and only one* tasks are selected and paid. In this case, to provide enough incentive for subjects, the experimental rewards are set relatively higher than with all-pay system. More precisely, in practicing random payment system, the expected payment with random payment system is set roughly equal to the one with all-pay system.

But, even though the expected payment with random payment system is equal to the one with all-pay system, can it give control over the subject's preference? Thus, examining and comparing these payment systems in the economic experiment is the subject matters in this section (see also Charness et al. 2016).

First, random payment system has been criticized by Holt (1986) and others that when a subject follow non-expected utility theory (particularly, violating independence axiom in expected utility theory), it is not incentive compatible. Also, random payment system may not induce ambiguity averse preference due to hedging over uncertain events when subjects are ambiguity averse (Bade 2014).

For games with repeated interaction (typically, infinitely repeated games), random payment system is also used. In infinitely repeated game experiments, discount factor is represented by the random termination probability. But, in such an environment, even though the random termination probability provides the same incentive compatibility constraint as prescribed in the discount factor, equilibrium path may be different from the original setting. Thus, random payment system is also problematic in such an environment.

But only random payment system should be criticized? Recent studies show that there is a case that all-pay system may not be incentive compatible.

According to induced value theory by Vernon Smith, if the subjects show other-regarding preferences, payment system may violate dominance precept. That is, the presence of other-regarding preference should be considered as the lack of experimental control over the subject's preference. It is actually the case even if we use all-pay system. Then, such an experiment is meaningless because of lack of control over the subject's preference? What justification is made for it, if we assume induce value theory is fundamental methodology in economic experiment?

On the other hand, confirming other-regarding preference in economic experiment is widely accepted research project in economic science. One reason behind it is because "new school" of behavioral economics gains its popularity in economics. As demonstrated in the previous section, "new school" of behavioral economics need not induced value theory.

Then, induced value theory is no longer valid methodology in the economic experiment? If so, why we should make payment to subjects? We try to answer these questions about payment systems in order.

3.2 Several Payment Systems

In this subsection, several payment systems are compared. Suppose that a subject takes part in an experiment where totally N person participate and make decisions in totally T tasks.

In all-pay system, *every* subject is paid and the amount paid is calculated for *every* T tasks. As we have already said, this is the gold standard of payment system in experimental economics. For all-pay system, *risk neutrality* should be assumed. If subjects are risk averse, there are several evidences that they show more *present bias* under all-pay system (Sherstyuk et al. 2013). Another concern for all-pay system is wealth effect, as we have already mentioned. That is, accumulated rewards up to the task K ($<T$) makes future rewards less attractive for a subject because of diminishing marginal utility (Chandrasekhar et al. 2011).

As for random payment system, there are two variations. One is *within-subjects* random payment system (wRPS) where *every* subject is paid and the amount paid is calculated for only K out of T tasks (typically $K = 1$). The other is *between-subjects* random payment system (bRPS) where only M subjects out of N are paid and the amount paid is calculated for only K out of T tasks ($M = K = 1$ is an extreme case.).

Random payment system is known as problematic in several experimental environments. For the experiment concerning *choice under risk*, if several decision problems (typically, lottery choices) are presented, the subjects may not consider that each decision problem is independent, but they view the set of decision problems as a compound lottery with random payment system. Then, if the independent axiom

Table 1 An Ellsberg urn problem

	Blue	Green	Red
Probability	30/90	60/90	
Prize	\$5	\$9	\$9

of expected utility theory is violated, random payment system is not incentive compatible and causes preference reversal (Holt 1986). There is also an evidence that the subjects are more risk averse under bRPS than wRPS (Laury 2005).

For *choice under uncertainty* experiment, random payment system is also problematic. That is, ambiguity averse subject may not reveal his preference because of the existence of an opportunity for hedging over uncertain events (Bade 2014; Baillon et al. 2015; Oechssler and Roomets 2013; Kuzmics 2013). This is illustrated by the famous *Ellsberg urn problem* as follows (an example below taken from Bade 2014).

Suppose that totally 90 balls are contained in an urn. 30 of 90 balls are certainly blue. 60 of 90 balls are either green or red. Then, an experimenter draws a ball from the urn. If your choice is blue and a blue ball is drawn, you get \$5. If your choice is either green or red and the respective ball is drawn, you get \$9 (see Table 1).

Suppose that you participate in two consecutive tasks in this situation. In the first task, you are asked to choose either blue or green, and in the second task, you are asked to choose blue or red. Then, if an ambiguity averse subject believe, for example, that the probability of drawing a green ball, $p(G)$, is 10/90 and the probability of drawing a red ball, $p(R)$, is 50/90 in the first task and that $p(G)$ is 50/90 and $p(R)$ is 10/90 in the second task.

The point here is that the ambiguity averse subject forms *pessimistic* belief over the combination of colors for the balls in the uncertain urn, that is, the chance to draw a ball of his favorite color from uncertainty urn (green or red) is less than the one to draw a ball of another color.

Then, given this belief, for the ambiguity averse subject, the expected payoff for choosing blue ball is $\$5 \times (30/90) = \$5/3$ while the expected payoff for choosing green or red ball is $\$9 \times (10/90) = \$1$. As the former is greater than the latter, the ambiguity averse subject is willing to bet on the blue ball in both tasks. Namely, if he confronts with an uncertain (ambiguous) situation, he will stick to a certain event (choice), that is, blue ball. This is called *ambiguity aversion*.

Then, what if random payment system is introduced in this situation? Suppose that either the first task or the second task is chosen with probability 1/2 after the experiment for calculating rewards. When the ambiguity averse subject takes into account of this payment system, he can devise the following combined choice for the first and the second tasks: to choose green in the first task and red in the second task. Then, the expected payment for this choice becomes $(1/2) \times (p(G) + p(R)) \times \$9 = (1/2) \times (60/90) \times \$9 = \$3$. As this is greater than the expected payoff for blue ball, the ambiguity averse subject will switch to choose an uncertain event (green in the first task and red in the second task). Thus, preference reversal occurs and

Table 2 Prisoner's dilemma stage game

1	2	
	C	*D*
C	1, 1	−1.5, 3
D	3, −1.5	0, 0

the ambiguity averse subject never reveals his ambiguity aversion preference when random payment system is introduced in the Ellsberg urn problem.

Random payment system also causes a problem in a game experiment with repeated interaction (an example below taken from Chandrasekhar and Xandri, 2011). Suppose that the following prisoner's dilemma stage game is infinitely repeated (see Table 2).

In this setting, when both players follow trigger strategies, mutual cooperation outcome (C, C) is sustainable if and only if the discount factor $\beta \geq 2/3$.

For testing this equilibrium prediction in the laboratory, the discount factor β is usually represented by *random termination probability*. That is, at the end of each stage game, experimenter (or, typically, a computer program) decides randomly whether the game continues to the next round. When the continuation probability is set equal to β, that is, the game ends at each round with probability $1-\beta$, equilibrium condition for mutual cooperation outcome (C, C) remains the same. But if random payment system is introduced in this environment, this might not be the case.

To see this, suppose that mutual cooperation outcome (C, C) was sustained up to the 9th round. With random termination probability, the game will end at 10th round with probability $1 - \beta$. Given that the opponent player keeps playing C along with equilibrium path induced by trigger strategy, playing C gives 1 payoff and playing D gives 3 payoffs. Then, if the game ends at 10th round, the expected payoff for playing C at 10th round is 1 and the expected payoff for playing D at 10th round is $\frac{9}{10} + \frac{1}{10} \times 3$ (as an outcome among ten rounds is chosen randomly). Likewise, the game will end at 11th round with probability $(1 - \beta)\beta$ and the expected payoff for keeping playing C is 1 and the expected payoff for playing D is $\frac{9}{11}+\frac{1}{11}\times 3+\frac{1}{11}\times 0$ (As you played D at the 10th round, your payoff for playing D at 11th round is 0 because your opponent follows trigger strategy and played D). This way, the expected payoff for playing D at and after the 10th round can be calculated as follows.

$$\sum_{t=0}^{\infty}(1-\beta)\beta^t\left(\frac{9}{10+t}+\frac{3}{10+t}\right) = 1.0116.$$

Thus, as this is greater than the payoff of keeping playing C, players have the incentive to deviate from mutual cooperation to D, when random incentive system is introduced. In other words, random incentive system makes players *time inconsistent*. All-pay system may also be problematic because of wealth effect.

Then, Chandrasekhar and Xandri (2011) propose another payment system that every subject is paid and the amount paid is based on the outcome *at last round* only. This is called "last round payment system." Unlike all-pay system, last round payment system works for any risk attitude. Unlike random payment system, last round payment system doesn't cause time-inconsistent behavior.

Sherstyuk et al. (2013) have compared last round payment system with other payment systems in the laboratory using infinitely repeated prisoner's dilemma game. As for the rate of mutual cooperation, there was no significant difference between experiments with all-pay and last round payment systems and both rates were significantly higher than the one with random payment system. For the percentage of always D strategy, it was significantly higher with random payment system than with all-pay and last round payment systems. Finally, as for the rate of tit-for-tat strategy, again there was no significant difference between experiments with all-pay and last round payment systems and both rates were significantly higher than the one with random payment system. Thus, the performance of last round payment system was equal to the one of all-pay system.

Then, can we conclude that last round payment system is a better option? I think there is still a concern for it. In an experiment, a subject might try to guess at which round the last round comes. The expected number of repetition in repeated prisoner's dilemma described above is easily calculated as $\bar{t} = 1/(1 - \beta)$. From this, the subject could adopt a strategy such that cooperating until round $t < \bar{t}$ and then deviating to D at and after round $\bar{t}$. As $\bar{t}$ is common knowledge among subjects, if subjects anticipate that other subjects follow that strategy, mutual cooperation may not be sustainable, as the backward induction argument for finitely repeated game is applied here. Thus, it could be possible that such consideration may cause a player to deviate from the equilibrium path.

3.3 Mechanism Design Approach for Several Payment Systems

As we examined in the previous subsection, no single payment system is flawless, at least from behavioral viewpoint. So, one may ask to characterize each payment system more systematic, theoretical way.

Azrieli et al. (2016) study several payment systems by mechanism design approach. They consider an experiment with multiple tasks, that is, the same subject takes part in several tasks. The individual choice experiment where each subject has to choose several pairs of lottery and game experiment with repeated interaction are examples. Then, they ask whether there is any incentive compatible payment system.

In their theory, D denotes the set of decision problems, X the set of alternatives, $P(X)$ the set of rewards over X, R a subject's preference relation over X, R^* preference over $P(X)$, M the set of announced choices, μ message function, and φ payment system. Then, the experiment with a payment system is represented in the following canonical form (Fig. 1).

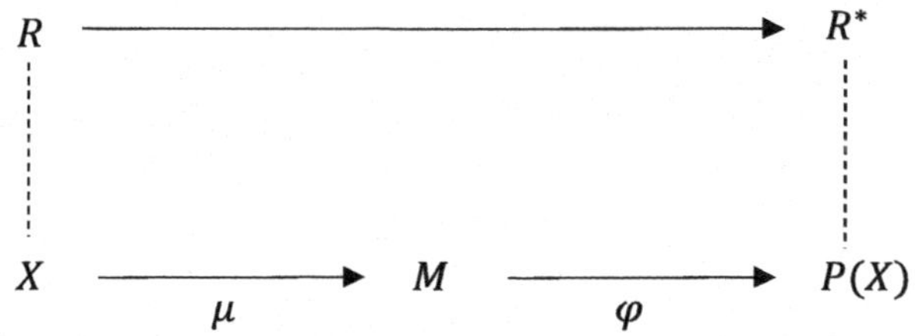

Fig. 1 Canonical form of the experiment with payment system

In this form, μ represents subject's choice from X accordance with his preference R over X. μ is called *truthful* if it chooses a maximal element in X. Then, payment system φ determines rewards $P(X)$, which is typically a lottery. So, $P(X)$ is probability distribution over X. The subject also has preference R^* over $P(X)$. If R^* corresponds to R, R^* is called an extension of R or *incentive compatible.*

Then, with which condition, random incentive system is incentive compatible? To state their characterization, we need the following definitions coming from decision theory.

Definition 1 Act is a function from the state space to $P(X)$, which represents a realization of the randomizing device to determine the payment. An act f dominates another act g if the payment under f is greater than or equal to the payment under g in any state.

Definition 2 (*Monotonicity*). If an act f dominates another *act* $g \Rightarrow fR^*g$, then extension R^* is monotonic.

Proposition 1 (Azrieli et al. 2016). *Random incentive system is incentive compatible if monotonicity holds.*

For all-pay system, the following definition is necessary.

Definition 3 (*Non Complementarity at the Top*). The sum of the payments under a choice μ is preferred to the sum of the payments under different choice ν.

The idea behind Non Complementarity at the Top (Ncat) is as follows. For example, even though the payment for a safe lottery x_i is preferred to the payment for a risky lottery y_i, portfolio preferences for the set of each type of lottery may be different, that is, it may be the case such that $\sum_i y_i R^* \sum_i x_i$. Ncat represents nonexistence of such portfolio effect.

Proposition 2 (Azrieli et al. 2016). *All-pay system is incentive compatible if Ncat holds.*

4 Conclusion

For obtaining experimental control over the subject's preference, monetary payment is assumed to be necessary according to induced value theory. But from the argument so far, any payment system has a limitation in inducing true preference. Then, no satisfactory payment system exists?

The answer is no. When an experiment is run *one and only one* round, arguments against those payment systems are not applicable. So, if we'd like to retain induced value theory, we should stick to the one-shot experiment.

The argument for one-shot experiment seems to be extreme. In fact, during hot debates between behavioral and experimental economists in 1990s, researchers of learning/evolutionary theory advocates repetition in the experiment to obtain "clean" experimental environment (e.g., Binmore 1999). But in the twenty-first century, research interests have been shifted to understand behavior in the first round decision. Quantal response equilibrium (QRE) proposed by McKelvey and Palfrey (1995), level-k (Stahl and Wilson 1995) and cognitive hierarchy models (Camerer et al. 2004) are representative models trying to describe subject's initial response in a novel strategic situation where he/she deviate significantly from rational choice. Those researchers think that learning/evolution may contaminate "pure" strategic thinking, and proposed models show good predictive power in the one-shot environment.

One may think that if we allow only one-shot experiment, it is too restrictive in designing and conducting a meaningful experiment. Especially, for researchers in studying individual choices such as eliciting risk and time preferences, without conducting multiple-choice experiments, it seems to be impossible to achieve their research goals. In those experiments, the multiple price list (MPL, Holt and Laury 2002) is so far the standard method for eliciting subject's risk attitude in the individual choice problem (a similar method is proposed by Coller and Williams (1999) for eliciting time preference).

With MPL method, subjects are asked to choose one of two lotteries with different prizes. Subjects are presented several lotteries in order. In each lottery, prizes are fixed but probability obtaining higher prizes in each lottery is gradually increased. For example, the prizes in Choice *A* are either 2 or 1.6 dollars and the prizes in Choice *B* are either 3.85 or 0.1 dollars. The probability of obtaining a higher prize in each lottery is increased from 10 to 100% by 10% (Table 3).

After all the choices are completed, subjects are paid one of their realized prizes according to their choices. That is, random payment system is used. In this experiment, a risk-neutral subject who initially chooses Choice *A* will switch their choices to Choice *B* at Lottery 4. A risk-averse subject will switch later. This switching point gives a measure for the subject's risk attitude. Then, if we are not allowed to run a multiple-round experiment for securing our payment method being valid, the MPL is no longer available. But there are several alternatives which require one and only one round. Becker, De Groot and Marschak (BDM, Becker et al. 1964)'s and Gneezy and Potter (1997)'s are such methods.

With the BDM method, the subject is given a lottery. Then, he/she is asked to sell it with a ask price, p. After that, an experimenter (buyer) chooses a bid price, b, randomly. If $p > b$, the lottery cannot be sold, then subject plays the lottery by him/herself and is paid realized prize. Otherwise, the lottery is sold and subject earns the bid price. It is well known that the BDM method is incentive compatible, that

Table 3 Lottery choices in the MPL method

Prize	Choice *A*		Choice *B*	
	\$2.00 (%)	\$1.60 (%)	\$3.85 (%)	\$0.10 (%)
Lottery 1	10	90	10	90
Lottery 2	20	80	20	80
Lottery 3	30	70	30	70
Lottery 4	40	60	40	60
Lottery 5	50	50	50	50
Lottery 6	60	40	60	40
Lottery 7	70	30	70	30
Lottery 8	80	20	80	20
Lottery 9	90	10	90	10
Lottery 10	100	0	100	0

is, equalizing p to certainty equivalence of the lottery is a dominant strategy for each subject. From the certainty equivalence, one can easily derive the subject's risk attitude.

With Gneezy and Potter (1997)'s method, the subject is given initial endowment, x. Then, he/she is asked to choose the amount y from x for investment. With probability p, k times the amount used for investment will be returned ($kp > 1$) and otherwise return is zero. Investing all the endowment x is the best policy for a risk-neutral subject because the expected return for investing $x + (kp - 1)y$ is greater than the one for not investing, x, as $kp > 1$. But a risk-averse subject will hesitate to invest. This way we can detect the subject's risk attitude.

For both the BDM and Gneezy and Potter (1997)'s methods, only one-shot experiment is necessary. So, devising a one-shot experiment for eliciting subject's risk attitude is possible. Of course, as is well known, both methods are not without limitation, but it is also the case for the MPL (see Charness et al. 2013).

Anyway, avoiding any concern about payment systems, designing and conducting a one-shot experiment will be a promising way to save the induced value theory. Of course, "new school" of behavioral economists may need not to worry about any payment systems, because the subject's preference is not controlled but is identified according to their experimental methodology.

References

Azrieli, Y., Chambers, C. P., & Healy, P. J. (2016). Incentives in experiments: a theoretical analysis. *Mimeo.*

Bade, S. (2014). Randomization devices and the elicitation of ambiguity averse preferences. *Mimeo.*

Baillon, A., Halevy, Y., & Li, C. (2015). Experimental elicitation of ambiguity attitude using the random incentive system. *Mimeo.*

Becker, G. M., Degroot, M. H., & Marschak, J. (1964). Measuring utility by a single-response sequential method. *Behavioral Science, 9,* 226–232.

Berg, D., Dickhaut, J., & O'Brien, B. (1986). Controlling preferences for lotteries on units of experimental exchange. *Quarterly Journal of Economics, 101,* 281–306.

Binmore, K. G. (1999). Why experiment in economics? *Economic Journal, 109,* F16–F24.

Camerer, C., Ho, T.-H., & Chong, J. K. (2004). A cognitive hierarchy theory of one-shot games. *Quarterly Journal of Economics, 119,* 861–898.

Chandrasekhar, A. G., & Xandri, J. P. (2011). A note on payments in experiments of infinitely repeated games with discounting. *Mimeo.*

Charness, G., Gneezy, U., & Halladay, B. (2016). Experimental methods: pay one or pay all. *Journal of Economic Behavior & Organization, 131,* 141–150.

Charness, G., Gneezy, U., & Imas, A. (2013). Experimental methods: eliciting risk preferences. *Journal of Economic Behavior & Organization, 87,* 43–51.

Coller, M., & Williams, M. B. (1999). Eliciting individual discount rates. *Experimental Economics, 2,* 107–127.

Gneezy, U., & Potters, J. (1997). An experiment on risk taking and evaluation periods. *Quarterly Journal of Economics, 112*(2), 631–645.

Holt, C. A. (1986). Preference reversals and the independence axiom. *American Economic Review, 76,* 508–515.

Holt, C. A., & Laury, S. K. (2002). Risk aversion and incentive effects. *American Economic Review, 92*(5), 1644–1655.

Kahneman, D., & Tversky, A. (1979). Prospect theory: an analysis of decision under risk. *Econometrica, 47,* 263–291.

Kuzmics, C. (2013). A rational ambiguity averse person will never display her ambiguity aversion. *Mimeo.*

Laury, S. K. (2005). Pay one or pay all: rndom selection of one choice for payment. *Mimeo.*

McKelvey, R. D., & Palfrey, T. R. (1995). Quantal Response Equilibria for Normal Form Games, *Games and Economic Behavior, 10,* 6–38.

Oechssler, J., & Roomets, A. (2013) Unintended hedging in ambiguity experiments. *Mimeo.*

Savage, L. J. (1954). *The Foundations of Statistics*, Wiley.

Shertyuk, K., Tarui, N., & Saijo, T. (2013). Payment schemes in infinite-horizon experimental games. *Experimental Economics, 16,* 125–153.

Smith, V. L. (1976). Experimental economics: Induced value theory. *American Economic Review, 66,* 274–279.

Smith, V. L. (1982). Microeconomic systems as an experimental science. *American Economic Review, 72,* 923–955.

Stahl, D. O., & Wilson, P. W. (1995). On player's model of other players: Theory and experimental evidence. *Games and Economic Behavior, 10,* 218–254.

Von Neumann, J., & Morgenstern, O. (1944). *Theory of games and economic behavior*. Princeton University Press.

Wakker, P. P. (2007). Message to referees who want to embark on yet another discussion of the random-lottery incentive system for individual choice. https://personal.eur.nl/wakker/miscella/debates/randomlinc.htm.

Billions of Dollars Worth of Experiments: Calibrating Clinical Trial Investments

Yusuke Narita

Today is the golden age of Randomized Controlled Trials (RCTs; equivalently, randomized experiments or A/B tests). RCTs are the society-wide standard of evidence; they are popular in business and politics (Siroker and Koomen 2013), as well as public policy (Gueron and Rolston 2013) and the social sciences (Banerjee and Duflo 2012). At their historical origin, RCTs started as safety and efficacy tests of drugs and medical treatments, i.e., clinical trials (Gaw 2009). Clinical trials are still a major application of RCTs and a necessary step in bringing new drugs and medical devices to the markets.

Clinical trials are high stakes and costly. First, a large number of individuals participate in clinical trials. For example, Narita (2018) finds that over 360 million patients worldwide participated in registered clinical trials between the years 2007–17. The same number just for North America is still over 210 million. This fact suggests that pharmaceutical companies spend a tremendous amount of money on clinical trials [especially because clinical trials are expensive (Morgan et al. 2011; Wong et al. 2014; Sertkaya et al. 2016; Martin et al. 2017)].

Nevertheless, there is little empirical evidence about how much the pharmaceutical industry as a whole spends on clinical trials. This lack of evidence may be due to data availability and quality issues: Many pharmaceutical companies still keep paper files, as opposed to digitalized data, which complicates the process of estimating trial costs. This lack of evidence is a serious omission, as the rising cost of clinical trials is one of the main obstacles that pharmaceutical companies face in the process of drug research and development.

I received research assistance from Soumitra Shukla, Qiwei He, and Esther Issever.

Y. Narita (✉)
Department of Economics, Cowles Foundation, and Y-RISE, Yale University, 37 Hillhouse Avenue, New Haven, CT 06511, USA
e-mail: yusuke.narita@yale.edu

T. Kawagoe and H. Takizawa (eds.), *Diversity of Experimental Methods in Economics*,
https://doi.org/10.1007/978-981-13-6065-7_8

In this essay, I attempt to fill this gap by calibrating the total clinical trial investments in North America. I focus on North America as most of the existing trial cost estimates are limited to North America. I combine Narita (2018)'s evidence about the number of registered clinical trials with several other studies about the average cost of a single clinical trial (Morgan et al. 2011; Wong et al. 2014; Sertkaya et al. 2016; Martin et al. 2017). The integration of these pieces of evidence informs us of how much the registered clinical trials cost in total.

1 Bottom Line

I report my estimates of the total North American clinical trial investments in Table 1. In particular, this table offers lower bound, upper bound, and average estimates for the total cost of clinical trials per year, from 2007 through 2016. The number of registered clinical trials in North America comes from Narita (2018)'s data. To translate this number into total trial cost estimates, I consider four different scenarios about the average cost of a single clinical trial, which is based on four pieces of research detailed below. I compute the total trial cost estimates by taking a lower bound, upper bound, and average estimate from each piece of research, and multiplying the estimate by the number of registered trials in that year.

The main takeaway from Table 1 is that the total annual cost of clinical trials in North America is estimated to be in an order of hundreds of billions of US dollars even if I use conservative lower bound estimates. In the following sections, I explain each part of this calculation as well as its caveats and limitations.

2 Number of Clinical Trials in North America

Narita (2018) assesses the number of clinical trials by assembling data on clinical trials registered in the WHO International Clinical Trials Registry Platform (ICTRP).[1] ICTRP is the largest international clinical trial registry and subsumes domestic platforms like ClinicalTrials.gov for the US.[2]

Narita (2018) processes his data as follows. He first uses the "date of registration" variable to define the year associated with each trial. Starting from the universe of all trials registered between January 1, 2007 to May 31, 2017, he excludes any outlier trial with a registered sample size greater than 5 million. For each trial, he defines its "Geographical Region" according to which country runs the registry including that trial. Many registries like ClinicalTrial.gov recruit subjects in multiple countries under the same trial ID, making it challenging to pin down the physical location of each trial.

[1] http://www.who.int/ictrp/en/, retrieved in May 2018.

[2] https://clinicaltrials.gov, retrieved in May 2018.

Table 1 Estimated total clinical trial cost (in million dollars)

Year	# of Trials registered in North America	Bound	Scenario 1	Scenario 2	Scenario 3	Scenario 4	Mean of scenarios 1–4
2007	13,383	Lower bound	$ 297,103	$ 615,618	$ 214,128	$ 588,852	$ 428,925
		Upper bound	$ 954,208	$ 8,019,094	$ 976,959	$ 1,543,060	$ 2,873,330
		Average	$ 517,922	$ 3,799,166	$ 449,669	$ 895,992	$ 1,415,687
2008	17,007	Lower bound	$ 377,555	$ 782,322	$ 272,112	$ 748,308	$ 545,074
		Upper bound	$ 1,212,599	$ 10,190,594	$ 1,241,511	$ 1,960,907	$ 3,651,403
		Average	$ 658,171	$ 4,827,947	$ 571,435	$ 1,138,619	$ 1,799,043
2009	17,149	Lower bound	$ 380,708	$ 788,854	$ 274,384	$ 754,556	$ 549,625
		Upper bound	$ 1,222,724	$ 10,275,681	$ 1,251,877	$ 1,977,280	$ 3,681,890
		Average	$ 663,666	$ 4,868,258	$ 576,206	$ 1,148,126	$ 1,814,064
2010	17,742	Lower bound	$ 393,872	$ 816,132	$ 283,872	$ 780,648	$ 568,631
		Upper bound	$ 1,265,005	$ 10,631,006	$ 1,295,166	$ 2,045,653	$ 3,809,207
		Average	$ 686,615	$ 5,036,599	$ 596,131	$ 1,187,827	$ 1,876,793
2011	18,239	Lower bound	$ 404,906	$ 838,994	$ 291,824	$ 802,516	$ 584,560
		Upper bound	$ 1,300,441	$ 10,928,809	$ 1,331,447	$ 2,102,957	$ 3,915,913
		Average	$ 705,849	$ 5,177,687	$ 612,830	$ 1,221,101	$ 1,929,367
2012	19,661	Lower bound	$ 436,474	$ 904,406	$ 314,576	$ 865,084	$ 630,135
		Upper bound	$ 1,401,829	$ 11,780,871	$ 1,435,253	$ 2,266,913	$ 4,221,217
		Average	$ 760,881	$ 5,581,365	$ 660,610	$ 1,316,304	$ 2,079,790
2013	20,515	Lower bound	$ 455,433	$ 943,690	$ 328,240	$ 902,660	$ 657,506
		Upper bound	$ 1,462,720	$ 12,292,588	$ 1,497,595	$ 2,365,380	$ 4,404,571
		Average	$ 793,931	$ 5,823,798	$ 689,304	$ 1,373,479	$ 2,170,128

(continued)

Table 1 (continued)

Year	# of Trials registered in North America	Bound	Scenario 1	Scenario 2	Scenario 3	Scenario 4	Mean of scenarios 1–4
2014	23,509	Lower bound	$ 521,900	$ 1,081,414	$ 376,144	$ 1,034,396	$ 753,463
		Upper bound	$ 1,676,192	$ 14,086,593	$ 1,716,157	$ 2,710,588	$ 5,047,382
		Average	$ 909,798	$ 6,673,735	$ 789,902	$ 1,573,928	$ 2,486,841
2015	24,221	Lower bound	$ 537,706	$ 1,114,166	$ 387,536	$ 1,065,724	$ 776,283
		Upper bound	$ 1,726,957	$ 14,513,223	$ 1,768,133	$ 2,792,681	$ 5,200,249
		Average	$ 937,353	$ 6,875,857	$ 813,826	$ 1,621,596	$ 2,562,158
2016	27,527	Lower bound	$ 611,099	$ 1,266,242	$ 440,432	$ 1,211,188	$ 882,240
		Upper bound	$ 1,962,675	$ 16,494,178	$ 2,009,471	$ 3,173,863	$ 5,910,047
		Average	$ 1,065,295	$ 7,814,365	$ 924,907	$ 1,842,933	$ 2,911,875
2007–2016	210,980	Lower bound	$ 4,683,756	$ 9,705,080	$ 3,375,680	$ 9,283,120	$ 6,761,909
		Upper bound	$ 15,042,874	$ 126,419,216	$ 15,401,540	$ 24,325,994	$ 45,297,406
		Average	$ 8,164,926	$ 59,893,002	$ 7,088,928	$ 14,125,111	$ 22,317,992
Average estimate of total trial costs for 2007–16							$ 4,379,233

Note: This table shows estimated total clinical trial costs (in million US dollars). See the remaining tables and the following references for the details of each scenario:

Scenario 1: Sertkaya et al. (2016)
Scenario 2: Morgan et al. (2011)
Scenario 3: Martin et al. (2017)
Scenario 4: Wong et al. (2014)

Based on this data, Narita (2018) finds that for 2007–2017, the total number of registered clinical trials around the world is over 290,000, making the sum of their sample sizes over 360 million (Table 2). North America runs the largest number of clinical trials, constituting over 210,000 trials, as shown in Table 1. This number provides the foundation for my calibration of the total clinical trial investments in North America.

3 Average Cost of a Clinical Trial in North America

To translate the number of trials into the total trial investments, the next step is to calculate the average cost of a single trial. Table 1 uses estimates based on four of the most well-known studies on estimating the average trial cost (Morgan et al. 2011; Wong et al. 2014; Sertkaya et al. 2016; Martin et al. 2017).

Scenario 1: Sertkaya et al. (2016)
Scenario 1 in Table 1 is based on Sertkaya et al. (2016). Sertkaya et al. (2016) estimate the average cost of a trial for each trial phase for each of the following 13 therapeutic categories: dermatology, endocrine, gastrointestinal, cardiovascular, immunomodulation, genitourinary system, hematology, central nervous system, oncology, respiratory system, anti-infective, ophthalmology, pain, and anesthesia. The data source consists of Medidata Grants Manager, Medidata CRO Contractor, and Medidata Insights data. Medidata Grants Manager is a database of over 250,000 investor grants, 27,000 protocols, and 1400 indications, providing expense information usually used for clinical trial budgeting. Medidata CRO Contractor is a database of thousands of negotiated outsourcing contracts. Medidata Insights is a database of clinical operational performance metrics. The authors analyze a total of 31,000 contracts, with around 600 contracts in each trial type (a combination of trial phase and therapeutic area), from the years 2004–2012.

Sertkaya et al. (2016) calculated the average cost per clinical trial, x_{jk}, by clinical trial phase, j, and therapeutic area, k, using the following equation (subscripts jk means the average for clinical trial phase j and therapeutic area k):

$$\begin{aligned}x_{jk} = &\text{ data collection management and analysis costs} + \text{IRB approval}_{jk}\\ &+ \text{IRB amendment}_{jk} + \text{source data verification}_{jk}\\ &+ (x_{jk}^{site} \times \text{number of sites per study}_{jk}) + \text{site overhead}_{jk}\end{aligned}$$

where

Table 2 Number of registered medical clinical trials

Number of registered clinical trials by year												
Total # of clinical trials registered	2007	2008	2009	2010	2011	2012	2013	2014	2015	2016	2017	2007–2017
	16,502	23,349	24,468	26,803	25,415	26,794	29,406	31,707	34,854	39,793	17,506	296,597
Trial phase												
0	–	–	–	2	2	–	15	8	10	6	–	43
I	1624	2359	2680	2537	2683	2598	2584	3476	2916	2975	1204	27,636
I and II	585	669	755	780	792	784	829	959	1022	1148	431	8754
II	2858	3239	3245	3217	3180	3190	3244	3182	3620	4526	1582	35,083
II and III	335	378	397	378	398	410	414	455	543	553	210	4471
III	2136	2634	2312	2686	2589	2567	2545	2304	3251	4193	1174	28,391
III and IV	11	12	22	20	29	14	44	43	41	24	14	274
IV	1755	2208	2067	2078	2146	2132	2269	2481	2647	2862	1005	23,650
Not Specified	7198	11,850	12,990	15,105	13,596	15,099	17,462	18,799	20,804	23,506	11,886	168,295
Per-trial sample size												
01–09	1049	1369	1461	1539	1652	1627	1805	1749	1467	1073	380	15,171
10–99	7197	9996	11,018	11,657	12,082	12,339	14,322	16,557	17,058	19,082	9194	140,502
100–999	6059	8882	9074	10,310	9500	10,121	11,005	11,260	13,265	15,784	6507	111,767
1000–9999	1051	1673	1422	1731	1495	1490	1632	1611	2018	2544	990	17,657
10000–99999	91	172	171	289	199	237	232	239	265	351	135	2381
100000 or More	9	17	10	39	26	33	43	60	64	90	37	428
Not Specified	1046	1240	1312	1238	461	947	367	231	717	869	263	8691

(continued)

Table 2 (continued)

Number of registered clinical trials by year												
Total # of clinical trials registered	2007	2008	2009	2010	2011	2012	2013	2014	2015	2016	2017	2007–2017
	16,502	23,349	24,468	26,803	25,415	26,794	29,406	31,707	34,854	39,793	17,506	296,597
Geographical region												
North America	13,383	17,007	17,149	17,742	18,239	19,661	20,515	23,509	24,221	27,527	12,027	210,980
Asia	452	1023	1978	2975	3633	2711	5031	6223	5759	6050	3892	39,727
Europe	2214	4880	4651	5579	2799	3840	2388	552	3191	4449	742	35,285
Oceania	453	439	690	507	697	450	1378	1329	1370	1287	742	9342
Latin America	0	0	0	0	47	132	94	94	313	480	103	1263
Registry Name												
CT.gov	13,383	17,007	17,149	17,742	18,239	19,661	20,515	23,509	24,221	27,527	12,027	210,980
EUCTR	2214	4880	4651	5579	2799	3840	2388	552	3191	4449	742	35,285
JPRN	370	639	1327	1927	2277	775	2908	3525	2798	2344	2099	20,989
CHICTR	61	279	332	439	685	1139	1138	1643	1839	2567	1036	11,158
ACTRN	453	439	690	507	697	450	1378	1329	1370	1287	742	9342
CTRI	9	86	308	597	658	785	949	1018	1091	1111	747	7359
RBR	0	0	0	0	47	132	94	94	313	480	103	1263
SLCTR	12	19	11	12	13	12	36	37	31	28	10	221

Notes This table provides summary statistics of clinical trials registered in the WHO International Clinical Trials Registry Platform (ICTRP, http://www.who.int/ictrp/en/, retrieved in May 2018). The sample consists of clinical trials registered there between January 1, 2007 to May 30, 2017. I exclude any trial with a registered sample size larger than five million

Table 3 Estimated average cost per clinical trial: scenario 1

Type	Aggregated phase 1–3 cost per trial
Dermatology	22.2
Endocrine	30.5
Gastrointestinal	32.7
Cardiovascular	34.4
Immunomodulation	34.5
Genitourinary system	35.2
Hematology	36.3
Central nervous system	37
Oncology	37.8
Respiratory system	40.5
Anti-infective	41.2
Ophthalmology	49.8
Pain and anesthesia	71.3
Average cost per trial	38.72

Notes This table shows estimated average clinical trial costs (in million US dollars) based on Sertkaya et al. (2016)'s Fig. 1 on page 121

$$
\begin{aligned}
x_{jk}^{site} &= \text{site recruitment}_{jk} + \text{site retention}_{jk} + \text{administrative staff}_{jk} \\
&\quad + \text{site monitoring}_{jk} + (x_{jk}^{patient} \times \text{number of planned patients per site}_{jk}) \\
x_{jk}^{patient} &= \text{patient recruitment cost}_{jk} + \text{patient retention cost}_{jk} + \text{physician cost}_{jk} \\
&\quad + \text{registered nurse and clinical research associate cost}_{jk} \\
&\quad + \text{clinical procedure cost}_{jk} + \text{laboratory cost}_{jk}
\end{aligned}
$$

Table 3 details Sertkaya et al. (2016)'s average cost estimate per trial for each trial type. Its dermatology estimate is the minimum of all trial types, thus providing the "lower bound" in Scenario 1 in Table 1 ($22.2 million). The "upper bound" cost value in Scenario 1 in Table 1 ($71.3 million) comes from the total cost of pain and anesthesia, which is the maximum cost value of all the trial types. Perhaps the most important cell in this table is the average or mean of per-trial costs across all trial types, which turns out to be $38.7 million.

Scenario 1 in Table 1 has a relatively low total cost estimate. This is probably be because the study draws only from hard data and uses no statistical modeling or estimation. In other words, this study likely underpredicts the average trial cost because there are other cost drivers that are not accounted for, as the raw data for those factors are unavailable. Additionally, the data draws from only a small sample of trials: those funded by the global pharmaceutical and biotechnology industry. The limited nature of their data may contribute to the low estimate, as well as the fact that this study only looks at phases 1–3. Another potential reason for underestimation is that, though the analysis was conducted in 2016, the data was collected from 2004 to 2012 and was not adjusted for inflation.

Scenario 2: Morgan et al. (2011)
Scenario 2 in Table 1 is based on Morgan et al. (2011). Their data source is English language research articles containing original drug development cost estimates, published from 1980 to 2009, inclusive. Among these research articles, the authors chose 13 articles based on criteria regarding the quality of methods, data sources, and study samples.

Table 4 displays Morgan et al. (2011)'s overview of many different analyses concerning the cost of drug development.[3] "Cash costs" represent the amount of cash spent directly on research and development. "Capitalized costs" reflect the direct cash spent on research and development, as well as the opportunity cost of engaging in drug development research. All of their numbers were adjusted to 2009's price level (which may also contribute to the relatively low-cost prediction). Their methods for cost estimation are as follows:

- Hansen and Chien, DiMasi, and DiMasi et al.: They estimate the average total cost per drug licensed for sale using data on costs, success rates, and durations of each stage of the clinical trials. Stage-specific cost data provide information about the average amount spent per stage of development, e.g., average cost per phase 2 of the clinical trials. Stage-specific success rates provide information about the average number of projects that must reach a stage. Stage-specific durations of investigation provide information about the average timing of different investments made. Combined, these data types produce an estimate of the average costs per successful clinical trial.
- Adams and Brantner: Adams and Brantner used econometric methods to model firm-level research expenditure as a function of the number of drugs a firm had under development at various stages of clinical investigation. This provides an estimate for the additional annual research expenditure required for a firm to investigate one drug at a given stage of development.

For my "lower bound" and "upper bound" predictions in Scenario 2 in Table 1, I used the minimum and maximum cost estimates among the studies Table 4 presents. Variation in the cost estimates likely comes from differences in methods, data sources, and time periods among the different research articles. I used Hansen and Chien's cash estimate of $46 million for the lower bound and Paul et al.'s cash estimate of $599.2 million for the upper bound. The average cost is determined by taking the simple mean of cash cost estimates across all the studies presented in Morgan et al. (2011)'s work, which comes out to $283.88 million.

[3]Morgan et al. (2011) measure the cost of drug development as a whole, and not simply the cost of running clinical trials. This is likely the reason that their estimates are so much larger than others. However, as clinical trials make up a significant portion of the cost of drug development, and their minimum estimate is comparable to the minimum clinical trial cost estimate of Wong et al. (2014), I have decided to include the useful information offered by Morgan et al. (2011) as another possible cost estimate.

Table 4 Estimated average cost per clinical trial: scenario 2

Research Articles	Cash	Capitalized
Hansen & Chien	46	73
DiMasi	81.5	127.5
DiMasi et al.	349	578
Adams & Brantner	343.7	602.7
Paul et al.	599.2	965.6
Average cost per trial	283.88	469.36

Notes This table shows estimated average clinical trial costs (in million US dollars) based on Morgan et al. (2011)'s Table 1 on page 8

A caveat is that none of the research articles summarized in Morgan et al. (2011) specifies the type of trial that they studied (which drugs were tested). None of the articles offer per-phase costs either. This makes it difficult to understand the sources of overly high or low costs.

Scenario 3: Martin et al. (2017)
Scenario 3 in Table 1 is based on Martin et al. (2017). Their data comes from 726 interventional studies conducted by seven major pharmaceutical companies all in the top 20 biopharma companies ranked by revenue in 2016. The authors examined the costs of trials that had a final clinical trial report (CTR) date in 2012–2015 and began in 2010 or later.

Martin et al. (2017) consulted the in-house finance departments from each of the drug development companies that they studied. Together they built the Clinical Financial Dataset (CFD), which tracks the cost of each clinical trial conducted by the companies studied. CFD tracks per-trial costs in specific areas that were determined by a top-down method that maintains consistency in the cost determination method used across companies. Their study is unique as it breaks down trial cost by four key cost areas: personnel, outsourcing, grant contracts, and other expenses. Total cost per clinical trial was calculated as the sum of costs in the following areas: direct costs (investigator grants and contract research organization (CRO) costs) and personnel costs (hours were gathered from companies' time reporting systems, which were then used to calculate personnel spending on individual trials). They use no modeling to determine the average cost per clinical trial.

Table 5 presents the resulting 25th percentile, median, and 75th percentile cost estimates. For the average trial cost of Scenario 3 in Table 1, I use the mean value provided in Martin et al. (2017). For the lower ($16 million) and upper ($33.6 million) bound estimates, I approximated the 25th and 75th percentiles of each phase and summed these costs to get a total cost.

It should be noted that Martin et al. (2017) define "cost" according to specific criteria: direct costs such as investigator grants and contract research organization (CRO) costs, personnel costs, cost of drug, etc. The specificity of Martin's criteria may contribute to a below-average cost estimate. Additionally, Martin et al. (2017)'s

Table 5 Estimated average cost per clinical trial: scenario 3

Phase	25th percentile	Median	75th percentile
Phase 1	2	3.4	5
Phase 2	5	8.6	20
Phase 3	9	21.6	48
Total	16	33.6	73

Notes This table shows estimated average clinical trial costs (in million US dollars) based on Martin et al. (2017)'s Fig. 2 on page 382

study only makes note of phase 1–3, so they may be losing cost information due to the absence of phase 4 costs. Finally, information on trial type is not available, which makes it difficult to understand the exact determinants of their lower cost estimate.

Scenario 4: Wong et al. (2014)
Scenario 4 in Table 1 is based on Wong et al. (2014). The data source is wide ranging: publicly available literature; interviews with experts, FDA personnel, drug sponsors, clinical research organizations (CRO), and academic clinical research centers; April 2012 FDA public hearing on Modernizing the Regulation of Clinical Trials and Approaches to Good Clinical Practice; and Medidata Solutions databases: Medidata Grants Manager, Medidata CRO Contractor, and Medidata Insights. Their method of cost estimation is essentially the same as the method in Scenario 1 (Sertkaya et al. (2016)).

The "lower bound" used in Scenario 4 in Table 1 comes from the cost estimate for "Genitourinary System" ($44 million), which is the minimum cost of all trial types represented in Wong et al. (2014)'s analysis. The "upper bound" estimate in Scenario 4 in Table 1 comes from the cost estimate for "Respiratory System" ($115.3 million), which is the maximum cost of all the trial types. The most important cell in Table 6 is the average cost ($66.9 million). This is the estimate used for the average column in Scenario 4 in Table 1.

There are a few caveats. Wong et al. (2014) and Sertkaya et al. (2016)'s model requires numerous data points such as phase durations, success probabilities, expected revenues, a discount rate, and a full range of itemized costs associated with clinical trials. In order to construct the model's "baseline scenario," they used itemized clinical trial cost data from Medidata Solutions. However, Medidata's data was from 2004 or later and had not been adjusted for inflation. Since the data points represented averages across a certain range of time, they could not be assigned specific years, and thus their team was unable to adjust them for inflation. Additionally, even data points adjusted for inflation, such as expected revenues obtained from a study by DiMasi, Grabowski and Vernon (2004), were only adjusted to 2008. All figures were adjusted using the producer price index for commodities in the category "Drugs and Pharmaceuticals".

Table 6 Estimated average cost per clinical trial: scenario 4

Type	Aggregated phase 1–3 costs per trial
Genitourinary system	44
Dermatology	49.3
Central nervous system	53.1
Anti-infective	54.2
Immunomodulation	56.2
Gastrointestinal	56.4
Endocrine	59.1
Cardiovascular	64.1
Hematology	65.2
Ophthalmology	69.4
Oncology	78.6
Pain and anesthesia	105.4
Respiratory system	115.3
Average cost	66.95

Notes This table shows estimated average clinical trial costs (in million US dollars) based on Wong et al. (2014)'s Fig. 3 on page 30

4 Summary

Clinical trials are a costly investment. For North America, for example, the average trial cost is believed to be tens of thousands of dollars per subject and tens of millions of dollars per trial (Morgan et al. 2011; Wong et al. 2014; Sertkaya et al. 2016; Martin et al. 2017). Multiplying the average cost by the number of subjects or trials (Narita 2018), this essay suggests that the total investments in clinical trials may amount to trillions of dollars for the last decade, just in North America (Table 1). This massive cost estimate raises a question of whether clinical trials are a cost-effective social investment to improve the health and knowledge of future generations. I leave this more challenging question for future work.

References

Banerjee, A., & Duflo, E. (2012). *Poor economics: A radical rethinking of the way to fight global poverty*, PublicAffairs.
Gaw, A. (2009). *Trial by fire: Lessons from the history of clinical trials*, SA Press.
Gueron, J.M., & Rolston, H. (2013). *Fighting for reliable evidence*. Russell sage foundation.
Martin, L., Hutchens, M., Hawkins, C., & Radnov, A. (2017). How much do clinical trials cost? *Nature Reviews Drug Discovery*, *16*, 381–382.
Morgan, S., Grootendorst, P., Lexchin, J., Cunningham, C., & Greyson, D. (2011). The cost of drug development: a systematic review. *Health Policy*, *100*(1), 4–17.
Narita, Y. (2018). Toward an ethical experiment. Working Paper.

Sertkaya, A., Wong, H.-H., Jessup, A., & Beleche, T. (2016). Key cost drivers of pharmaceutical clinical trials in the United States. *Clinical Trials, 13*(2), 117–126.

Siroker, D., & Koomen, P. (2013). *A/B testing: The most powerful way to turn clicks into customers*. Wiley.

Wong, H.-H., Jessup, A., Sertkaya, A., Birkenbach, A., Berlind, A., & Eyraud, J. (2014). Examination of clinical trial costs and barriers for drug development https://aspe.hhs.gov/report/examination-clinical-trial-costs-and-barriers-drug-development.

New Wine into Old Wineskins? *Methodenstreit*, Agency, and Structure in the Philosophy of Experimental Economics

Ivan Boldyrev

Experiments have become part and parcel of today's economics. Experimental evidence is used to update and to refute economic theories, but also helps in formulating new theories or policies. Experimental evidence and (quasi)experimental designs are becoming increasingly popular in many fields of applied economics (Angrist and Pischke 2010). The consequences of this transformation are deep enough to prompt methodological reflection at least as wide-ranging and radical, as the change itself. In this discussion, seemingly outdated distinctions may gain a new significance and inspire more general questions on the structure and perspectives of current economic science.

In this paper, I will briefly defend two claims that, I believe, put the "experimental turn" in economics into the broader historical and philosophical perspective.

First, I argue that the adoption of experimental method should be seen as part of the general tendency of recent economics to become more empirical. It helped decisively to recognize the context-dependence of economic agency and economic rationality. This tendency invites us to rethink current economics in view of the famous *Methodenstreit* and to ask anew how it can be not just a social, but a cultural and an historical science. Thus, apart from marking a turn in the intellectual history of economics, experiments demonstrate *the ways economics itself may turn (in)to history*.

Second, and related issue, concerns the relevance of experimental economics for policy. Here, I suggest that it is instructive to look at the current debates in view of a classical *agency-structure dualism* familiar from social theory. It is this dualism—implying both tension between and attempts to reconcile agency and structure—that is invoked when discussing policy prospects of experimental (and behavioral) research. In particular, what exactly should be changed as a result of a given policy (be it in view of promoting the welfare or increasing efficiency, or similar

I. Boldyrev (✉)
Department of Economics, Institute for Management Research, Radboud University, Nijmegen, The Netherlands
e-mail: i.boldyrev@fm.ru.nl

T. Kawagoe and H. Takizawa (eds.), *Diversity of Experimental Methods in Economics*,
https://doi.org/10.1007/978-981-13-6065-7_9

concerns economists address)? Answering this question by referring to the interplay between agency and structure may additionally illuminate important methodological aspects of experimental economic research.

1 Going Local

There is one basic feature most economic experiments share—they are situated events, happening in a particular environment, limited in space and time and providing only partial generalizations, or "the library of anomalies". But is this feature so unique?

It has been 20 years since Avner Greif, in defending new approaches to economic history, observed the profound change in economic *theory*—a change that, since that time, has only become deeper. Both micro- and macroeconomists, Greif argued, had abandoned the search for "a single universally applicable economic model" (Greif 1997: 401) and instead produced a plethora of contextualized specific models in order to capture the complexity of ever-changing economic world. Indeed, the way from general equilibrium to game theory (Rizvi 1994) in microeconomics and from the unified "rational expectations" approach to the current perplexity over "right" macroeconomic theories in view of the recurrent critiques of the "dominant" DSGE paradigm (Korinek 2017) all demonstrate that economics is becoming more local and ad hoc (see a nice older text by Amable et al. 1997) and, importantly, more *empirical* (on various facets of the "empirical turn" see, in particular, Hamermesh 2013; Backhouse and Cherrier 2017).

The "experimental turn" fits very nicely into this picture. An important tendency in experimental economics, observed by various authors, is the shift from the theory-testing function to direct application of experiments in different real-world situations (Guala 2007; Santos 2011). This change is often tackled as a re-assessment of inductive reasoning (see, in particular, the interpretation of experiments as "exhibits" in Sugden 2005); the relative emancipation from the primacy of theory (Backhouse and Cherrier 2017); or as a turn to "performativity" (Guala 2007; Callon and Muniesa 2007; Herrmann-Pillath 2016). Thus, experiments are often seen as tools to comprehend or transform *a qualitatively changing historical reality*, without strong claims to universal "external validity". This entails the plurality of particular causal mechanisms and regularities isolated and revealed by experiments and the uncertainty as to which particular combination of those mechanisms is at place in each specific case under consideration.

These developments remind very much of the older debate in economics, namely, the famous *Methodenstreit* between Carl Menger and Gustav Schmoller representing, respectively, Austrian and Historical School. What interests me in this debate is less the idea of a "correct" method—deductive or inductive—but rather the different ways to understand *the subject matter of economic theory*. In this respect, *Methodenstreit* demonstrated the major opposition between understanding economics as a universal science of rational behavior and as an historical science dealing with particular values and cultures. Note that at stake was the context-(in)dependence of economic action, and not the very ability of economists to make generalizations (allowed by both sides of the debate).

Now, if economics today seems to move away from universal theories, what are we to make of experiments in this context? According to Plott (1991), experiments should help reject (and, perhaps more problematically, confirm) *universal* economic theories, of which they merely provide particular examples. But what if theories themselves are not of universal validity, what if they are designed and tested more or less ad hoc, locally in space and time—that is, in culture and history? If we assume that *economics in general* now embraces more local and specific analyses, moving from one big theory or paradigm to a set of models tailored to account for particular causal mechanisms, than experiments, both in their theory-testing and in their more autonomous, theory- or market-generating functions should appear as more local, too.

To be sure, economics now cannot fully subscribe to the approach of the German Historical school. Neither can it fully renounce its universalist aspirations. But the tension involved in *Methodenstreit* and the historical approach in general open up a new methodological perspective on economic experiments and suggest seeing them not only as tools to establish generally ("externally") valid results and comprehend the nature of human rationality, but also as a series of culturally and historically situated attempts to provide contextualized and partial generalizations. Those generalizations would then *describe* as much as *explain* and could be seen as parts of more comprehensive narratives and explanations involving further empirical methods, abstract modeling and, perhaps, following again the legacy of the *Methodenstreit*, insights from history and from other human sciences, such as anthropology. This latter interdisciplinary collaboration seems a particularly uneasy task, although not unknown to economic experimentalists (see, for example, the famous study in Henrich et al. 2004).

All this moves experiments closer to *case studies*. Again, this hardly amounts to identifying the two, but demonstrates local and—in this sense—historically situated nature of experimental results. Seen in this light, many important issues in the methodology of experimental economics, such as the problem of reproducibility of experimental results, the sensitivity of those results to particular contexts, or the "performativity" of experiments—can be discussed with this "pole" of history in mind. In the limit case, no result would be fully reproducible and every experiment, like every country or age discussed by the *Historical school*, would be unique as an "exhibit" of particular culture in a particular time period.

2 What Policy? Agency, Structure, and History in Appraising Experimental Economics

Once we pose the problem of universality and address the issue of historical and cultural relativism in the context of economic experiments, the question immediately arises as to what kind of universal validity one might expect from experimental research and, in particular, what its foundation could be.

One way of thinking about this problem consists in confronting "the social" with "the natural", the historical and cultural relativism with the immutable or else very slowly changing laws of human nature that would allow broader generalizations and arguably reduce the heterogeneity of human cultures to some harder—and thus universalizable—facts about the workings of the human mind. With all simplicity of this opposition, it is, as many others, alive and matters for many different contexts. One of them concerns the policy implications of experimental research.

In his instructive paper addressing different ways to link experimental results to policies, Lee (2011) distinguishes three programs in this respect: the "heuristics and biases" program of Daniel Kahneman, Amos Tversky and Richard Thaler; the "fast-and-frugal-heuristics" program associated mostly with Gerd Gigerenzer; and the experimental-market-economics program advanced initially by Vernon Smith. Lee's question is: what kind of normative claims do these programs imply and what might their respective policy proposals be? However, underlying this question is another one: what exactly—"agency" or "structure" (or, perhaps, both)—should be changed in order to make human behavior more "optimal" or "rational"? Should we hope for improving individual decision-making or should we more emphasize its institutional context?

The "heuristics and biases" program assumes inherent human irrationality while suggesting the importance of changing structural (institutional) constraints of irrational action. In this perspective, agency does not really matter, for it cannot be really changed quickly and in a predictable way, but the structure does. The "fast-and-frugal-heuristics" program stresses the mutual dependence and co-evolution of agency and structure that both turn out to be malleable and subject to improvement. Finally, the experimental markets program clearly focuses on the "ecological rationality" of intersubjective, institutional structures and not primarily on cognitive capacities of individual agents. These distinctions echo previous classification of "technological" (institutions-focused) and "behavioral" (agency-focused) experiments (Santos 2007).

The interplay of agency and structure can become a tension that is involved in defining the boundaries of economic approach. When Gul and Pesendorfer (2008) make their case "for mindless economics"—that is, roughly, for economics different from and independent of natural science—they repeatedly claim that the aim of standard economic analysis is "to analyze institutions (sic!), such as trading mechanisms and organization structures, and to ask how those institutions mediate the interests of different economic agents. This analysis is useful irrespective of the causes of individuals' preferences" (Gul and Pesendorfer 2008, p. 8). The new *Methodenstreit* initiated by Gul and Pesendorfer is somewhat similar to the older one, because it involves a social science—economics—again, as in the nineteenth century, in need to justify its own, particular type of rationality, and its own ontology providing the right to generalize irrespective of neuroscientific facts.

Note how both experimental economists focusing on markets and psychology-oriented behavioral scientists situating their normative concerns between changing agency and structure clearly tend towards *irreducibility of "structure"*—that is, cultural norms in which human action is embedded and which preclude us from deriving any universal laws of economic action. Even the psychology-inspired fast-and-frugal-heuristics program actually mostly addresses claims of the type "if heuristic x says to do y, and if x is more effective/fast/frugal than other heuristics in environment E, and one is in environment E, then do y" (Hands 2014). In other words, even here *rationality becomes local and context-specific*. The behavioral experiments run by the adherents of nudging are equally geared toward institutional control—and institutional transformation, allowing for more rational outcomes. Thus, even those who think they are dealing with "human nature", have society and culture at the back of their heads. The same is, of course, true for market-based experimental approaches that start from the rules to be implemented.

This is precisely the way how *in this context* the distinction between agency and structure corresponds to the previous one, between universalism and historical/cultural specificity. I say "in this context" because many agency-focused accounts would surely stress the cultural and historical embeddedness of human action and consider it to be fully compatible with methodological individualism. I will not go into details here, but the only aspect I wish to highlight is precisely the link between the analysis of institutions and the spatial and temporal heterogeneity of societies. This link brings us back to economics as an historical science.

3 Conclusion: On Re-contextualization

Is it worthwhile to rethink experimental economics in view of some old-fashioned methodological debates? I think the answer is yes, and the reason is that these seemingly outdated debates are still on the agenda, and it is an important methodological task to recognize them in their new clothing. Economics today is still a social science that should be open to history and description, to qualitative and interpretive approaches that allow to grasp the complexity of real economies embedded in cultures and polities.

What could be the implications of this perspective on economic experiments? Answering this question necessarily involves some speculation, as in any other attempt to delineate the tendencies in the development of complex intellectual and academic practices. That is why these implications are to be taken *cum grano salis*.

Perhaps the most immediate and significant one follows directly from the inductivist tendency in economics I sketched above. Abandoning the pretense of universalism amounts to the re-evaluation of more partial and small-scale studies. Experimental design would then be more tailored to fit particular aims of more local explanations and policy concerns. There would be less emphasis on reproducibility/robustness of results across various cultures and contexts and more on tracing in detail particular causal mechanisms at work in the contexts under scrutiny.

This widening of methodological perspective obviously allows for more interdisciplinarity. Once no economic model appears to be universally valid, more qualitative approaches become equally legitimate. Ethnomethodological and interpretive work in sociology, various anthropological and ethnographic approaches, discourse analysis and, of course, history—all might contribute to the problems at hand. Note, that here, history can be tackled not as the reproduction of the same, but rather as a set of disciplines conveying the view of contingency and complexity of happenings, of the multiplicity of factors (that is, of course, uneasily reconciled with economists' quest for parsimony of assumptions and unambiguity of conclusions). In this sense, the search for more valid explanations could consist less in comparing how the same formal structure works in qualitatively different contexts, but rather in looking at whether the particular local regularity is revealed by other empirical methods. Qualitative approaches gain additional significance once we admit that the same formal rules and norms can be perceived and interpreted by economic agents differently in different cultures.

Needless to say, this perspective does not amount to pure relativism. The heterogeneity and multiplicity of various approaches should not prevent us from making generalizations and revealing regularities. The older problem of the Historical school—the lack of "theory"—should be reinterpreted in the light of new developments. For current experimental economics does not arguably possess a unified "theory", either—rather, it is a set of experimental designs and results that together convey a certain understanding of human behavior across various contexts. In fact, context-dependence of economic action and rationality has been one of the major implications of behavioral experiments over the last decades! In this sense, experimental economics itself legitimizes its own "re-contextualization".

References

Amable, B., Boyer, R., & Lordon, F. (1997). The *ad hoc* in economics: the pot calling the Kettle Black. In A. D'Autume & J. Cartelier (Eds.), *Is economics becoming a hard science?* (pp. 252–275). Cheltenham: Edward Elgar.

Angrist, J. D., & Pischke, J.-S. (2010). The credibility revolution in empirical economics: How better research design is taking the con out of econometrics. *Journal of Economic Perspectives, 24*(2), 3–30.

Backhouse, R., & Cherrier, B. (2017). The age of the applied economist: The transformation of economics since the 1970s. *History of Political Economy, 49*(annual suppl.). 1–33.

Callon, M., & Muniesa, F. (2007). Economic experiments and the construction of markets. In D. MacKenzie, F. Muniesa, & L. Siu (Eds.), *Do economists make markets? On the performativity of economics*. Princeton: Princeton University Press.

Greif, A. (1997). Cliometrics after 40 years. *American Economic Review, 87*(2), 400–403.

Guala, F. (2007). How to do things with experimental economics. In D. MacKenzie, F. Muniesa, & L. Siu (Eds.), *Do economists make markets? On the performativity of economics*. Princeton: Princeton University Press.

Gul, F., & Pesendorfer, W. (2008). The case for mindless economics. In A. Caplin & A. Shotter (Eds.), *The foundations of positive and normative economics*. Oxford: Oxford University Press.

Hands, W. D. (2014). Normative ecological rationality: Normative rationality in the fast-and-frugal-heuristics research program. *Journal of Economics Methodology, 21*(4), 396–410.

Hamermesh, D. (2013). Six decades of top economics publishing: Who and how? *Journal of Economic Literature, 51*(1), 162–172.

Henrich, J., Boyd, R., Bowles, S., Camerer, C., Fehr, E., & Gintis, H. (Eds.). (2004). *Foundations of human sociality: Economic experiments and ethnographic evidence from fifteen small-scale societies*. Oxford: Oxford University Press.

Herrmann-Pillath, C. (2016). Performative mechanisms. In I. Boldyrev & E. Svetlova (Eds.), *Enacting dismal science: new perspectives on the performativity of economics*. Palgrave McMillan: New York, NY.

Korinek, A. (2017). Thoughts on DSGE Macroeconomics: Matching the moment, but missing the point? Available at SSRN https://ssrn.com/abstract=3022009.

Lee, K. S. (2011). Three ways of linking laboratory endeavours to the realm of policies. *European Journal of the History of Economic Thought, 18*(5), 755–776.

Plott, C. R. (1991). Will economics become an experimental science? *Southern Economic Journal, 57,* 901–919.

Rizvi, S. A. T. (1994). Game theory to the rescue? *Contributions to Political Economy, 13*(1), 1–28.

Santos, A. C. (2007). The 'materials' of experimental economics: Technological versus behavioral experiments. *Journal of Economic Methodology, 14,* 311–337.

Santos, A. C. (2011). Experimental economics. In J. B. Davis & W. D. Hands (Eds.), *The Elgar companion to recent economic methodology*. Cheltenham: Edward Elgar.

Sugden, R. (2005). Experiments as exhibits and experiments as tests. *Journal of Economic Methodology, 12,* 291–302.

Creating Social Ontology: On the Performative Nature of Economic Experiments

Carsten Herrmann-Pillath

1 Introduction

Experimental economics has become the new methodological gold standard in economics, as far as the empirical validation of economic hypotheses is concerned. There are different variants of the experimental approach, reaching from computer simulation to field studies. In this paper, I concentrate on one variant exclusively, which is laboratory studies of human choice. This stays at the core of economic theory, which many see as the study of choice under constraints, following Robbins' classical definition. There is a strong alliance between the experimental approach and behavioural economics, which goes back to the use of experiments in testing economic hypotheses about rationality and optimization. On a first, though superficial sight, therefore experiments are often associated with the search for alternative economic models of choice, facing the many deviations between experimental results and the predictions of standard economic theory.

The experimental method is an essential element of what I call the 'naturalistic turn' in economics. Naturalization means first, that methodological standards and methods of the natural sciences are increasingly employed in economics, as epitomized in the institution of the 'lab', and secondly, that these methods refer to hypotheses that advance empirical claims about 'reality' in general and about human nature in particular.[1] The latter relates to human individuals as bodily beings, such as in the context of the more specific subfield of neuroeconomics, in which the experimental approach is aligned with theories and methods from the neurosciences. In this paper, I reflect on the naturalism of experimental economics, building on insights from philosophy and science and technology studies, among other inspirations. My

[1] This definition follows the conception of naturalism in the philosophy of mind, see Papineau (2009).

C. Herrmann-Pillath (✉)
Max Weber Centre for Advanced Social and Cultural Studies, Erfurt University, Erfurt, Germany
e-mail: carsten.herrmann-pillath@uni-erfurt.de

T. Kawagoe and H. Takizawa (eds.), *Diversity of Experimental Methods in Economics*,
https://doi.org/10.1007/978-981-13-6065-7_10

aim is to establish an epistemological framework for experimental economics that allows for deducing more specific principles of evaluating experimental results in terms of their reference to the real world.

This effort builds on existing research that has highlighted the performative dimensions of experiments: Every experiment is a performance that is staged by the interactions between the researchers and the subjects of the experiments.[2] So, a fundamental methodological issue in experimental economics, taken very serious by the research community, is how far the experiments actually reflect reality, in the sense of the external validity of the experimental results. Regarding this question, serious experimenters employ whole batteries of methods that allow for establishing their empirical claims. I do not consider the details here but raise the more fundamental question what naturalism of experiments means in the context of their performativity.

With the naturalistic turn, economists have adopted the stance of modern natural science in assuming a clear-cut separation between the subject and the object of research: Here, the term 'modern' refers to the sciences as they emerged and unfolded in the nineteenth and twentieth century. The subject is the scientist; the object is 'nature'. Conceiving human individuals as natural beings means that the assumption is taken for granted that human behaviour is governed by certain regularities which are universal, in the sense of the covering law conception of scientific theories.[3] The purpose of research is to discover these regularities, present theoretical formulations, and proceed with the empirical testing of these general hypotheses. So, the standard rationality assumption of economics is no longer regarded to be an axiom that does not submit claims about real human individuals, but as a general hypothesis which can be disproven by experiments. Violations of the rationality assumption result into the construction of new models of human decisions, such as prospect theory and the loss-aversion hypothesis, which can be subjected to new experimental tests. The new theories are in turn evaluated in terms of the covering law notion of scientific theories.

The problem with this approach is that the separation between subject and object and the implicit assumption of natural invariances of behaviour appears to be internally contradictory if human individuals are the object of research. The subject/object divide is the more general setting in which the nature/culture divide is also located. The covering law approach to human behaviour implicitly suggests that there are natural invariants of behaviour which transcend cultural variability. However, if we

[2]This view has been thoroughly developed by Guala (2007). In experimental economics as such, the notion of performativity has not yet arrived, even though in the methodological debates, following similar debates in psychology, the problem of the interaction between experimenters and experimental subjects looms large (Levitt and List 2007). This is mostly seen as a potential source of failure, therefore experimental economists typically try to minimize this interaction. I will argue that performativity is a general property of any experiment, and not a dysfunctional phenomenon.

[3]Although experimental economists rarely refer their methodological debates to concepts of the philosophy of science, reference to the covering law approach to theories is implicit in the majority of their statements, right from the early times, such as in Smith's (1976) influential paper. For a more recent statement by a leader of the field, see Camerer (2015: 252), who refers to 'general laws', also citing Smith.

assume, as many would do, that culture is, in fact, the most essential differentia specifica of the human species in the natural world, which in fact also enables the creation of human science, we could no longer maintain the separation between subject and object as posited by the naturalistic methodology. In simplest terms, 'nature' is, in fact, an expression of 'culture', insofar as nature is only accessible via science as a cultural activity. This applies to experiments involving human actors, since we would expect that their behaviour is deeply shaped by cultural factors. This is exactly what performativity means: If experiments are factually testing cultural phenomena, there are principled limits to establishing external validity in terms of the complete generalization over human 'nature'.[4]

I will radicalize this reasoning further in questioning the naive naturalism of experimental economics also in the context of the natural sciences. This results into what might be called 'enlightened' or 'reflexive naturalism'. The problem of the entanglement of subject and object of research can be also seen as reflecting the fact that nature is always being constructed by the observers, especially in the context of laboratory experiments. This does not mean that the construction becomes arbitrary and empirical validation hollow. These issues have been most systematically explored in the philosophical work on fundamental physics, especially quantum theory. In this paper, I submit a specific epistemological perspective that builds on this work, thus relating the performativity notion with most advanced philosophical evaluations of one of the core fields in 'post-modern' natural science: Here, 'post-modern' is used in an unusual way, as I consider physics after the discovery of quantum mechanics as transcending modern physics in the sense of classical physics. By this conjunction of two different strands of philosophical work, I achieve a 'reflexive turn' in naturalism. In other words, and in the context of Bruno Latour's treatment of the term 'modernity', I refer to classical physics as 'modern' in terms of the clear demarcation between subject and object, or nature and culture, and quantum physics as genuinely modern or 'post-modern', in terms of discovering the entanglement of subject and object as a phenomenon of the real world, and not merely a problem of subjectivism and hence of epistemology. This idea builds on Karen Barad's 'agential realism' which I recommend as the proper framework in evaluating the empirical significance of laboratory phenomena displaying performativity.

The paper continues with the discussion of the performative properties of economic experiments, which on first sight would define a fundamental difference to experiments in the natural sciences. My workhorse is reflecting on the exclusive use of monetary incentives in designing experiments. However, in relying on Barad's reception of Niels Bohr's view on quantum mechanics, I argue in the third section that in fact performativity is a property of experiments in both domains, once we adopt

[4]My discussion is deeply influenced by Latour's (2012) work on the modes how humans approach the world they live in and create worlds which are ontologically diverse. As in his earlier works, where Latour questioned the genuine 'modernity' of modern thinking, the idea is central that modern naturalism is naive in not reflecting upon the fact that what we perceive as 'nature' is actually created by ourselves, as we cannot go behind our own science in understanding what nature 'is'. Hence, a genuinely modern view must be reflexive. However, this view does not lead towards subjectivist constructivism, as I develop below, and which transpires from Latour's influential laboratory studies.

a new ontological perspective on what ‘reality’ means. I show that this perspective is very fruitful for resolving even empirical issues in experimental economics. Section 4 presents further extensions of the argument, and Sect. 5 concludes.

2 Experiments as Performances

One of the most important features of experiments involving human actors is that the experimenter needs to safeguard unequivocally that the subjects undergoing the procedure play the same game as designed by the experimenter, and that there is no variance across the population in these perceptions. So, experimental work always needs to de-contextualize the contingent cognitive models by which the subjects perceive and interpret the experiment. This problem is clearly recognized by the experimental community, yet mostly conceived as regular phenomenon that replicates similar issues in experimental work in the natural sciences. De-contextualization would correspond to experimental isolation of phenomena and causal factors and control of environmental impacts on the experiment. As in the natural sciences, the idea is that isolation result in the identification of specific causal mechanisms that also work in the world outside the lab, though being often hidden by a manifold of mediating and disturbing impacts of the environment, which, in the case of human test persons, also includes their supposed internal states, especially cognitive models.

Evidently, this approach implies that there are stable features of human nature which are universal with regard to species characteristics, and which can be isolated in the experimental setting: the regularities uncovered by the experimental methodology are seen as being ‘real’ in the sense of existing also outside the lab. I think that this naive transfer of epistemological beliefs common in the natural sciences is highly problematic. Let me illustrate this by discussing a specific aspect of economic experimental methods, the use of money as an incentive. My argument proceeds in two steps: In this section, I take the conventional, that is ‘modern’ view of the sciences for granted and show that the phenomenon of performativity undermines its transfer to experimental economics. In the next section, I substantially extend this reasoning in arguing that ‘post-modern’, hence genuinely modern science as represented by quantum mechanics reveals that the phenomenon of performativity is, in fact, a defining feature of reflexive naturalism.

Economic experiments differ in many important respects from experiments employed by other human sciences, in particular, psychology. These differences have boiled down to a set of methodological standards which are mandatory for every researcher in economics; their violation would immediately result into a rejection of the research by pertinent journals. One of these rules is the requirement that in the study of choice, monetary incentives must be used which need to be sufficiently strong to supersede other disturbing impacts of costs such as investing effort into keeping attention. Originally, this recommendation goes back to Vernon Smith’s ‘induced value’ method which had more limited scope, since it mainly applied for market experiments, so that money would be involved in both experiments and real-world markets; in addition, money was not suggested as the exclusive incentive that might be used, as long as certain general properties would be shared with money. However, today using money as a mandatory incentive in designing economic experiments is justified by the ideas that first, monetary incentives are interpreted as reflecting underlying utilities; second, that they are strong enough to override disturbing factors in determining choices, such as pure negligence; and thirdly, the use of money also seems to safeguard the generalization of experimental results, as this incentive is commensurable across different subjects. So, it is an important element in supporting the claims of economists criticizing psychological research as often resulting in highly diverse experimental results which cannot be integrated into a more general theoretical framework.[5]

In experimental practice, money is indeed highly salient, beyond the experimental setting in the narrow sense.[6] Most experimental work is done at universities engaging students as subjects. For the students, income generated by the experiments can be an attractive option for earning additional income. The monetary incentives are systematically arranged, such as distinguishing between different instalments (show-up fees, pay-offs and so forth), and they are also used as sanctions: Subjects who do not follow the rules formulated by the experimenter can easily lose their claims. So, the money incentive is an important means to suppress deviant behaviour in the lab, imposing the experimenter's exclusive interpretation of the rules on the subjects. The use of money as an incentive also needs to be seen in the context of other measures that aim at safeguarding the generalizability of results, such as the anonymization of subjects, as far as their self-perception is concerned. That means, the lab is a Benthamite panopticon: The experimenter can observe all actions taken by the subjects, but the subjects themselves do not communicate or even see other participants and focus exclusively in what they see on the computer screen. Before the experiment is implemented, they are meticulously instructed about the rules and their tasks, becoming highly aware of the consequences of deviant actions. Before the experiment is started, subjects are being tested whether they correctly understand the instructions, so that a convergent understanding of the experimental setting is guaranteed.

Considering these universal characteristics of the economic lab procedures, their highly artificial nature is salient, especially in the sense of imposing the characteristic attitudinal stances and cognitive patterns of the rational actor on the participants, such as full and transparent information, highly structured rule-guided behaviour, and focus on quantified pay-offs as incentives. The material infrastructure of the lab further enhances this artificiality, thus signalling de-contextualization. This is an important difference to paper-and-pencil experiments in the field, which otherwise observe the same methodology. So, we might conjecture that in the field the

[5]For a concise statement on the alleged superiority of the economic approach, see Erev and Greiner (2015).

[6]My description of experimental procedures follows Böhme's (2016) meticulous ethnographic records on how experiments are done, thus does not simply refer to the methodological standards, but to the practices. As in Muniesa and and Callon's (2007) seminal study of auctions, this ethnographic perspective is necessary in order to identify the performative workings of experiments.

probability of implicit contextualization is larger so that subjects might interpret a certain task differently from the meaning intended by the experimenter. For example, a public-good game might be interpreted as a wager, thus weakening the salience of cooperation opportunities; this interpretation might be nurtured by receiving environmental cues from familiar contexts.[7]

So, the use of monetary incentives in economic experiments is seen by economists as safeguarding generalization and enabling the isolation of causal relationships determining behaviour. However, one could also argue that the use of money fundamentally constrains the universalization of laboratory results. This is because the entire standard experimental set-up is a very strong priming procedure, according to the standard understanding of psychology. Priming starts with advertising the experiments as an opportunity for earning pecuniary income. In methodological debates, this is mostly seen positively, as the subjects do not primarily focus on the experiment as such, so that apparently the lab situation becomes like other everyday life conditions, that is, an ordinary part-time job. However, this argument can be also inversed: The use of pecuniary incentives may turn the experiment into a performance that transfers monetary contextualization in everyday life circumstances to the experimental setting. This possibility emerges from many studies of money priming in psychology, which also use the experimental method, yet following the methodological standards of psychology.

Considering this rich literature, the entire economic research using experiments may not generate any results that could generalize over any specific behavioural regularity that becomes observable, precisely because the subjects are being primed with money. Hence, from the perspective of psychology and social sciences, economic experiments would only identify behavioural regularities which are contextualized by the use of money also in the real world. Whereas economists assume that money is neutral with reference to behaviour, because it just reflects underlying utilities, psychological and sociological research has clearly shown that money primes trigger very substantial changes in behaviour.

Interestingly, this psychological research vindicates many hypotheses originally elaborated in Georg Simmel's magnum opus on the 'Philosophy of Money'.[8] In this book, broadly spoken, Simmel suggested that, historically and psychologically, the institution of money causes fundamental transformations in two dimensions, namely the cognitive and the emotional, which correspond to social processes of rationalization and individualization. Rationalization is supported by money making alternatives of choices commensurable in quantitative terms and in allowing for

[7]This example is taken from Karlan (2005). The contextualization typically happens when subjects perceive the structure of the game as being similar to constellations of social interaction that they are familiar with in their everyday life. This applies for even the simplest games, such as the ultimatum game. The classical study of this phenomenon is Henrich et al. (2005). Tellingly, in his detailed defence of experimental economic methodology as the king's way to generate information about general regularities in behaviour, Camerer (2015: 263) treats this problem of endogenous contextualization only very superficially, simply claiming that it is always possible to find appropriate controls in the econometric testing.

[8]Simmel (1907). On this and the following, see Herrmann-Pillath (2016a).

arbitrary divisions and manipulations of values. Individualization results from the fungibility of money and other goods and assets, hence the emerging dis-embedding of choices from social contexts. Many of these Simmelian insights have been vindicated by recent psychological research.[9] Most importantly, whereas Simmel mainly analysed the historical and cultural psychology of money working in the longer run of societal transformations, psychologists study what economists call 'frame shifts' which operate on a short-term- and even instantaneous basis. For example, priming people with money leads to less cooperative stances, supports self-reliance, and triggers increasing social distance between individuals. These results fit into the larger context of research on incentives and on the relative importance of social versus individual preferences. There is ample evidence that extrinsic motivation, especially in terms of pecuniary incentives, crowds out intrinsic motivation. Similarly, pecuniary incentivization may trigger frame shifts, such as viewing a social interaction in terms of exchange, and less in terms of mutual moral commitments. However, and concurring with sociological research, even the form of priming with money depends on the specific way of framing of the use of money, such that the same monetary artefact is interpreted in a different way, depending on contextualization via cognitive states. This fact is also well-known to experimental economists (for example, in ultimatum games test persons responds differently to the same monetary pay-offs if the money used in the game was previously distributed in alternating ways, such as lotteries, remuneration of solving simple tasks, or arbitrary allocation by the experimenter). So, one cannot even speak of one single type of incentive when considering the role of monetary incentives but must take into consideration that money can be categorized in various ways by the experimental subjects, implying that there are no unequivocal and generic effects of the money incentive.[10]

This substantial research, therefore, suggests with high plausibility that the prescribed methodology of experimental economics effectively results in a specific framing of individual behaviour which would correspond to basic behavioural assumptions of economics. This is salient from the fact that often deviations from economic predictions become less pronounced once subjects learn how to play the games of the experiments. This learning, in fact, indicates increasing de-contextualization (or, re-contextualization in terms of the money prime). Economists conventionally interpret this as successful isolation of regularities of behaviour.

I advance another interpretation: What subjects factually learn is how to perform the experiment properly, supported by completing the frame shifts that are triggered by the monetary incentives. Given the empirical evidence that we have about the effects of money on behaviour, the methodological prescriptions of experimental economics do not result in universal regularities of behaviour but only in regularities that are specific to the money frame, taking the possibility into consideration that

[9]For exemplary studies, see the work by Katherine Vohs and colleagues, Vohs et al. (2006, 2008). For many more references, see my previously cited paper.

[10]As an example of money activating different frames, see Kouchaki et al. (2013). The classical sociological study of various categorizations of money is Zelizer (1997). Zelizer explicitly criticizes Simmel for assuming general social and psychological effects of money. So, her argument would apply for economics with a vengeance.

monetary incentives can also be categorized into different mental accounts by the subjects. This is a case of strict performativity of economic theory: First, using money as an incentive is justified by economic theory exclusively, since all other human sciences would endorse the case for diversity of human motivation and incentives; second, the money frame triggers behavioural dispositions and tendencies which at least support the convergence of observed behaviour with predictions generated by economic hypotheses. So, we can even speak of strong performativity, however, without referring to economic theory in the narrow sense, as in the original literature about performativity of economics. In this original approach, economic theories diffuse into the real world and result in behavioural changes that converge with the theory. In case of experimental economics, what transpires is certain fundamental cognitive and emotional dispositions that relate with the institution of money but may at the same time become isolated and systematized by economics. However, this may also include all practices and knowledge that relate with the use of money in society.[11]

Reflecting on this analysis, however, we can also reach an additional conclusion: We can be fully justified in generalizing the results of experimental economics as long as in the real world the same kind of framing applies. This was the original approach by Vernon Smith in doing experiments on artificial markets: Here, the market frame would apply both in the experiment and in the field. So, generalizability would not refer to the direct transfer of behavioural regularities of individuals from experimental subjects to individuals in any other circumstance in the field, but only to those regularities as being contextualized in the experiment, so that what generalizes is regularities cum context. This observation paves the way to reconsidering the naturalistic stance in experiments in a much more radical fashion.

3 Performativity and the Principle of Complementarity

I will now push my philosophical analysis one step further in radically questioning the implicit ontological and epistemological assumptions of experimental economics; in doing this, I refer to the transition from classical physics to quantum physics. I rely on the work of Karen Barad who presents a philosophical extension of what she calls Niels Bohr's 'philosophy-physics'. I think that this work is highly relevant for better understanding the performativity of economic experiments. The crucial point emerges that the performative nature of economic experiments is not just a specific condition applying for human subjects, thus possibly reinstating the divide between the human world and nature, but that any kind of experimental work is performative, in both in the natural sciences or the human sciences. This idea leads to what I have called 'reflexive naturalism'.

[11]On the different types of performativity, see the seminal work by MacKenzie (2007). My broader conception concurs with the notion of 'economization' advanced by Çalışkan and Callon (2009).

Barad's approach stays in the tradition of laboratory studies that often have highlighted the constructivist dimensions of laboratory work and have focused on the intermingling of 'scientific' and 'social' factors, eventually discarding this artificial separation as a methodological, or even ideological construct.[12] Yet, as has been salient in Latour's contributions, this does not necessarily mean eschewing a realist ontological position. Relying on Bohr's work, especially his methodological reflections, offers the solution to this apparently paradoxical position.

The gist of the argument easily comes to the fore when considering the debates about the so-called Copenhagen interpretation of quantum mechanics, especially the controversy between Bohr and Heisenberg.[13] Whereas Heisenberg adopted the uncertainty principle, Bohr proposed the complementarity principle (another term is principle of indeterminacy). According to the former, phenomena such as the wave-particle dualism emerging in laboratory experiments are interpreted in an epistemological way, pointing to the fundamental limitations of human knowledge in ascertaining states of elementary particles in the classical dimensions of position, velocity and so forth. This is the subjectivist interpretation of the use of quantum probabilities, which are conceived as reflecting fundamental epistemological limits to observation. In contrast, Bohr adopted an ontological interpretation of the quantum formalism in arguing that the different possible states of an elementary particle are complementary. Bohr's view requires to adopt a fundamentally different ontology in eschewing the standard separation between subject and object, which is still maintained by Heisenberg. In place of this, Bohr suggested that the fundamental ontological units are 'phenomena' that realize in an experimental setting. The notion of phenomenon means that subject and object are ontologically entangled, which is, however, not merely an abstract ontological proposition, but boils down to the specific material setting, the arrangements and the practices of the experiment.

According to Bohr, reality is constituted by the experiment, and there is nothing such as an immutable and fully autonomous object that could be separated from the phenomena emerging in the laboratory. For Heisenberg, the object is out there, but we are fundamentally uncertain about its states; for Bohr, there is no such thing as an 'object' in the real world: reality is constituted by complementary phenomena which materialize in certain well-defined experimental settings. However, this does not result into a radical-constructivist questioning of the status of reality. The point is that under strict control of the laboratory setting, a series of experiments leads to results that relate with complementary phenomena which exhaust all relevant information about the underlying domain of reality, cast into the terms of classical physics, as far as the description of the experimental results is concerned. For Bohr, quantum physics did not supersede classical physics, but both retain a systematic connection, as the experimental work, the observations recorded, the manipulations

[12]The starting point of Barad's (2007) argument is Bohr's analysis of the role of experiments in physics. On the central role of laboratory studies in understanding science, see Doing (2008).

[13]For more detail on this, see Faye (2014). Barad also puts much emphasis on the Heisenberg/Bohr controversy, which was deeply driven by philosophical concerns. I closely follow Barad's exposition and extensions.

of the experimenter, and so on, all are cast in the concepts of classical physics. So, despite the contra-intuitive theoretical propositions of quantum mechanics, there is a fundamental ontological continuity even with pre-scientific experience, as far as this is conceived in classical terms. So, when considering phenomena as the substance of reality, quantum mechanics as a theory supersedes classical physics as a theory, but the ontological continuity between classical concepts and quantum physics is maintained. This also implies that there is no ontological fissure between micro and macro.

So, the essential insight of Bohr's reflections on quantum mechanics is that in the quantum world, the traditional naturalistic notion of the object having exactly defined properties that are independent from the experimental setting must be discarded. This is what Barad denotes as 'intra-action' between subject and object, thus unveiling the performative nature of quantum physics. This notion generalizes over Bohr's philosophy-physics in the sense that the ontology of phenomena is no longer a special aspect of physics, but, and quite naturally so, is an aspect of universal ontology. Phenomena emerge via intra-action, which means that objects are not ontologically separate from subjects, but that in a phenomenon, subject and object are entangled (the common term 'inter-action' would suggest that both exist independently and then enter interaction). This entanglement happens via the material settings and practices that enable and realize intra-action. Barad calls the resulting philosophical position 'agential realism', thus establishing conceptual bridges with positions developed, for example, by Actor-network theory.[14] In a phenomenon, we cannot simply assign epistemological agency only to the subject, thus elevating the human agent to a special position. Epistemological agency is embodied in the intra-action between subject and object.

I suggest that agential realism is most powerful in interpreting the practices and results of experimental economics, enabling the transition from naive to reflexive naturalism. In the conventional views on economic experiments, researchers clearly assume that experimental subjects as the objects of the inquiry have certain properties that are immutable and independent from the experimental setting. This assumption seems necessary in maintaining the methodological value of the experiments that claim to generate results which have validity beyond the walls of the lab. This corresponds to the epistemological position of classical physics, and hence naive naturalism which separates between the researcher as the subject and the material world as the object of inquiry.

So, I argue that, conventionally, experimental economics is naturalistic in the classical or 'modern' sense, maintaining the epistemological stance of approaching the object of research as being an entity that has stable properties independent from the experimental setting, and which are simply identified by the experimental procedures. So, the question is, what would it mean to reconsider the methodology of experimental economics in terms of a 'post-modern', or, genuinely modern and

---

[14] In Latour's realist interpretation of laboratory practices, he also overcomes the conventional subject/object divide in assigning agency to objects, too (see Latour 2005: 63ff). Barad does not discuss possible connections to ANT in more detail.

reflexive naturalism which focuses on phenomena as entanglements of subjects and objects in experiments?

In experimental economics, the classical position is implicit in the notion of preferences. Experimental subjects are conceived as 'having' preferences which are stable and do not change when they are subject to the experimental procedures. For example, when researchers conduct experiments employing public goods games, they would like to know how far human individuals have social preferences, in comparison to individual preferences. This is one of the most prolific fields in experimental economics, as this is a crucial question in considering the empirical validity of the fundamental economic model of rationality and choice.[15] However, it is important to notice that this effort partly misconceives the status of preferences in modern economic theory, as formalized in Samuelson's 'revealed preference' concept. Here, a preference is not what individuals have as properties of objects, but preferences are a mathematical way to describe their observed behaviour. Interestingly, we could already interpret this view in terms of agential realism, as we could argue that therefore preferences are descriptions of behavioural regularities as being contextualized in a specific environment. On the contrary, experimental and behavioural economics clearly tend to see preferences as properties that individuals have, as this is a necessary condition for transferring the results of the lab to the field.[16]

If we reconsider this procedure from the viewpoint of Bohr's and Barad's philosophical position, we would immediately conclude that this is a misplaced assumption, reflecting naive naturalism. According to the position of agential realism, we would expect that the preferences that individuals are believed to have are continuously being constructed by the interaction between researcher and test persons during the intra-action that is enabled and realized in the lab. However, this does not imply that the results of the laboratory do not reflect 'reality' outside of the lab. In fact, outside of the lab, the same principle applies, namely that people do not 'have' preferences as immutable and stable properties, but that preferences emerge in social contexts and interactions, which, as these are performative, must be properly seen as 'intra-actions', too, or, if the parlance of Actor-network theory is employed, as 'agencements'. In other words, I argue that the economic experiment has the same methodological status as an experiment that uncovers quantum regularities in identifying phenomena as entanglements of subjects and objects.

We can now re-evaluate the methodology of experimental economics in terms of reflexive naturalism. I have referred to the example of social and individual preferences because this offers an illuminating analogy to the wave-particle dualism in quantum mechanics. Elementary particles do not have the properties of waves or particles, but depending on the experimental set-up, these phenomena emerge, thus being complementary descriptions, both together constituting reality. I think that the same applies for the dualism of individual versus social preferences: Human beings

---

[15]For important discussions and analytical overviews of this research, see Levitt and List (2007) and Bowles and Polonía-Reyes (2012).

[16]For a pertinent discussion of the methodological status of preferences in economic theory, see Ross (2005: 104ff).

do not have these preferences, but they emerge in certain contexts, thus implying that their specific type of agency emerges via intra-action.

It is highly illuminating referring to the work of the philosopher Tuomela here. Without going into details, suffice to introduce his distinction between the 'I mode' and the 'We mode' of human agency. Tuomela argues partly naturalistically, claiming that human agents have the property to switch between the two modes, depending on contextual triggers, which he explains by evolutionary biology and the necessity to enable cooperation in human groups, while maintaining fundamental individual incentives (Tuomela explicitly refuses to assign ontological status to supra-individual entities). The 'I mode' corresponds to the standard 'a-social' view of economics, thus focusing decisions on the interests and motives of the individual. In the 'We mode', people would directly take the position of a certain reference group to which they assign themselves. In economics, a related view has been developed in terms of so-called 'team preferences'. Hence, the 'We mode' should not be confused with notions of 'agreement' between individuals (such as social contracts, bargaining, etc.), but means that individuals take the perspective of the group in adopting individual decisions. Formally, that means, for example, that the pay-offs in strategic games are directly merged into group-level pay-offs in the individual decision calculus. The notion of 'We mode' is tightly connected with the concept of collective intentionality which also plays an important role in philosophical theories about human sociality and institutions.[17]

Tuomela's view means that we cannot apply one single explanatory framework exclusively to explaining social phenomena. Standard economics adopts methodological individualism and would only argue in terms of the 'I mode'. However, in the real world, this effort would necessarily fail in many instances, because there is also the possibility that people act in the 'We mode'. However, this is by no means a stable and fixed relationship: Even the same individual can switch between the 'I mode' and the 'We mode', depending on context, and even instantaneously.[18] Accordingly, we cannot expect that in the lab either of the two modes would emerge as the exclusive one. However, we can suggest another interpretation: Namely, that the exact control of environmental factors in the lab would allow for identifying the modes in a pure form, provided that the relevant triggers are present.

I believe that the analogy to Bohr's complementary principle is most salient here: We can think of alternative experimental settings in which even the same people may manifest 'I mode' or 'We mode' behaviour, depending on context, and considering the intra-action between cues created by the experimenter and cognitive responses by the subjects, which can also vary probabilistically. These experimental observations are

[17]Tuomela (1995, 2007). For the notion of team preferences, with a game-theoretic formalization, see Sugden (2000). The literature on collective intentionality is overviewed by Schweikard and Schmid (2013). This establishes a conceptual bridge between Tuomela and Searle; Searle (1995, 2010) plays an important role in the philosophical grounding of the performativity concept. Hence, we can put agential realism in a larger context of philosophical debates also closely related to economics, which I cannot pursue further here.

[18]Interestingly, this can be experimentally shown in research on altruism, see Kirman and Teschl (2010).

complementary, meaning that experiments that would show individual optimization do not justify extending this result to the real world outside the lab. Yet, the result catches reality in the sense that under similar environmental conditions, people will manifest this property. This observation does not weaken the methodological value of experiments, but to the opposite, strengthens it. According to agential realism, it is the experiment which allows for demonstrating the complementarity principle in the controlled and purest form. Barad calls this 'diffraction', meaning that in the real world, human behaviour will oscillate between individual and social preferences in a complex and even unpredictable way, and that experiments allow for observing diffractive patterns in a controlled fashion.[19]

There is an excellent example for this principle of complementarity in psychological experiments on human sociality, which also includes deep methodological reflections, namely the work by the Japanese psychologist Toshio Yamagishi. Yamagishi has proposed an 'ecological approach to culture' to refer to the fact that in experiments about human values there is no fixed property that deterministically causes individually oriented or social-oriented behaviour. In psychology, the economic notion of preferences corresponds to the notion of 'values'. In cross-cultural research, many scholars adopt a value-based approach, meaning that individuals of a particular culture are seen as having certain values that distinguish them from individuals of other cultures. Interestingly, this view is also mostly adopted in recent economic research on culture, where culture is defined as values transmitted cross-generationally in populations, thus appearing to be a stable property that members have and share. In contrast, Yamagishi argues that individuals do not have these stable and fixed properties but that these are triggered by certain environmental cues. So, in a battery of experiments comparing Japanese and US American subjects he shows that the standard view is false comparing the 'collectivism' of the Japanese with the 'individualism' of the Americans in terms of culture-based values. For example, in an anonymous setting that does not give any cues about what a group-oriented behavioural standard might afford, the Japanese act as individualistic as the Americans. Differences occur once there are cues about what a group-oriented behaviour might be. So, the differences between Americans and Japanese appear to be related to more fundamental cognitive tendencies, which have been labelled 'field independence' versus 'field dependence'. Field dependence involves stronger awareness of contextual factors and environmental cues in choosing certain actions.[20]

---

[19]There is no space to go into more details here, see my discussion in Herrmann-Pillath (2016b), referring to the overview by Bowles and Polonía-Reyes (2012). In this work, I present a semiotic model that introduces the notion of 'bimodality' which seems to be very close to the principle of complementarity. This systematizes Bowles and Polonía-Reyes' observation that incentives always work in a twofold way, namely directly triggering a certain behaviour, but also providing information about contextual conditions of choices which result into a specific framing of the situation. For example, changing a negative social incentive (such as moral outrage) into an apparently similar pecuniary negative incentive (a fine) might shift the frame to a market exchange interpretation, so that the fine might even increase the incidence of deviant behaviour because individuals think they pay for it, so giving it legitimacy.

[20]Obviously, this might also be interpreted as a fixed property of subjects, though of a more abstract kind. So, Yamagishi's approach needs further scrutiny. Yamagishi (2012) is an extensive survey of his

In the context of the current discussion, we can just concentrate on the essential insight that Yamagishi's research clearly vindicates Tuomela's philosophical ideas: Collectivism, altruism, social preferences and related concepts refer to the 'We mode', and individualism, individual preferences and so on refer to the 'I mode'. The ecological approach to culture means that people switch between the modes depending on the experimental setting: The same Japanese subjects act strongly individualistic or strongly collectivistic, across different experimental designs which give different cues on behavioural alternatives.

Interestingly, one of the leaders in the field of experimental economics, Vernon Smith, has also suggested the notion of 'ecological rationality' in his Nobel lecture, referring to very similar ideas.[21] I suggest that this view matches with Bohr's complementarity principle: Ecological rationality implies that human individuals have both individual and social preferences, and which of them prevail depends on the contextualization. In the lab, researchers evoke certain behaviours in a controlled way. But that does never mean that one pattern can be exclusively generalized. To the contrary, we must recognize that human individuals manifest both individual and social preferences in a complementary way. Behaviour is a phenomenon in the Bohr-Barad understanding.

This is the reflexive-naturalistic view on economic experiments, which may be powerful to resolve many methodological debates over experimental economics. As I mentioned previously, it seems to tie up with the notion of revealed preferences, as we would approach preferences as revealed by an experiment as phenomena that emerge by the experimental intra-action. They are not properties of individuals. However, the agential realist view does not imply simple behaviourism, as in the original notion of revealed preferences: We do not keep reference to the object as a 'black box', but radically eschew reference to an object at all.[22]

---

work. On the concept of field-dependence, see Nisbett (2003). Interestingly, this is often explained in terms of agricultural ecologies and production settings, thus would reflect an interaction between cognitive structures and material environments, which have resulted in cognitive path-dependencies. I discuss these issues in detail in Herrmann-Pillath (2017).

[21] Smith (2003).

[22] I cannot delve into further discussions of the philosophy of science discourse that is pertinent here, but just keep it within the limits of Barad's view. However, I mention that there is a close affinity to Ladyman and Ross's (2007) 'ontic structural realism' which also eschews reference to objects and highlights generative powers of structures which can be grasped by concepts and formalism, as well as statistical methods. This is of direct interest here, because Ross has also proposed an externalist view on neuroeconomics and behavioural economics which argues against full reduction to internal properties of individuals.

4 Distributed Cognition and the Production of Social Ontology

In the context of the methodological debates about modern physics, the notion of 'experimental metaphysics' has been suggested. We can transfer this into the context of economics in suggesting that an economic lab is a place where social ontologies are experimentally created. This is the elementary basis for extending the results of the lab to the field: Social ontologies created in the lab connect with social ontologies outside the lab via the similarity of performative mechanisms that work in both contexts. This is indeed the way how many economists think about the empirical validity of the lab: What counts is not what we learn about the individual behaviour in the lab, but how the artificially created environments intra-act with the individuals in producing phenomena; phenomena are the stuff of social ontology. Thus, external validity of the lab results depends on identifying similar patterns of intra-action, hence similar mechanisms of performativity.[23]

This view is most salient in the many ways how experiments are also used in market design. In this case, experimenters do not primarily claim to describe reality but aim at transforming reality, such as in designing auctions which have previously been tested in the lab. However, this is only a special case, which relies on the effort to achieve a similar level of environmental control in the field as in the lab, in order to produce the expected results. We can also ask whether the environmental conditions in the lab can be also identified in the real world, which requires observational isolation of the respective mechanisms. So, we would not ask whether real people have the properties that they are supposed to have in the experiment, but whether the entire experimental setting is replicated in an analogous way in the real world.[24]

The most straightforward example here leads us back to the origin of experimental economics, namely the study of experimental markets in the lab aiming at discovering properties that markets also have in the real world. This was the main focus of Vernon Smith's work. Coming back to my discussion of the performative role of money, this approach clearly does not pose any methodological troubles: If people are primed with money in the context of artificial markets, so they are in real-world markets. So, one of the conditions for transferring lab results to the field is fulfilled.

It is important to notice that in the work on artificial markets another perspective emerges that ties up with my discussion. This is that market experiments confirm

[23]As an example for an economist's sophisticated reflection about this, see Kagel (2015). Kagel shows that the external validity of experiments very much depends on the way how learning processes are contextualized in the lab, and to which extent this contextualization matches with field conditions.

[24]On the relationship between experiments and market design, see Roth (2008). It is interesting to notice that market design can be also directly based on 'mechanism design', which is a purely theoretical field of economics, in the first place. Often mechanism design analysis is directly referred to the real world, without applying experiments in order to empirically validate the mechanisms. In my view, if mechanism design is systematically combined with experiments, we gain important insights into performativity.

views on markets that emphasize their computational properties.[25] In artificial markets that also involve artificial agents, the properties of the latter can be reduced even to the level of 'zero intelligence' robots which just implement some simple decision rule. This is interesting as the question loses much significance which properties human agents have in the real world and when interacting on real markets. Smith's notion of ecological rationality comes very close to recent developments in cognitive sciences which have highlighted the distributed nature of human cognition. That means, again, that information processing and knowledge accumulation does not happen 'within' human individuals, but in the interaction between individuals and certain parts of their environment. The notion of 'extended mind' makes this point most articulate: Human mind is no longer seen as being located or embodied in the brain, but as extending far beyond the brain, including artefacts, social networks and so on. This also means that human agency, as enabled by cognition, is distributed in the same way (which matches with a fundamental proposition of ANT).[26]

I briefly touch upon this other strand of literature because it further supports the position of agential realism. In referring to experimental economics, this also shows that there are essential methodological fissures between different forms of experiments. Comparing artificial markets with artificial agents on the one hand, and even artificial markets with real human agents on the other hand, the former tends towards recognizing the role of distributed cognition and distributed agency, whereas the latter sticks to the idea that agency is exclusively located within the individuals. Therefore, I argue that the agential realist view also allows for the methodological synthesis of otherwise diverging strands of experimental economics.[27]

Finally, elsewhere I have suggested that economic explanations might follow the methodological standards which have recently developed by the so-called 'constitutive explanations' or mechanism approach in the philosophy of science. A special kind of mechanism that is essential in social ontology is performative mechanisms. Now, if we conceive of experiments as being performative, we can redefine their status as an empirical method. Experiments are the king's way to identify performative mechanisms in pure form, precisely because the contextual conditions are controlled to the maximum possible degree. I suggest that a further development of agential realism, in the context of experimental economics, might move into the direction of grounding practices and empirical methods in the constitutive explanations framework.[28]

---

[25] See Mirowski and Somefun (1998). On the following, see the overview by Plott and Smith (2008).

[26] The seminal paper in the analytical philosophy of mind was Clark and Chalmers (1998); in cognitive science, Hutchins (1995). For a recent overview, see Clark (2011).

[27] Davis (2010) gives a detailed and illuminating overview of the emergence of different strands of behavioural and experimental research in economics, as far as the implied notion of the individual is concerned. These historical developments deserve much attention, as they have deeply shaped the current understanding of experiments.

[28] Herrmann-Pillath (2016b). For a comprehensive introduction into this approach in the philosophy of science, see Craver and Tabery (2015).

5 Conclusion

My reasoning ended with what is possibly a surprising conclusion. The notion of performativity emerged in the humanities and apparently would undermine any kind of naturalistic essentialism that guides the empirical claims that experimental and behavioural economists submit. If we adopt the stance of reflexive naturalism, this judgment falls apart. Experiments are one of the most reliable ways to empirically identify performative mechanisms and hence the processes by which social ontologies are produced in the real world. This is also the basis for how experiments can guide the design of policies and institutions in the real world: The experiment can suggest particular ways how to create 'social worlds' within particular contexts and with particular aims.

What is clearly refuted by my analysis are any claims of experimenters that by means of experiments we can identify stable properties that human individuals have under any circumstances, such as individuals having particular 'preferences' or 'values'. This applies for both the individual and the population level, be it culture or even species level. In one sense, and superficially, this seems to reinstate the nature–culture divide. But the position of agential realism, based on Bohr's and Barad's physics-philosophy, leads us to recognize that nature is a product of culture, and vice versa, or, more specifically, that what constitutes reality is entanglements of subjects and objects in phenomena. In this view, the idea that individuals have stable properties is simply meaningless. As I have argued, again surprisingly, this view concurs with the revealed preference approach in economics, though reinterpreting it substantially.

One more specific insight of my discussion is, however, that experiments in psychology and economics should be distinguished neatly, and probably the fact that economic experiments rely on money as an incentive is truly significant here. Economists mostly believe that this is one device that makes economic experiments more reliable and robust in generating insights into any kind of human behaviour. In my analysis, economic experiments do just that, generate insights into economic behaviour, and most reliably in market or market-type environments. So, it seems to me that investigating into the entire realm of human sociality by using the specific approaches of economic experiments is misguided, as far as claims on generalization and universality are concerned. Yet, this does not diminish the empirical significance of economic experiments, to the contrary. Overstretching their reach undermines their empirical claims, which should be re-interpreted as identifying particular performative mechanisms in economic contexts.

References

Barad, K. M. (2007). *Meeting the universe halfway: Quantum physics and the entanglement of matter and meaning*. Durham: Duke University Press.

Böhme, J. (2016). 'Doing' laboratory experiments: An ethnomethodological study of the performative practice in behavioral economic research. In I. Boldyrev & E. Svetlova (Eds.), *Enacting dismal science. new perspectives on the performativity of economics* (pp. 87–108). New York: Palgrave Macmillan.

Bowles, S., & Polanía–Reyes S. (2012). Economic incentives and social preferences: substitutes or complements? *Journal of Economic Literature*, *L*(2), 368–425.

Çalışkan, K., & Callon, M. (2009). Economization, part 1: Shifting attention from the economy towards processes of economization. *Economy and Society, 38*(3), 369–398.

Camerer, C. F. (2015). The promise and success of lab-field generalizability in experimental economics: A critical reply to levitt and list. In G. R. Fréchette & A. Schotter (Eds.), *Handbook of experimental economic methodology* (pp. 249–295). Oxford: Oxford University Press.

Clark, A. (2011). *Supersizing the mind: Embodiment, action, and cognitive extension*. Oxford: Oxford University Press.

Clark, A., & Chalmers, D. J. (1998). The extended mind. *Analysis, 58,* 10–23.

Craver, C., & Tabery, J. (2015). Mechanisms in science. In E. N. Zalta (Ed.), *The stanford encyclopedia of philosophy* (Winter 2015 ed.). Retrieved from http://plato.stanford.edu/archives/win2015/entries/science-mechanisms/.

Davis, J. B. (2010). *Individuals and Identity in Economics*. Cambridge: Cambridge University Press.

Doing, P. (2008). Give me a laboratory and I will raise a discipline: The past, present, and future politics of laboratory studies in STS. In E. J. Hackett, O. Amsterdamska, M. Lynch, & J. Wajcman (eds), *The handbook of science and technology studies* (pp. 279–297). Cambridge, MA, USA and London: MIT Press.

Erev, I., & Greiner, B. (2015). The 1-800 critique: Counter-examples, and the future of behavioral economics. In G. R. Fréchette & A. Schotter (Eds.), *Handbook of experimental economic methodology* (pp. 151–165). Oxford: Oxford University Press.

Faye, J. (2014). Copenhagen interpretation of quantum mechanics. In E. N. Zalta (Ed.), *The stanford encyclopedia of philosophy* (Fall 2014 ed.). Retrieved from http://plato.stanford.edu/archives/fall2014/entries/qm-copenhagen/.

Guala, F. (2007). How to do things with experimental economics. In D. MacKenzie, F. Muniesa, & L. Siu (Eds.), *Do economists make markets? On the performativity of economics* (pp. 128–162). Princeton and Oxford: Princeton University Press.

Henrich, J., et al. (2005). 'Economic Man' in cross–cultural perspective: behavioral experiments in 15 small-scale societies. *Behavioral and Brain Sciences, 28,* 795–855.

Herrmann-Pillath, C. (2016a), Constitutive explanations in neuroeconomics: Principles and a case study on money. *Journal of Economic Methodology, 23*(4), 374–395.

Herrmann-Pillath, C. (2016b). Performative Mechanisms. In I. Boldyrev & E. Svetlova (Eds.), *Enacting dismal science: New perspectives on the performativity of economics* (pp. 53–86). New York: Palgrave McMillan.

Herrmann-Pillath, C. (2017). *China's economic culture: The ritual order of state and markets*. Abingdon and New York: Routledge.

Hutchins, E. (1995). *Cognition in the wild*. Cambridge and London: MIT Press.

Kagel, J. H. (2015). Laboratory experiments: The lab in relationship to field experiments, field data, and economic theory. In G. R. Fréchette & A. Schotter (Eds.), *Handbook of experimental economic methodology* (pp. 339–359). Oxford: Oxford University Press.

Karlan, D. S. (2005). Using experimental economics to measure social capital and predict financial decisions. *American Economic Review, 95*(5), 1688–1699.

Kirman, A., & Teschl, M. (2010). Selfish of selfless? The role of empathy in economics. *Philosophical Transactions of the Royal Society B, 365,* 303–317.

Kouchaki, M., Smith-Crowe, K., Brief, A. P., & Sousa, C. (2013). Seeing green: mere exposure to money triggers as business decision frame and unethical outcomes. *Organizational Behavior and Human Decision Processes, 121,* 53–61.

Ladyman, J., Ross, D., Spurrett, D., & Collier, J. (2007). *Every thing must go: Metaphysics naturalized*. Oxford: Oxford University Press.

Latour, B. (2005). *Reassembling the social: An introduction to actor–network.theory*. Oxford: Oxford University Press.

Latour, B. (2012). *Enquête Sur Les Modes D'existence: Une Anthropologie Des Modernes*. Paris: La Découverte.
Levitt, S. D., & List, J. A. (2007). What do laboratory experiments measuring social preferences reveal about the real world? *Journal of Economic Perspectives, 24*(2), 31–64.
MacKenzie, D. (2007). Is Economics performative? Option theory and the construction of derivatives market's. In D. MacKenzie, F. Muniesa, & L. Siu (Eds.), *Do economists make markets? On the performativity of economics* (pp. 54–86). Princeton and Oxford: Princeton University Press.
Mirowski, P., & Somefun, K. (1998). Markets as evolving computational entities. *Journal of Evolutionary Economics, 8*(4), 329–357.
Muniesa, F., & Callon, M. (2007). Economic experiments and the construction of markets. In D. MacKenzie, F. Muniesa, & L. Siu (Eds.), *Do economists make markets? On the performativity of economics* (pp. 163–189). Princeton and Oxford: Princeton University Press.
Nisbett, R. (2003). *The geography of thought: How Asians and Westerners think differently…and why*. New York: Free Press.
Papineau, D. (2009). Naturalism. In E. N. Zalta (ed.) *The stanford encyclopedia of philosophy* (Spring 2009 ed.). Retrieved from http://plato.stanford.edu/archives/spr2009/entries/naturalism/.
Plott, C. R., & Smith, V. L. (2008). Markets. In Charles R. Plott & V. L. Smith (Eds.), *Handbook of experimental economics results* (Vol. 1). Amsterdam: North-Holland.
Ross, D. (2005). *Economic theory and cognitive science: microexplanations*. Cambridge, MA, USA and London: MIT Press.
Roth, A. E. (2008). What have we learned from market design? *Economic Journal, 118,* 285–310.
Schweikard, D. P., & Schmid, H. B. (2013). Collective intentionality. In E. N. Zalta (Ed.), *The stanford encyclopedia of philosophy* (Summer 2013 ed.). Retrieved from http://plato.stanford.edu/archives/sum2013/entries/collective-intentionality/.
Searle, J. R. (1995). *The construction of social reality*. New York: Free Press.
Searle, J. R. (2010). *Making the social world: the structure of human civilization*. Oxford: Oxford University Press.
Simmel, G. (1907). *Philosophie des Geldes*, 2nd ed., reprint 2009. Cologne: Anaconda.
Smith, V. L. (1976). Experimental economics: Induced value theory. In The American Economic Review (Vol. 66, No. 2). Papers and Proceedings (pp. 274–279).
Smith, V. L. (2003). Constructivist and ecological rationality in economics. *The American Economic Review, 93*(3), 465–508.
Sugden, R. (2000). Team preferences. *Economics and Philosophy, 16,* 175–204.
Tuomela, R. (1995). *The importance of us: A philosophical study of basic social notions*. Stanford: Stanford University Press.
Tuomela, R. (2007). *The philosophy of sociality*. Oxford: Oxford University Press.
Vohs, K. D., Mead, N. L., & Goode, M. R. (2006). The psychological consequences of money. *Science, 314,* 1154–1156.
Vohs, K. D., Mead, N. L., & Goode, M. R. (2008). Merely activating the concept of money changes personal and interpersonal behavior. *Current Directions in Psychological Science, 17*(3), 208–212.
Yamagishi, T. (2012). Micro–macro dynamics of the cultural construction of reality. A Niche construction approach to culture. In M. J. Gelfland, C. Chiu, & Y. Hong (Eds.), *Advances in culture and psychology* (Vol. 1, pp. 251–308). Oxford and New York: Oxford University Press.
Zelizer, V. A. (1997). *The social meaning of money*. Princeton: Princeton University Press.

Printed by Printforce, the Netherlands